Twayne's United States Authors Series

EDITOR OF THIS VOLUME

Mason Lowance

University of Massachusetts

Solomon Stoddard

TUSAS 295

Facsimile of a Funeral Elegy, circa 1664, in Solomon Stoddard's autograph from his college notebook.

SOLOMON STODDARD

By RALPH J. COFFMAN

Northeastern University

TWAYNE PUBLISHERS

A DIVISION OF G. K. HALL & CO., BOSTON

Published in 1978 by Twayne Publishers,
A Division of G. K. Hall & Co.
All Rights Reserved

Printed on permanent/durable acid-free paper and bound
in the United States of America

First Printing

To Hope and Edith

Library of Congress Cataloging in Publication Data

Coffman, Ralph J.
    Solomon Stoddard.

    (Twayne's United States authors series ; TUSAS 295)
    Bibliography.
    Includes index.
    1. Stoddard, Solomon, 1643–1729.
BX7260.S816C63   285'.8'0924 [B]   78-5520
ISBN 0-8057-7198-0

Contents

About the Author

R. J. Coffman is a graduate of Harvard University, where he received a Ph.D. directed by Alan Heimert for "Gardens in the Wilderness: Studies in Stuart Puritan Reforms and the Diversity of New England Puritanism, 1604–1650," which he is preparing for publication. He received the B.D. from Andover Newton Theological School, where he submitted a thesis on the religious philosophy of Samuel Taylor Coleridge to Gerald Robertson Cragg and Dean George Peck. He also holds an M.S. in Library Science from Simmons College and an Ed.M. from Boston University.

He has published articles on such topics as bibliography, information science, and early American history and literature. He is author of *Samuel Taylor Coleridge: A Bibliography of His Library*, which is an in-depth analysis of the intellectual sources of Coleridge's Romanticism. Mr. Coffman's specialties are the evolution of early American society and the sociointellectual background of Anglo-European Romanticism. He is currently a member of the faculty at Northeastern University.

Preface

When Solomon Stoddard, minister of the First Church of North-ampton, Massachusetts, died after six decades of service in 1729, he left behind a rich legacy. Sensitive to the climate of his own changing society, he constantly sought to address the spiritual anxieties of his age, and in the process he helped prepare the way for a new order of society through a rhetoric of action and a religion of equality. The youth found his method and message exciting, as Thomas Clap, the future president of Yale College, recorded in his notebook:

When I was about seventeen years old . . . I read *A Treatise Concerning Conversion* by Mr. Stoddard of Northampton, upon which I thought I had never really been converted and was under much concern and distress for over a month or two, after which I thought I was enabled by the spirit of God to lay hold upon Christ. . . . And some short time after this, on May 15, 1720, I joined to the church in Cambridge and found at times a great delight and satisfaction in the ways of religion.[1]

Gradually, Stoddard's fame as a revivalist spread abroad: when the great English Evangelist George Whitefield passed through North-ampton in the fall of 1740 on his American tour he noted that he had just traversed the "land of the great Stoddard." Through subtle ramifications, Stoddard's rhetoric and religion, too, spread afield into secular thought and in a sense facilitated the reception of revolutionary ideas in America.

In his outward bearing, he conformed to the role of the Puritan minister. He scorned powdered periwigs or any other ostentacious dress. He wore a black cassock with narrow sleeves and buttons down the front and two slits extending upward to the hips for convenience in riding. Black knee-length breeches, rather narrow, terminated in white stockings and black blunt-toed, single buckled shoes. By the standards of his day, he was considered a tall man, and his bearing was accentuated by the steeple crown hat he wore in his travels. Known to strangers as a dignified, hence acceptably austere, individual, in private conversation and to his friends he displayed wit, charm and a dash of humor. He loved his favorite pipe which was regularly packed with the finest Virginia tobacco, freshly mixed in London. He was a devoted father who, judging by his record, did not impose his own profession on his sons although he did welcome ministers as prospective sons-in-law. Although a country parson, he lacked not the Hebrew, Greek and Latin of the Mathers, but instead of ornamenting his wisdom he preferred plain language and originality. Although he penned two poems at Harvard as a student (one in Latin), he was only a sometime poet with little knack or desire for framing a wilderness baroque poetry, as did his neighbor in Westfield, Edward Taylor. His own genre was the sermon for which he painstakingly developed a revival rhetoric. Not a man locked into the thought-forms of the past, he respected tradition and distilled those elements from many thinkers in a distinctive syncretism, which, because he was both a pragmatist and a visionary, exhibits the tension between the head and the heart, discipline and doctrine, in often tentative solutions.

Indeed, the tension between the head and the heart, discipline and doctrine, is basic to understanding the nature of his achievement and the extent and subtlety of his influence. The method used in this study of Stoddard attempts to establish the intellectual and social roots of his thought and their intellectual and social repercussions. Although many have tried to probe the basic tension in Stoddard's thought, all have presented their analyses from necessarily fragmentary perspectives, since there has never been a full-length study of the *process* of his development. This is understandable but regrettable since the immediate foreground to the Great Awakening has not been considered attractive by students of Colonial America.

The purpose of this study is to understand Stoddard as one of the foremost early American religious thinkers—the man who actually brought to an end the reign of disciplinarian Puritanism in Massachusetts. Since its church-state platform had been established in the fall and winter of 1633–1634 by the Reverend John Cotton and John Winthrop, the colony had suffered deep religious and political division over the issues of doctrine (the articulation of experiential religion) and discipline (the institutionalization of experience into codes of community acceptance—church membership and political enfranchisement). Cotton's Code had directly connected doctrine and discipline in the concept of regenerate magistracy, but others, led by the Reverend Thomas Hooker, believed in a more moderate solution and were forced into founding another colony where they would be free to implement their ideals. This colony was Connecticut. The geneses of these two Puritan ideologies of Massachusetts and Connecticut are imbedded in the dark corners of their founders' previous English existence, where the implementation of ideology remained academic in the midst of the oppressive climate of Archbishop William Laud's church and Charles I's autocratic rule. Yet, stemming from this tantalizingly elusive period of early Stuart Puritanism, two trajectories converged on Stoddard's coming to Northampton, Massachusetts—the socio-religious backgrounds of both his family and the families of his Northampton townsmen. We shall witness the uncanny coalescence of English men and women in the gathered communities of the American wilderness, each with unique but overlapping sets of political and religious values, and how these values prepared the way for Stoddard's first American revolution—to be sure, a bloodless, but decisive turning point in American history. What happened, in effect, was that Stoddard implemented in western Massachusetts a different form of the Connecticut solution, but, since it was perpetrated within the boundaries of Cotton's Code, it could not be disregarded by the established oligarchies. By this act he called the bluff of those disciplinarian Puritans now led by the house of Mather. Thus was made manifest to the world the deep and abiding ideological division between the two major groups within non-separating Congregationalism, a division long known to the primary actors in the wilderness experiment but officially disregarded for reasons of vulnerability of colonial charters to revocation by the Crown. Stoddard's release of the subterranean wellsprings of doctrinal Puritanism precipitated Royal censure, as those who were hostile to years of oppression by Cotton's Code gathered 'round him. In formulating his position Stoddard looked not only to his spiritual progenitors in America but also to the Continental Pietists. Out of his quest for a truly experiential religion unfettered by secular pressures of the state was born a distinctly American revivalism that spread across early New England in sporadic waves until the time was ripe for his grandson to initiate the movement now known as *the* Great Awakening. Stoddard, however, was the first American doctrinal revivalist, and it is in the climate prepared by his work that the real sources of the Awakening, at least in the north, are to be found.

Stoddard's life exhibits the uncertainties of his age. Actually he underwent three distinct periods of development, treated in chapters two through four: first, as a champion of sacramental discipline and its renewing power; secondly, as a shrewd ecclesiastical statesman who also developed a new strategy for revival preaching; and thirdly, as a true Evangelical who espoused the Word as the central datum of the church and the itinerant minister as the chief apostle of that datum. In this last period Stoddard rejected completely the hierarchy of discipline over doctrine that had come to characterize the very essence of Puritanism in particular and the magisterial Reformation in general. This presents Stoddard ultimately as a true innovator, but he was not cut from tradition entirely. Rather, he used those elements of other systems and structures to fashion his own formulations which tend to be open-ended. It is hoped that this approach to the ever-changing quality of Stoddard's thought will stimulate others to investigate this very dynamic period of American history too long neglected.

Stoddard has been the object of either praise or criticism as father-figure or prophet, but little of his ambiguity has been appreciated. The first assessment of Stoddard's contribution came from the pen of his archrival, Increase Mather, who cast him as Pope Stoddard, the ecclesiastical prince of the Connecticut River Valley. Over the years Mather's assessment persisted. Williston Walker, the great Congregational historian, followed, as did Perry Miller, the incisive scholar who rescued Puritanism from neglect and used Mather's epithet as the basis of his vignettes. Of course, Stoddard the Pope refers not only to the extent of his power but the quality of that power. Was he really a pope-like disciplinarian or was he an Evangelist? James Walsh, for instance, has argued in the affirmative, that his dislike of binding covenants and rigid membership policies actually led him to espouse Presbyterian discipline instead, a hierarchical framework which would be imposed on church government as well as on doctrine. Others have not been as receptive to the view that he merely shifted from one disciplinarian structure to another. For instance, E. Brooks Holifield, traced the renaissance of sacramental doctrine in the latter seventeenth century and how Stoddard contributed to this overthrow of discipline. Thomas A. Schafer noted the impact that Stoddard's revivalism had on the youths of his day, providing social as well as religious outlets for generations who, repressed at home by paternal rule and relegated in church to second-class membership, were not encouraged to partake of the divine offer of spiritual renewal. The extent of Stoddard's actual influence has also received attention. For instance, Paul R. Lucas found little direct evidence for his scepter-wielding authority, yet Rober G. Pope discovered a general pattern of revivals that swept through New England parished prior to 1700. Were they the products of Stoddardean Evangelicalism? Most likely, not. But between 1715 and 1730 another series of awakenings spread across western New England during the height of Stoddard's eminence. In examining these revivals we find that the parishes were connected in some way to Stoddard, either by itinerant ministers of his Hampshire Council or by parish ministers through familial relationship.

In seventeenth-century New England, religion cannot be understood apart from society, nor society apart from religion. For this reason, this study attempts to probe beneath institutional and intellectual history to uncover family and kinship networks that may have some deeper bearing on Stoddard's contribution than merely the superficial narrative can offer. In order to fully explore this possibility the English origins of both Stoddard's family and those of the first settlers of Northampton are examined for the study of the emigrations of family clusters from Stuart England to New England sometimes reveals that political and religious allegiances coincide with obscure English backgrounds. Only then can a fuller appreciation of ideological diversity in Puritan New England and its significance for Stoddard (and, indeed, every other Puritan minister) be understood.

Therefore, chapter one begins with Stoddard's own family, its English roots and its colonial connections. Through his father's four marriages he was related to prominent gentry families who were, in turn, interrelated through English backgrounds. Stoddard's own children also provided him with a vast network among whom were seventeen ministers. We shall see how his father's own life was riddled with ideological controversy, since his first wife was related to John Winthrop and the magisterial proponents of a strict order of Congregational government, while he was of a more independent mind. This provided the genesis of the head/heart, discipline/doctrine tension in Stoddard's family life, and we shall examine how this dialectic continued throughout his early years.

Of course, this tension was basic to Puritanism. Since the first settlers had landed during the Great Migration of the 1630's, ruling oligarchies had wrestled with the conundrum of grace and order, the heavenly and the earthly church. Resolution of the dilemma of identifying the visible saint was absolutely crucial in a society that was predicated on rule by only the elect. Yet, the elect were known only to God. Visible marks of righteous living could be misleading. Something more was needed. Enter John Cotton, for years the vicar of St. Botolph's cathedral in Boston, Lincolnshire, sensitive, a true mystic—yet also a statesman. Confronted by John Winthrop and other leaders in the fall of 1633 with the prospect of Massachusetts' errand of the pure being dissolved as more and more disbelievers entered the haven ports of the colony, Cotton looked to a colleague in Rotterdam, Hugh Peter: he had instituted a test of conversion there. Almost as though echoing Descartes' simultaneous discovery, "Cogito, ergo sum," Cotton framed his premise, "If you know (your experience of conversion), then you are (a visible saint)."

Stoddard as a boy found Cotton's harsh discipline perhaps fine for a mystic but it was too strong for his spirit. He had not seen the Light, he had not felt the grace. So his life rolled on uneventfully except for his studies, and even when he was in college he still remained outside the church and the state as did all of his siblings. As a microcosm of society, the Stoddard family quietly slipped into that uncertain complacency lamented in the jeremiads of declension in meetinghouses across the countryside. Thus, Stoddard's religious concerns were born of a deeply personal quest for assurance that lasted until his twenty-seventh year.

When Stoddard set foot in Northampton in 1669, his own struggle with Cotton's Code recapitulated, in microcosm, the collective experience of the Northampton townspeople. Chapter two begins by presenting evidence that his invitation to preach there was no chance affair; rather it illustrates the uncanny coincidence of social and ideological patterns in the formation of early New England towns. Each family in the town had connections with moderate Congregational opponents of Cotton's Code. As we trace the origins of these moderates who championed doctrine over discipline we can at last grasp the ideological roots of Stoddard's supporters and understand the special religious climate that prevailed in the Connecticut River Valley at his coming. The coincidences of these patterns help explain why a city-bred college graduate who was not a church member should seek a pulpit on the Massachusetts frontier, in an obscure, isolated and infant village, recently torn by religious controversy, and why the unique assortment of Northampton settlers should select an untried, unconverted novice as their pastor after they had just been through a trial by fire with their recently deceased, staunchly conservative pastor.

Initially, as we shall see, Stoddard tried to live by the accepted discipline of Massachusetts, allowing children of church members to receive baptism and to enter a state of education. Its effect was brief, however, and apathy prevailed. It was clear that new methods were needed to stimulate the people not only to become members of the church but in the process become members of the colony. More than half of the adults in Northampton were outside of the church and town community. If he could not look to his colleagues for advice, at least he could resort to the words of his Harvard tutors who had introduced him to Presbyterians and Independents from whose thought he could be free to select elements to fit his situation.

All lines seem to converge on November 5, 1677, the day when he ceased to record degrees of church membership in his record book. Opening the doors of the meetinghouse, he accepted all good-living adults into the church. All were in theory able to participate in the sacraments, the supreme symbol of full acceptance into the community in seventeenth-century Massachusetts. This marked what is possibly the single most important date in American social and intellectual history since 1633 when Cotton had imposed his code on the Colony, the code Stoddard had now silently overthrown. However, in place of Cotton's code, Stoddard offered a new formalism: just as before there was an established order but of a different kind, Stoddard now became a champion of sacramental discipline. The two Protestant rites of initiation had become the cornerstones of religion and society supplanting Cotton's emphasis on the regeneration experience, and, indeed, detracting from the preached Word as a vehicle of grace. From 1677 to 1700 Stoddard maintained this posture, while, at the same time, developing the rhetoric of revivalism.

Chapter three exposes Stoddard as pope of the instituted church in which the sacraments were balanced with preaching of the Word. This period is characterized by the strife of the controversy with the Mathers and in the development of alliances to combat their opposition to innovation. Besides the intrigue and Mather's expulsion from the presidency of Harvard, this was a period full of growth for Stoddard: when he finally emerged at the other end of the first decade of the eighteenth century his ultimate mission was fully formed.

Chapter four begins with Stoddard the Evangelical, the man who has just jettisoned the sacraments as co-equal with the Word as a channel of grace. Doctrine had finally won out, and with it the appreciation of the minister as the apostle to the people, all the people. The trend, now observable in his thought, was away from the discrete church communities so neatly isolated from each other as had been the vision and the dream of the first strict Congregationalists. One step to its dismemberment was the erosion of the parochial appointment of ministers. A council was established which provided, in effect, an itinerant ministry. New missions were established for the Indians. Preaching of the response of the heart as well as the head to religion became common. Gradually, but unmistakably, the youth began to find religion as something more than a creed of paternalistic duties.

Stoddard's achievement was his pragmatic method of combining doctrine and discipline in response to changing social conditions. Ultimately, of course, he was a defender of doctrine over discipline, of heart over head, and in this respect his career is embued with the uncanny qualities of those, as Hegel once noted, who have stood at the crossroads of history. He was, simply, the right man at the right moment, a sensitive product of his society who sought to understand it and who was not afraid to minister to its maladies. His medicine, confided to his successor, finally erupted society's festering wound in the Great Awakening. No provincial pulpiteer, Stoddard sensed the cosmic magnitude of his mission when he noted the decline of Protestantism and the expansion of Catholicism. The new course for the Reformation, he felt, was neither a Protestant church devoid of two sacraments to all but the pure nor a Catholic cathedral replete with seven. The evolution of Christianity was at stake and now appeared ready for a new order, just as it had when Cotton had set foot in Boston in 1633. When Stoddard set foot in Northampton in 1669 a portal in God's plan was already opening.

Acknowledgments

Several individuals have been especially helpful in the preparation of this study, and my thanks to them: (Miss) Maureen Weinstock, Weymouth, Dorset; R. Sharpe France of the Lancashire Records Office; I. P. Collins, Somerset Records Office; (Mrs.) Jeanne Strong, Los Altos, Calif.; P. I. King, Northamptonshire Records Office; K. W. Newton, Essex Records Office; Anthony J. Camp, Society of Genealogists, London; William Joyce of the American Antiquarian Society; Ralph Lazzaro of Harvard Divinity School; Ralph Crandall of the New England Historic and Genealogical Society; Juliette Tomlinson and Ruth McIntyre of the Connecticut Valley Historical Museum; Robert Anderson of Harvard; Stanley Greenberg of the Forbes Library, Northampton; Winifred Collins and Aimee Bligh of the Massachusetts Historical Society; Marcia Dorey of Middleton Congregational Church; Professors Alan Heimert and George Huntston Williams of Harvard; Gerald Robertson Cragg and George Peck of Andover Newton Theological School; Dean Roland H. Moody and Albert M. Donley and my staff Ruth Eastman, Erna Lasman and Marianne Pfaff, of Northeastern University. To my mother, Edith, goes my appreciation for reviewing what seemed endless pages and to my wife, Hope, for daily encouragement and love.

RALPH J. COFFMAN

Marblehead, Massachusetts

Chronology

1643   Solomon Stoddard born on September 27 in Boston, Massachusetts, the second son of Anthony and Mary (Downing) Stoddard.

1647   Mary, his mother, dies on May 16. In August his father marries Barbara Clap.

1648 (ca.)   Enrolls in the elementary school in Boston.

1653   Enrolls in the Cambridge grammar school.

1655   Barbara, his first stepmother, dies on April 15.

1657   Father marries Christian Eyre.

1658   Enters Harvard College in September when he is not yet fifteen.

1662   July, graduates Bachelor of Arts and in September enrolls for the A.M.

1664   Writes a funeral elegy on the death of a friend, possibly Samuel Eliot, son of the Indian Apostle, John Eliot.

1665   Defends successfully a thesis with President Charles Chauncy on August 8 and graduates A.M.

1666   Appointed a Fellow of the college on November 25.

1667   Appointed Librarian of the college in March, but soon leaves Cambridge to be the chaplain to ex-Governor Searle of the Barbados, where he preaches to the dissenters for two years.

1669   Returns to Boston, prepares to sail for London, but is invited to preach at Northampton, Massachusetts, in November.

1670   Given a formal call to be pastor of the church in Northampton, which he does not accept immediately. On March 8 marries Esther (Warham) Mather of Windsor, Connecticut, the widow of his predecessor, Eleazer Mather.

1672   Accepts the call as pastor on February 7 and ordained on September 11 after having experienced his effectual calling. Adopts the Half-Way Covenant in November, but discontinues it six months later. Beginning of the first phase of career, that of a sacramentalist.

1673   Westfield church members, with Edward Taylor's backing, ask Stoddard to allow David Wilton to move to their town to help gather a church. Successfully resists losing Wilton, one of his staunchest supporters. The beginning of controversy between Stoddard and Taylor.

1675   As King Philip's War spreads, Stoddard succeeds in securing colonial troops to protect the towns of the Connecticut River Valley against the threat of Indian raids. Northampton embroiled in the Parsons-Bridgman witchcraft trial.

1677   November 5. Distinction between full and Half-Way church members ceases to be recorded at Northampton, marking the first revolution in American history.

1679   Stoddard and seventeen other ministers petition the General Court for an ecclesiastical synod. Stoddard submits his first public defense of "Stoddardeanism" at the Reforming Synod—"Nine Arguments against Examinations Concerning a Work of Grace before Admission to the Lord's Supper"—and is rebutted by Increase Mather's "Confutation." First religious awakening in Northampton.

1680   The Reforming Synod has its conclusions published, and Stoddard wins the victory of the day.

1683   Second religious awakening at Northampton; stepmother Christian dies.

1685   Delivers the Boston lecture June 21 on Gal. 5:17; June 26 dines with Sewall. *The Safety of Appearing* completed on October 19 and Increase Mather and Samuel Willard asked to write prefaces to it, but refuse.

1687   Anthony Stoddard dies in Boston as "the most ancientest shopkeeper in town." *The Safety of Appearing* published in Boston despite the opposition of the Mathers, and almost immediately Edward Taylor issues his criticisms of it.

1688   Stoddard replies to Taylor's criticisms.

1690   The Galatians sermon, "The Lord's Supper as a Converting Ordinance," preached on October 5, marking the mature period of Stoddardean sacramentalism, characterized by the doctrine of converting ordinances. Edward Taylor issues his "Animadversions" on Stoddard's sermon. The Cambridge Association formed to protect the Bay from Stoddard's ideas. Stoddard silent during the trial of four Indians at Northampton.

1696   Third religious awakening at Northampton.

1698   *The Tryal of Assurance.* On August 23 Sewall journeys to Northampton, lodges with Capt. Aaron Cooke and accompanies Stoddard the next day to hear Isaac Chauncy deliver a lecture at Hadley.

1699   The Reverend Benjamin Colman leads the Brattle Street Church in opposing the Mathers by drafting "A Manifesto."

1700   *The Doctrine of Instituted Churches* published in London after Increase Mather's *Order of the Gospel* is published in Boston. Benjamin Colman pens a witty reply to Mather in *The Gospel Order Revived.* Beginning of pamphlet war with Increase Mather. Beginning of the second phase of Stoddard's career—Pope of the instituted church.

1701   The Massachusetts General Court dismisses Increase Mather as the president of Harvard College and appoints the Reverend Samuel Willard of Boston as the vice-president and acting president. *The Necessity of Acknowledgement of Offences* preached at the July 3 lecture in Boston.

1703   *God's Frown in the Death of Useful Men* preached in January as the funeral sermon for Col. John Pynchon of Springfield and Northampton. At the Massachusetts General Court on May 26, *The Way for a People to Live* delivered. *The Sufficiency of One Good Sign* supposedly preached at the Boston lecture on May 30. Not one copy has survived.

1705   *The Danger of Speedy Degeneracy* preached to the General Court on July 5. A proposal for a Massachusetts ministerial association drafted at a meeting of clergy in August, but Stoddard fails to endorse it.

1706   The lecture at Boston preached by Stoddard on November 7.

1707   *The Inexcusableness of Neglecting the Worship of God* delivered to the Hampshire County Inferior Court on December 17. Simultaneously Governor Gurdon Saltonstall of Connecticut endorses the Saybrook Platform. On July 3 at Boston Stoddard preaches from Micah 1:5, "What is the Transgression of Jacob?" On July 8 Sewall journeys as far as Watertown with Stoddard on his return to Northampton.

1708   At the Boston lecture on July 8 *The Falseness of the Hopes of Many Professors* is delivered, at which Samuel Sewall is present. Stoddard returns home on July 12. Increase Mather answers the lecture in *A Dissertation.* In October the Saybrook Platform becomes law in Connecticut.

1709   *The Appeal to the Learned* published as a pointed refutation of Mather's *Dissertation*. This, in turn, is answered by Mather in *An Appeal of Some of the Unlearned.*

1710   On July 5 Stoddard and William Williams preach at Harvard commencement in Massachusetts Hall. Stoddard's stepmother Mary (Baker) (Savage) Stoddard dies at 7 A.M. on July 18.

1711   The Hampshire Association, based on Stoddard's *Doctrine*, is formed by Stoddard and the Reverend William Williams.

1712   The fourth religious awakening at Northampton. The Hampshire Association begins weekly lectures and an exchange of pulpits. *Those Taught by God the Father* delivered at the Boston lecture on July 3. Stoddard, William Williams and Ebenezer Pemberton dine with Samuel Sewall on July 5. On December 3, *The Efficacy of the Fear of Hell* preached to the Hampshire County Inferior Court at Northampton. Beginning of the Evangelical phase of Stoddard's career.

1713   Stoddard preaches at Harvard commencement in Massachusetts Hall on July 1. On July 2 preaches at the lecture in Boston. On July 5 offers a sermon for Samuel Sewall's son, Joseph.

1714   Increase Mather signals the death of his feud with Stoddard by offering to write a preface to the *Guide to Christ*. On July 2 Stoddard preaches in Boston, and on the tenth he and Simeon, his stepbrother, dine with Samuel Sewall. On July 13 Solomon takes a trip in his brother Simeon's coach.

1715   The Hampshire Association tries its first case. On September 1 Stoddard preaches the Boston lecture. Samuel Sewall present.

1716   On September 4, a Tuesday, Samuel Sewall travels to Northampton, spends two or three hours with Stoddard before dining with them. Stoddard accompanies Sewall as far as Pascomack on the way to Springfield.

1717   *Three Sermons Lately Preached*. On December 9 Samuel Sewall receives Stoddard's letter of condolence for Judith Sewall's illness. Sewall deeply touched.

1718   *The Presence of Christ* delivered on January 1 as the ordination sermon for Joseph Willard at Swampfield. On July 3 Stoddard preaches the Boston lecture, and on July 5 he dines with his nephew, the Reverend William Cooper, and Samuel Sewall. The fifth religious awakening at Northampton. *The Examination of the Power of Fraternity. The Duty of Gospel Ministers* delivered as the Brookfield ordination sermon on October 16 for Thomas Cheney.

1719   *The Way to Know Sincerity* delivered at the Boston lecture on July 2 and appended to *A Treatise Concerning Conversion*, reprinted in 1735 as *The Nature of Saving Conversion*. Samuel Hall, a Yale graduate and divinity student, goes to Northampton to study for the ministry under Stoddard.

1720   Fifty-eight sermons (September 1719 to May 1720), preached by Stoddard and recorded by Warham Williams in his notebook. Later, Williams will emulate their style.

1722   *An Answer to Some Cases of Conscience* indicates Stoddard's Evangelical attitude to Indian missions.

1723   The Reverend Salmon Treat, minister of Preston, Connecticut, solicits a sermon preached on May 19, *Defects of Preachers Reproved*, for publication at New London. On August 9, Stoddard's last publication issued, *Question: Whether God is Not Angry*. On August 23 Increase Mather dies.

1725   Israel Chauncy chosen as Stoddard's assistant in December but leaves by the following August.

1726   Jonathan Edwards, Stoddard's grandson, invited to preach for the month of August as a trial period. On November 21 he is given a "call" by the church.

1727   The Reverend John Williams preaches at Edwards's ordination on February 22.

1728   Edwards preaches "The Excellency of Christ" showing that the tension in Stoddard's thought between reflection and action was basic to his own.

1729   Stoddard dies February 11 at the age of eighty-six. William Williams, his son-in-law, preaches the funeral sermon at Northampton. At Harvard commencement in July Benjamin Colman presides over memorial services.

CHAPTER 1

Puritan Pronaos

I Genesis

SOLOMON Stoddard was born into an extensive network of Puritan families, conditioning the environment in which he was reared, and this provides one vantage point for viewing the significance of his later achievement. His mother, Mary, was the daughter of lawyer Emanuel Downing and Anne Ware, whose father was the secretary of the Irish dominion. In 1620, when Mary was born, the Downings lived on Castle Street, Dublin, near Anne's father, Sir James, with whom Emanuel was an associate. After Mary's mother died in 1621, the Downings returned to Suffolk County, England, where Emanuel married John Winthrop's sister, Lucy, in April 1622, at Groton Manor. Emanuel continued his preparation for the bar in Dublin and settled with his family in London in 1625 as a lawyer of the Inner Temple and attorney of the Court of Wards with his brother-in-law, John Winthrop. Together, these men and their families assumed leading roles in militant Puritan activities. In 1633 Mary and her sister Susan emigrated with Governor William Coddington to Boston, Massachusetts, where she was accepted immediately as a church member.[1]

Living with the Winthrops in Boston, Mary revealed an individualism which her son Solomon would also exhibit. In an age in which marriages were often contracted by gentry families, Mary, a "lusty, strong woman," longed to marry for love. Although her stepmother had sought to encourage engagement with eligible Boston youths, Mary resisted, pleading to her father on November 27, 1635, that she did "earnestly desire to submit [herself] in all duty and obedience" to her parents' wishes, "but I desire to await upon him that can change my heart at his Will. . . ." Four years later Mary finally met the right man.[2]

Anthony Stoddard, a wealthy linen draper from St. Michael Le Quern, London, arrived in Boston in the spring of 1639. His economic status and his religious convictions immediately marked him for leadership positions in the town, but acceptance into the community was not automatic. First, he was admitted as an inhabitant of Boston by the selectmen on August 26, 1639. Then, a month later, the Reverend John Cotton examined his state of religion, and he was approved to be a member of the church, and he was granted land by the town. The following May he became a freeman, after taking an oath of allegiance to the colony. During this period Anthony Stoddard and Mary Downing were married. Their first child, Benjamin, was baptized by the Reverend John Cotton on August 23, 1640.[3]

Although Anthony had married into a prominent gentry family and was financially self-sufficient, he was also a merchant at a time when the mercantile image had been tarnished by scandal. When he set foot on Boston soil, he the reverberations of the Antinomian controversy were still discernible in the chill harbor air. Antinomianism, a precursor of Quakerism, denied that civil or moral laws applied to individuals possessed with Inner Light. Some Boston merchants rallied to this religion of Anne Hutchinson, a middle-aged follower of John Cotton, because being exempt from law they could charge prices higher than the magistrates would allow. Consumer opposition to this abuse was sharpened by a period of spiraling inflation, while ministers and magistrates considered Antinomianism a threat to their authority. In a series of church and court trials, the Inner-Light leaders, including Anne Hutchinson, were excommunicated and banished, and several of their followers voluntarily exiled themselves. Even in their disgrace these *laissez-faire* merchants prospered; many doubled their landholdings and became the new ruling elite of Rhode Island.[4]

The Bay was not rid of controversy, however. In 1639 Robert Keayne, a forty-four-year-old freeman of the London Merchant Tailor's Guild, received a damaged shipment from London in his Boston shop on Cornhill. To recoup losses he inflated the retail price of some house nails to twopence over their actual value. When the magistrates discovered this markup, he was judged an Antinomian and fined £200, and the church threatened excommunication even though he had been a loyal member.[5]

When Anthony Stoddard was appointed constable, the stage was set for his own trial by fire. In September 1641 twenty-year-old Francis Hutchinson, son of Antinomian Anne, distraught by the banishment of his mother and her recent massacre by the Pequots, publicly castigated the Boston church as a "strumpet" for its autonomy in passing such harsh sentences and its lack of concern for Evangelicalism. The Reverend John Wilson, pastor of the church, excommunicated him and the Court of Assistants imposed a fine of £50 and banishment. Francis defaulted on the fine, and Governor Winthrop, disturbed by the possibility that Francis would arouse popular sympathy, charged Constable Stoddard with his arrest.[6]

Anthony hesitated and attempted to have the case turned over to the Boston elders, arguing that it was injudicious of the state to deal "with a member of the church before the church had proceeded with him." He felt that Francis was young to have suffered the loss of his mother, especially in such circumstances, and that his reaction in church could be viewed as an expression of grief. Certainly, Stoddard reasoned, heresy was more in the province of ecclesiastical censure than in the jurisdiction of civil law. The magistrates did not share Anthony's opinions because they saw Hutchinson's actions as a threat to the order of society: they fined Stoddard 13⅓ s. for having challenged their authority. Church and state were so intimately bound together in early Boston that censure in one entailed, almost automatically, censure in the other. Therefore, Anthony was brought before a disciplinary meeting of the Boston congregation, where he "freely and very affectionately" confessed "his error and contempt of authority." This recantation did not end the magistrates' surveillance of his activities, however, and within two years he was brought before the Quarterly Court on charges of usury "for selling cloth at an excessive rate." Although tried and acquitted, never did he reveal that he had ever been intimidated by the government. Indeed, Anthony's son, Solomon, would follow a complementary career in opposing the rigid code of Massachusetts orthodoxy.[7]

On September 27, 1643, when Solomon was born, conflict and controversy were woven into the very fabric of his home life, and his youth was punctuated by the duties of tribal religion: family prayers and Bible-reading, catechetical training, and parental and civil obedience in which the Fifth Commandment's exhortation was broadened to include honoring "All . . . superiours, whether in family, school, church or commonwealth."[8]

Anthony Stoddard's position in the community continued to improve, despite the loss of his wife, Mary, in June 1647, six months after he had been chosen as selectman of Boston. Anthony was an eminently practical man who was not content to leave his family motherless for long; in less than three months he married the wealthy widow Barbara (Clap) Weld. Barbara, one of the Puritan Claps of Devonshire who had connections with the moderate Puritan Dorchester Company, had emigrated in 1633 with sister Susan and uncle Edward from Selcomb Regis, a small coastal town twelve miles from Exeter, where the Reverend John Warham had lectured. Admitted to Warham's church in new Dorchester in 1636, she subsequently married Joseph Weld, a prominent Roxbury merchant, by whom she had a son, Daniel, and two daughters. Barbara, like her second husband, was an outspoken critic of the magistrates' decisions and was not afraid to go on record for her beliefs. Anthony's second marriage to another well-connected Puritan family provided him with an additional set of relationships which only further enhanced his position in the Bay.[9]

In 1648 Solomon and Daniel entered the Boston elementary school, which had been founded to protect the literacy of the second generation without which "that old deluder, Satan" would have kept "men from the knowledge of Scriptures." The selectmen of each town had been ordered by the General Court to provide facilities whereby male children could learn to "read and understand the principles of religion and the capital laws of this country."[10]

In Puritan Boston the elementary school was devoted to inculcating religion, and each pupil, young Solomon Stoddard included, was required to recite the fundamentals of faith before his classmates:

> Question: What is the resurrection from the dead which was sealed up to you in baptism?
> Answer: When Christ shall come to His Last Judgement.
> Question: What is the last Judgement which is sealed up to you in the Lord's Supper?
> Answer: At the last day we shall all appear before the judgement seat of Christ . . . and . . . receive an reward. . . .
> Question: What is the reward that shall then be given?
> Answer: The righteous shall go to life eternal and the wicked shall be cast into everlasting fire with the devil and his angels.[11]

The terrors of the unconverted state as the Reverend John Cotton exposed them to tender minds must have been strong *Milk for Babes*, indeed, and the catechism probably made a lasting impression on Solomon. As he gradually matured, he failed, as did most of his friends, and all of his brothers and sisters, to give a relation of his religious experiences to the Boston congregation. Throughout their youth the Stoddard children, although part of a Puritan dynasty in the Bay, never took communion with their parents. Understandably, the Lord's Supper became somewhat of a terrifying obstacle.

The Boston elementary school, convinced that Solomon should be promoted, graduated him in 1653. Instead of attending Boston grammar school, he was sent to board at Elijah Corlet's in Cambridge, considered to be superior.

Forty-three-year-old Corlet, son of a London chandler, had matriculated at Lincoln College, Oxford, had been ordained a deacon, and had graduated subsequently Master of Arts from Puritan Cambridge. While enrolled there he served as schoolmaster at Framlingham, Suffolk, and at Halstead, Essex, in which posts he undoubtedly taught the children of New England emigrants. When he finally emigrated to new Cambridge and established a grammar school on Water (now Dunster) Street, his reputation, therefore, preceded him, and in September 1642 he was formally commended by the government "for his abilities, dexterity and painfulness in teaching and education of the youth under him." Secure in this position, he married Rebecca Cutter, the daughter of a Newcastle merchant, and had three children by the time Solomon became his pupil.[12]

II *Anthony Stoddard and Moderate Congregationalism*

In 1651 parental anxiety intensified for offspring who had not established their godly role in the community by becoming members of the churches and citizens of the colony. The Platform of 1648 had hardened the distinction between those merely in a state of education and those in a state of grace, and in 1651 the General Court endorsed a six-year-old confession of faith which refused leniency in admitting children of church members to communion. This was the second phase of a controversy which had begun in 1634, and Anthony Stoddard became embroiled in it, as all of his own children were counted now among the unregenerate.

In 1634 the Reverend John Cotton, taking his cue from the Rev-

erend Hugh Peter of Rotterdam, had institutionalized a test for
regenerate church membership in new Boston and made it the basis
of civil enfranchisement. Henceforth in Massachusetts Bay, church
membership was essential to becoming a citizen of the colony. This
variety of urban conventicle Puritanism, "strict Congregationalism," clashed with the moderate Puritanism of the boroughs
such as Norwich, Springfield, Dorchester, and Exeter, which followed the example of the Reverend John White, the leader of the
Dorchester Company. White had employed a catechism of
"Ten Vows" in his Dorchester, Dorset, church in 1628 as a means of
conversion. He requested all parishioners to assent to his baptismal
"Vows" before taking the Lord's Supper. Hugh Peter used White's
"Vows," however, to exclude the unworthy from his Rotterdam
Congregation in 1633, and John Cotton set a similar test for regen-
eration in 1634 with the added dimension that citizenship in the
holy commonwealth also depended on it. Dissent split the colony.
In 1635 a Norfolk group under the Reverend Peter Hobart left
Charlestown and founded Hingham, where no religious test was
required for citizenship or church membership. Similarly, in 1636
the Reverends Thomas Hooker of Cambridge and John Warham of
Dorchester founded Connecticut Colony, where the prerequisite of
church membership was rejected and men were enfranchised by the
vote of the freemen. Hooker, a native of Chelmsford, Essex, had
connections with the moderate Puritan Braintree Company; and
Warham, the lecturer of Exeter, Devon, had connections with the
moderate Puritan Dorchester Company, as we have seen.

At the heart of the Hooker-Cotton controversy was the theology
of preparation and conversion. Because Puritans distrusted the
emotions (in contradistinction to Catholic theologians), many maintained that man's whole personality had to be remade through
stages of preparation before conversion. Thomas Hooker accepted
the logic of the morphology of preparation, but at the same time
denied the absolute identification of true conversion. John Cotton,
unlike Hooker, rejected sequence in the order of salvation and instead preached spiritual ecstasy, which envisioned that faith and
justification coincided and that conversion was a cataclysmic interior
event that did not necessarily correspond to outward marks of
sanctification. However, because Cotton believed that the success
of the church's mission in New England depended on its purity, he
had instituted his test for conversion, an order of discipline basically

inconsistent with his doctrine. Hooker totally rejected Cotton's incongruous combination of discipline and doctrine: the created faculties should be focused "upon God in the use of the means" of grace, but salvation was a supernatural act and it was folly to predicate citizenship in a commonwealth on a presumptive test of God's work. Thus, moderate Puritans invaded the Connecticut River Valley from the north and east.

Preeminent among Valley pioneers was William Pynchon, Jr., one of the three original petitioners for the settlement of Northampton. His English roots reveal important clues about the political and religious posture of western Massachusetts settlers, as they would affect Stoddard and his family. Born in 1590, Pynchon was the elder son of a landed gentleman who owned property in Springfield, Essex, not far from Chelmsford, where Thomas Hooker lectured. The Pynchon family was modestly wealthy, and through kinsman Sir Edward Pynchon of Writtle Manor, in addition to their own lands, two farms were leased to them which increased their annual income. Through Lady Elizabeth Pynchon Weston, a first cousin, who was the wife of Sir Richard Weston, a court official of James I who later became the Earl of Portland, the Pynchons of Springfield had connections with peers and the royal courts. When William's father died in 1610, William Jr. became heir to the Springfield holdings, sharing the interest in the properties at Writtle, Roxwell, Broomfield, and Chignall with his brother, Peter, and six sisters. The magnitude of the annual income from these lands can be estimated from the property in Broomfield, of which William was requested to set aside £93 annually for his brother and six sisters.

Although Pynchon did not formally matriculate at his father's alma mater, New College, Oxford, he did have connections with members of the college who frequented Essex County. Foremost of these was none other than the Reverend John White, who had gone down to New College with William, Sr. White's nephew, Josias, held a farm at Roxwell near the Pynchons', and through a continuing relationship between the Whites and the Pynchons, William nurtured a militant moderate Puritanism. In 1620 and 1624 he served as church warden. This was supposedly the local post representing the bishop, and hence he had been responsible for reporting irregularities in the diocese, such as nonconformist offenses to the Canons of the church. Perhaps because he joined the militantly Puritan Massachusetts Bay Company in 1628 and simultaneously refused to pay the lay subsidy of Charles I levied on him by Parliament, he was not reappointed as warden, for his true religious allegiances had been exposed.

Pynchon was not to be intimidated either by bishop or king and certainly not by the governor of Massachusetts. Sympathetic to White's moderate Puritanism, he came to the rescue of two neighbors from Roxwell, John and Samuel Browne, charged by Governor John Endicott, a strict Congregationalist, with being "factious" and unsound in their worship at Salem. The Brownes had protested discontinuance of the Book of Common Prayer and resisted signing the church convenant, so they were deported to London, where they were submitted to the arbitration of the Massachusetts Bay Company. Immediately the Brownes enlisted Pynchon's support, to no avail, however. They lost their case.

Pynchon was, above all, a practical man. In 1630 he emigrated to Roxbury, helped found the church, and established fur trade with the Maine coastal Indians. By 1634 he averaged four hundred pounds of beaver pelts annually. Although he was away from his home most of the year, his Roxbury land was still taxed, unfairly, he thought, and he refused payment. Nor did he much like covenant religion and Cotton's Code as it had just been imposed. Simultaneously with Hooker's migration to Connecticut, Pynchon moved to Springfield. Recalcitrance to strict Congregationalism persisted, and in 1650 his book, *The Meritorious Price of Our Redemption*, challenged the religious basis of citizenship that was law in Massachusetts. In the same year he was one of the three who petitioned the General Court to settle Northampton, a few miles upstream from Springfield on the Connecticut River. He was successful, but when his book was condemned by the General Court and all known copies were burned on Boston Common, he was forced out of the colony. He returned to Writtle manor, leaving the fur trade and two secret copies of his book to his son, John.[13]

Some, in Boston, appreciated Pynchon's moderate Puritanism, and among these was Anthony Stoddard, who objected to the Court's harsh treatment of him. Religion and politics should be kept separate, he argued. Church censure was one thing, sedition was another. His plea fell on deaf ears. Anthony was jailed for insolence to the governor even though by this time the merchant was one of the most prominent men in Boston: his estate was now worth in excess of £1,000 and he had held the position of deputy and selectman for several terms. However, his independent attitude displayed in the candid criticism he aimed at the government cost him power in the community. He lost the post of deputy.

Anthony Stoddard's opposition to Massachusetts' strict Congregational government was, therefore, a basic ingredient in the household atmosphere in which Solomon was raised. Stoddard considered himself an entrepreneur like Pynchon and both had the same attitude to the separation of church and state. Both felt there were issues which were only ecclesiastical and which had no political relevance. Of course their ideas were opposed by strict Congregationalists—but young Solomon would follow his father's footsteps.

III   *Honor First and Reason Rule*

In 1655, shortly after the death of Barbara (Clay) (Weld) Stoddard, Anthony took as his next wife twenty-seven-year-old Christian Eyre. This marriage was as financially successful as his two earlier ones. In England, Christian had lived a comfortable life on her father's estate, which comprised two houses, a stable, gardens, and an orchard. When she emigrated to Watertown in 1635, Dr. Simon Eyre, a surgeon, immediately established his prominence in the community by becoming a selectman, a representative, and a town clerk. Soon after Christian married, she received her portion of her father's estate and was due to inherit a sizable portion of the estate of her mother's brother, William Paine, a Boston merchant. Solomon, through this marriage, gained another set of connections with Boston gentry and seven brothers and sisters.[14]

In 1658, three years after his father's third marriage, Solomon was "judged ripe" for college by Master Corlet, and matriculated at Harvard that fall, joining his stepbrother Daniel, now a sophomore. The requirements for admission were fluency in Latin (in which all classes were taught), reading knowledge of Greek, and "skill in making verse;" but the main thrust of higher education was "to know God and Jesus Christ and answerably to lead an honest, sober and godly life."[15]

The course of study was not only rigorous but also rigid:

In the first year after admission for four days of the week all Students shall be exercised in the Study of the Greek and Hebrew Tongues, only beginning Logic in the morning towards the latter part of the Year unless the

Tutor shall see cause by reason of their ripeness in the Languages to read logic sooner. Also they shall spend the second year in logic with the exercise of the former languages, and the third year in the principles of ethics and the fourth in metaphysics and mathematics still carrying on their former studies of the week for rhetoric, oratory, and divinity.[16]

Judging from Stoddard's library the college syllabus can be reconstructed, which reveals, in part, the ways in which his mind was shaped during these years.[17]

The eclectic climate of Harvard's curriculum had been established in 1655 by President Charles Chauncy, Professor Emeritus of Trinity College, Cambridge. As an eminent Hebraist and Classical scholar, Chauncy believed that "All truth, whosoever it be that speaks it, comes from the God of Truth. Who can deny that there are found many excellent and divine moral truths in Plato, Aristotle, Plutarch, Seneca, etc.; and to condemn all pel-mel will be an hard censure. . . . If one abolishes all the learning that the heathen men have uttered out of the light of nature, it will be a great oversight." It became a dictum at the college that the Classical tradition was a satisfactory handmaiden to the Scriptures. The rich panoply of ancient myths provided a luxurious complement to biblical typology, and New England Puritans soon began to amalgamate Classical myth and Scripture types in their formulation of that first American dream—the errand of the faithful remnant into the vast western wilderness. Thus, Nathaniel Ward depicted his Simple Cobbler of Agawam as a mighty hero battling the fierce demons of the heretical underworld such as the Anabaptist-Potamides, the Erastian-Dryades, and the Seeker-Heliconiades. Even such practical pioneers as Captain Edward Johnson Chronicled the Great Migration as a flight of more than mortal beings from a once godly kingdom now ruled by "proud prelates whose Pythagorean philosophy" of unjust rule" "caused the king to lose his life." Steeped in the classical tradition, Stoddard learned those two vast compendia of ancient lore, the *Iliad* and the *Odyssey*, the powerful rhetoric of Isocrates, and the Greek florilegia collected by Reusner. Cicero's *De Officiis*, so highly praised by the German reformer Philip Melancthon, continued to be regarded as one of the bulwarks of Christianity on almost the same level as Augustine's *City of God*. However, the Cicero known to Stoddard was not the advocate of democracy who espoused that the consensus of all was the natural voice of the nation, but rather, it was the righteous citizen of the *Sententiae* who merely praised the virtues of the good man. Similarly, Ovid's *Metamorphoses* was filtered through Scripture and anything objectionable to the Puritan commonwealth was omitted. For instance, the creation story in *Metamorphoses* when blended with Isaiah 40 produced the motto of a 1664 Boston calendar: "Though all other animals are prone and fix their gaze upon earth, He gave to man an uplifted face, and bade him stand erect and turn his eyes to heaven." The Horatian epistles, similarly, were viewed as providing a genial reiteration of a Puritan's expected code of behavior. Already, in this colonial curriculum, one notices how the rationalistic, disciplinarian basis of strict Congregationalism was becoming mere moralism.[18]

The logic studied at Harvard midcentury, although preserving Burgersdijk's Scholasticism, reflected the influence of Peter Ramus, the French Plato, who believed that the world was filled with the ordered hierarchy of eternal ideas, and that a logic, of dichotomies correctly applied, could reveal the structure of ideas by a method called "rhetorical invention." As a Christian Platonist, Ramus believed that ideas were *a priori* to human thought and both Scripture and nature embodied them. Whereas an Aristotelian scholastic might argue in syllogistic form "All A is B; C is A: Therefore C is B," a Ramist would appeal to Scripture in the *middle term:* "C is either B or not-B; *but not-B contradicts the Bible:* Therefore C is B." Because of this account-book presentation of knowledge, Ramism won a favored position in the schools of Protestant merchants in Europe, and among Puritans in old and New England.[19]

Since Ramism reduced rhetoric to logic, it was extremely compatible with the Puritan plain style of preaching, and Stoddard studied Alsted, Heerebort, Makilmenaens, Talon and Dudley Fenner. While scholastic logic demanded that a lecture or sermon begin with a definition, "rhetorical invention" started with a proposition of an *a priori* truth. This was divided into a few lesser heads so that the general truth could be more readily comprehended, and finally the sense was made plain through familiar examples. This method, by always proceeding from the most to the least general, insured that every man not only could understand but also could remember the structure of a preacher's argument. Stoddard would use this technique of outlining his own sermons by first sketching the main points of doctrine and then supplying the particular illustrations.[20]

During his junior and senior years, Solomon began his study of ethics, metaphysics, and mathematics. Ethics was really casuistry, the art of applying moral judgments to one's actions. For Solomon, the casuist *par excellence* was the Reverend Doctor William Ames, professor of theology at Franeker, who had inspired the militant Puritanism of the Massachusetts Bay Company in London. His study of metaphysics included not only Augustine, Aquinas, and Suarez but also Calvin, Makowski, Cocceius, Ursinus, and a host of polemicists such as Parker, Hommius, and Vossius. Just as he learned from Keckerman. Arnold, Norton, Rivet, and Grotius that Reformed thought lacked uniformity, even in covenant theology and church government, so too did he learn that the Copernican view of a heliocentric universe (first taught at Harvard in his sophomore year) was opposed by both Protestants and Catholics alike. Similarly, faculty psychology which had traditionally regarded man as composed of unconnected faculties, was taught alongside Descartes' theory that the act of thinking was linked to the state of being (I think, therefore I am) which permitted a more integrated view of emotion and reason in the human personality. The undergraduate education Stoddard received, therefore, reflected a changing worldview in which an outworn neoscholasticism was juxtaposed with a new Cartesian view of man espoused by Digby and White and a Copernican view of the universe espoused by Heylyn. This Harvard education established the basic tension in his thought between the head and the heart, discipline and doctrine.[21]

Moreover, this tension was reinforced by his delayed maturity. All the Stoddard children were outside the church, and in 1657 the first overtures were made to extend the discipline of the church to all baptized children. Stoddard's father objected because he realized this sealed the second-class status of his son in the eyes of society, but to no avail. Then, in 1661, ministers John Norton (John Cotton's successor) and John Wilson proposed to extend the covenant to all baptized adult children, and "a great willingness appeared both in youth, maids, men and women" as they "did openly manifest their desire to acknowledge their relation to the church according to the covenant of God which they plighted in their parents." Anthony Stoddard and Edward Hutchinson opposed this development, not because they opposed broadening the admissions policy of the church, but because they realized that the Half-Way Covenant preserved second-class citizenship for their children. Yet, many disagreed with Anthony. As most of the second generation failed in becoming church members like their parents, many hoped that a special status could be reserved for them. Strict Congregationalists like Increase Mather upheld the value of a relation of one's conversion experience as proof of visible sainthood. They supported a Half-Way membership for righteous children of those who had been baptized as infants but who had not become members themselves, because it excluded them from full communion and thereby protected the purity of the church. Moderates like Jonathan Mitchell, Stoddard's tutor at Harvard, felt that some individuals who had been baptized in their infancy possessed saving faith even though they were unable to express their experience to the church or minister, and Half-Way membership would at least allow them and their children to be under the church's discipline.[22]

Solomon graduated A.B. in June 1662, just as the Half-Way Synod was making it possible for baptized and righteous individuals to confer their status to their children. Solomon was probably aware that the effects of the decision were far from liberalizing, since it formally acknowledged two classes of citizens, the enfranchised full members and the nonenfranchised Half-Way members. He did not pursue Half-Way status himself. In Connecticut, for instance, the problem was less dramatic, since men were enfranchised irrespective of their religious affiliation.[23]

When Solomon enrolled for the A.M. in the fall of 1662, ostensibly he had chosen a career in the ministry, and this was reflected by his great earnestness in studying "divinity" under tutor Mitchell. Although he had listened to him preach in the Old College for four years past and for four years he had heard him coax and constrain him to "Lie in the way of the Spirit in the use of *the means*," Stoddard remained one of the unregenerate. His spiritual condition weighed heavily on his mind as he began his next three years of study, for it reflected his failure to achieve maturity.

Mitchell was an excellent instructor who was dedicated to encouraging young men in the ministry. He had developed a "Model for the Maintaining of Students and Fellows of Choice Abilities" and he considered Stoddard one of these students who could cope with "difficulty, hardship, and self-denial." Well aware that "God will not give us such men by miracle," he worked his students hard. Solomon measured up to these expectations. He was attentive and conscientious and every word his tutor preached he recorded, reflected on, and remembered. He also used his father's money to buy books that Master Mitchell recommended. Books were a dear commodity at Harvard, but Anthony was generous: the price of only nineteen of these books that Solomon recorded was £8 13s., nearly half a year's tuition, room, and board.

Mitchell, a free spirit in an age when orthodoxy ruled the Bay, was one of the few New England ministers who encouraged "the institution of all ordinances for the conveying of grace (Matt. 28:18)." Mitchell had developed this view from reading Erastus, Prynne, Humphrey, and Cameron—Solomon followed in his footsteps. Thomas Erastus (1524–1583), the first Englishman to advocate the theory that sacraments could induce grace, was followed by John Cameron (1579–1625), the Scottish minister of the Protestant church of Bordeaux, who developed a theory of hypothetical universalism that held although Christ died for the elect, only those who actively believe will be saved. Alluding to Plato's allegory of the cave, Cameron quipped that although the sun may shine on all men, those who close their eyes are blind to its light. William Prynne (1600–1669), the Independent, added to Erastus' theory by distinguishing two varieties of conversion, one related to rational assent, the other related to participation in the sacraments, and John Humphrey, a Somersetshire nonconformist, went so far as to advocate "free admission" to the Lord's Supper for any righteous person: "want of grace" should be no "hindrance to communion."[24]

Jonathan Mitchell not only included these theologians in the regimen for study of divinity each Saturday at Harvard, but also incorporated their thoughts and rhetoric into his own eclectic sermons to Solomon and his classmates. Thus, he echoed his English colleagues when he likened the Lord's Supper to "a door of safety":

It is the summary message of the Gospel to come in His name. 'Tis the duty of you that do [believe], to renew your belief and of them that never believed now to begin.

With what are we vivified? 1. 'Tis a feast we are invited to. Luke 14:16, 17, 22. 2. The invitation to the feast is taken kindly. . . . Think but of the wrath of . . . Satan, the guilt of thy own conscience. *Why now Christ open a door to safety.* 3. . . . What, you that are invited? Why, we are helpless, vile creatures, as vile as sin can [be unli]ke you."[25]

This sermon, and others that Solomon actually recorded, made such a lasting impression that he later entitled one of his works *The*

Safety of Appearing in Christ's Righteousness in emulation of the ideas he had learned from his tutor.

It is understandable how a young student at the infant college on the Charles could have become enamored of open communion and, indeed, of an open community, at a time when church and colony were divided over the protection of institutional purity—not the chief end of religion or politics as Mitchell taught. In his college notebook young Solomon reflected. He had just learned Empedocles' paradox, God is like a circle whose center is everywhere and whose circumference is nowhere. How like it was to Descartes' principle of *concursus Dei*, which claimed that every action in the world is caused by the immediate action of God. Perhaps God had not retreated from creation as the jeremiads claimed. Perhaps, He only operated in mysterious ways. Man should reflect on the mystery of creation and not try to understand the unknowable. Affection, not reason, was the key to religion. "Considered in themselves," Solomon cautioned, the affections "have always an incomplete, imperfect act of the will or volition, joined with them," but considered as an object of God's love, "they are something that lies between a firm purpose of the soul and the execution of that purpose." Since Christ was the fusion of the timeless Logos and mutable flesh ("the Word was made flesh not by alteration but by union") only Christ has the power "to forgive sins as mediator." Natural affections are incapable of perceiving this truth because they "are necessarily accompanied with change and mutability," but religious affections, which have as their object the immutable, are "in God." Man has a "distinct communion" with God revealed "in our religious approach to Him," either by calling "on the name of Christ" or on the father in his name.[26]

Like Cameron, Stoddard indicated that "all graces are alike absolutely purchased for us but not alike absolutely received by us." The will remains absolutely free to choose the good. "The first grace is bestowed upon us absolutely & without condition, and this grace is the condition of the following priviledges as to the order of communication. . . . The elect, before they believe, have a right to what Christ purchased for them *ex foedere Dei et Christi* [out of the covenant of God and Christ] but not a subjective personal right or right which is actionable." In other words, men have no control over their election, which was antecedent to "the purchase of faith by us," but if they are in a potential state of election it is up to them to make the choice. Thus, Stoddard studied the results of the Synod of Dort of 1611 and sided with those who stood against double predestination. While an individual might have been chosen to election, he believed (with Cameron) that there was also a requirement to actualize his potentiality. He cautioned that "we must carefully distinguish between the covenant between the father and the son," which was totally unconditional, and the covenant of grace and mercy confirmed to the elect, which required man's involvement.

Ecclesiology, or the government of the church, was another aspect of "divinity" at Harvard and Mitchell once again opened the gates to unusual paths for Solomon. As one of the first assignments Solomon was required to read Samuel Rutherford, a prominent Scottish Presbyterian who espoused the national comprehensiveness of the church, a position diametrically opposed to Massachusetts' Congregational autonomy and exclusiveness. Rutherford had defended Scottish Presbyterianism against John Cotton in several polemical tracts, maintaining that authority did not rest in particular congregations, but in the national church from which it devolved to presbyters and elders. Solomon read the arguments and judged them to have a certain merit. Rutherford also objected to the Massachusetts practice of limiting church membership and freemanship to the visible saints. Stoddard's familiarity with this noted Scottish theologian and his supporter, Daniel Cawdry, provided him with a broad background from which to select those elements which later would form the platform of his own eclectic citadel.[27]

IV   An Elegy (1664)

The tension between the natural and the converted state plagued Solomon's decision to become a preacher in the Bay Colony, and as the summer of 1664 passed he realized he would have to begin his first ministerial duties without ever having been accepted into a church in Massachusetts. Of course, to a Puritan there was always a necessary doubt that one had faith, and even the most obvious visible saint did not take election for granted, for, in truth, there was no way to certainty: the best clue to assurance was doubt. The Puritan view of death reflected this uncertainty: death was both a punishment and a reward, darkness for the damned and release for the regenerate. At death Puritans were humbled at the awesome prospect of damnation even though, like Increase Mather, they may have earlier envisioned that death was deliverance from the harsh New England existence.

Not far into the fall term on November 1, 1664, Solomon's friend Samuel Eliot died—"A most lovely young man eminent for learning and goodness, a fellow of the College and a candidate for the ministry." In remembrance of his friend, the son of John Eliot, the Indian missionary, Stoddard offered a panegyric in his college notebook (see Appendix 1) which reflected the tension in a soul that quested after salvation but failed in achieving any assurance. For this reason, it is a crucial document in understanding young Stoddard's spiritual nightmare. Superficially, it appeared to emulate standard elegiac form and content. The Puritan practice of commemorating dead heroes in funeral elegies illustrates how praise of esteemed qualities both reinforced and promoted community ethical awareness. Solomon, as a student of Ramus, knew that poetry was "not distinct art by itself", but depended on logic. Since logic in a poem, as in a sermon, should reflect the order of creation and the history of redemption, elegies depicted and racapitulated one's spiritual growth from preparation to salvation: vocation to justification, adoption, sanctification, and glorification—this was the broad framework on which the fabric of the Puritan elegiac genre was stretched and painted—the great drama of salvation. Elegiac style, unlike the plain style used in sermons, permitted classical allusions and rhetorical devices to support biblical texts; indeed, often classical examples were used as parallels to Scriptural "types." Just as the Old Testament events and characters prefigured their New Testament fulfillments, so too Graeco-Roman *exempla* adumbrated their Scriptural counterparts.[28]

The rhyming couplets of the poem were crude, often imperfect, and the rhyme scheme was formless, even though some rhymes were repeated (11. 1–2, 31–32; 13–14, 15–16, 19–20; 27–28, 33–34). The meter was also uneven and mixed. Stoddard depicted the qualities of the deceased in generalities with which no Puritan would have disagreed: the hero was of considerable "worth" (1. 6), unmarried (1. 12), virtuous (1. 16), a patron of learning (1. 22), too youthful to have died (1. 23), with an active, keen mind (11. 33–34). If one compares these qualities with those that Daniel Gookin selected to describe Samuel Eliot, little difference is apparent. Gookin said he "gave abundant demonstration of his piety, gravity, and excellent temper." Similarly, Cotton Mather, in speaking of Eliot, said he was "a most lovely young man, eminent for learning and goodness. . . ."[29]

However, if we look to the praise of the hero's spiritual qualities, a difference between Stoddard's encomium and others, such as the Reverend John Wilson's 1663 lament for John Norton, the pastor of the Boston church, is noticeable. While both shift from bereavement to joy, Wilson used the tonal change to elucidate Norton's elect state;

> Nothing, but things at Gods right hand,
>   and heavenly Mansions
> Was in his thoughts, at home, abroad,
>   breath'd in's expressions.[30]

whereas Stoddard suggested that "the prize" of being heaven-born was attributable to both divine election and natural abilities:

> He was the darling of the graces light,
> both learning's patron and her favorite. (11. 21–22)

The three graces bestowing rewards on the good citizen recalled the Renaissance humanist idea of immortality. Furthermore, it was not Satan who was depicted as "the worst of fiends" but Circe, Ulysses' sorcerer enchantress. In Stoddard's early elegy a Homeric worldview and ethos nearly replaced Puritan belief and ritual:

> His years soon sold o're yet in them he gat,
> the basis of a never fading state,
> his heaven born soul aspiring him unto,
> who gave it rise & leaving earth below,
> ascends those heavenly mansions of above
> to eternity and renders earth his due. (11. 23–28)

Stoddard completed his paeon of grief without one Scriptural example, which places his poem in an unusual position within the Puritan elegiac tradition. While the classical context within which he constructed the encomium had an implicit Christian translation (the graces were God's grace, Circe was the devil, and the prize was salvation), it is significant that Stoddard, unlike John Wilson, for example, did not make these identifications patent. Did this reflect his continuing spiritual anguish and failure to become a member of the Boston Church?[31]

V   Tripos Verse *(1665)*

Before being granted the master's degree by President Charles Chauncy on August 8, 1665, Solomon and the other candidates were required to defend a "question in philosophy" that they had chosen. The purpose of these exercises was to demonstrate a knowledge of the classical languages, the scholastic philosophy of the medieval schoolmen, and an ability to versify arguments in the manner of the tripos verses which were standard fare at Cambridge University.[32] Solomon chose as his *questio* the affirmative of "Whether God's punishment of sin is a necessity of nature?" (See Appendix 2).

The theme of these two quatrains and a couplet in mostly iambic heptameter related the Christian concepts of original sin and atonement to the classical concepts of hubris and punishment. Solomon interpreted two mythological examples within the framework of atoning grace. The Gigantes, the mortal offspring of Uranus, attempted to win immortality by overthrowing the Olympian gods, but when they failed they were imprisoned in the abyss of eternal darkness. Icarus, too, had challenged the gods when, escaping from the Minotaur with his father, Daedalus, he flew too close to the sun and his fabricated, waxen wings melted, plunging him into the sea subsequently named after him. Both the Gigantes and Icarus had challenged "the things most high" and Stoddard's prayer-poem, addressed to "primal Wisdom" (1.1), beseeched God to "Teach us to reflect and to be prudent—Perceive that we have not dared/ to subdue the fates and God has so willed it" (11. 5–6). Although "nature demands justice to punish those that are evil" the weapons she uses in punishment are "the goodness of God" not the wrath of Zeus (11. 7–8). Although man lives in a world profoundly deep in sin, it is amazing "That so many guilty of sin can be saved" through God's goodness (1. 10). At this early stage in his career, Solomon emphasized the capriciousness of divine benevolence; later he would stress the unaccountability of God. Now he emphasized the terror of God's power; later he would exalt and praise the beauty of the divine. At this stage he used classical myths filtered through a Christian lens; later he would remain entirely Scriptural in his approach. Even at this stage, however, he was arguing for a view of salvation that stressed a capacious love of God for man, a broadened view of election, much like that of John Cameron and Mitchell. Salvation was not offered to the few, but to the many (1. 10), an idea adumbrating the thrust of his later Evangelicalism.[33]

Usually, completion of the A.M. resulted in a choice of a permanent career in the ministry, but Stoddard remained undecided, Instead, he continued to study divinity in unabated earnestness. In November 1666 he was chosen as a fellow of the college and was hired shortly after as its first librarian. The library was a treasured room in the Old College and only three men in Cambridge had keys to it, Master Mitchell, President Chauncy, and the librarian. Solomon was entrusted with sweeping the floor daily, dusting the huge folios, and charging them out to seniors and graduate students. Undergraduates were expected to study elsewhere. The job gave Solomon many hours each day for reflection and reading.

Still excluded from church and state, and "Growing out of health by reason of too close an application to his studies, he was prevailed on to take a voyage to Barbados, with Governor Daniel Serle as his chaplain, where he preached to the dissenters in that island." There, in all probability he met the nonconformist minister John Oxenbridge, a native of Northamptonshire and a moderate Puritan who might have encouraged him to go to England. In any event, Stoddard returned to New England "in about two years" and prepared to leave for London, but a turn of events launched him into a career which would wrench him from obscurity into the limelight of controversy.[34]

VI *The Later Phases*

From this point on Stoddard's career moved through three distinct phases. Already having had the basic tension between discipline and doctrine firmly established through his college education, he was confronted with the task of working out his theology in the world of practical experience. Invited to preach at Northampton in November 1669, he won the congregation and they called him to act as their second minister the following March. Stoddard sensed the community was sympathetic to his views and almost immediately he married his predecessor's widow, by whom he would have twelve children. Of these, one son, Anthony, would follow his father into the ministry, while five daughters, Mary, Esther, Christian, Sarah, and Hannah, would marry clergymen.

Stoddard began his ministry cautiously by following the established order of discipline of Massachusetts' strict Congregationalism: he accepted the Half-Way covenant into his church. This conservative move might have assured that the degrees of full and partial members of his church and town would be preserved, as was a practice in eastern-Massachusetts towns dominated by the Mathers. Such, however, was not to be the case, for Stoddard was unimpressed with the fleeting success of this order of discipline.

Soon he was tested as a leader of his flock, when neighbor Edward Taylor, in attempting to gather a church at Westfield, sought to lure some of Stoddard's staunch supporters to that town as the founders of a meetinghouse there. Stoddard resisted encroachments on his community's solidarity and incurred Taylor's displeasure. He also protected his town from Indian raids during King Philip's War by petitioning Boston magistrates with the awful consequences of their withdrawal of militia support from the area. During this period the town was also torn apart internally as the original oligarchy was threatened by men of lesser rank over competition for wealth and social prestige, a contest which exploded in a witchcraft trial. During these proceedings, Stoddard remained silent, evidencing ambivalence to the charges of witchcraft raised against one of his supporters.

Then, on November 5, 1677, silently and without warning, the first revolution in American history began. On that day Stoddard simply stopped recording whether his parishioners were either full or Half-Way members of the church in Northampton. The brashness of the action was matched by the modesty of the revolutionary—the Northampton minister had just introduced the beginnings of modern democracy into America by cutting the Gordian knot of Massachusetts' charter that limited citizenship to those who were judged truly regenerate Christians by their pastors.

In an effort to promulgate his good news, he openly advocated a Reforming Synod for the renewal of religion. Seizing the right moment, he mounted the platform in the fall of 1679 in Boston and for the first time defended his revolution before an audience stunned by the novelty and audacity of his ideas. His opponents were brilliant but xenophobic, strict Congregationalists to a man. Moreover, his ideas were not mere theories: they had been applied at Northampton and his church was already experiencing the first of its revivals—more salt in the wound than his adversaries could bear;

led by Increase Mather they went down to defeat. In 1680 Stoddard's revolutionary ideas were published in the Synod's conclusions.

The continuing success of Northampton practices culminated in a second revival three years later, and by 1685 Stoddard was a permanent fixture at Harvard commencement in Cambridge, where he delivered his first published sermon. It took two years for *The Safety of Appearing* to reach the press, however, and when it did, it coincided with the symbolic demise of the first generation: his father died in Boston as "the most ancientest shopkeeper in town." Strict Congregationalists Increase Mather and Edward Taylor again objected to Stoddard's church discipline which failed to distinguish between visible saints and the unconverted. Privately, Stoddard offered his defense to Taylor's criticisms.

On October 5, 1690, the end of Stoddard's first phase as Sacramentalist was heralded when the Northampton pastor exhorted his congregation that "The Lord's Supper" was, in fact, "a Converting Ordinance." From 1679 to 1690 Stoddard had maintained a widened church order while implicitly allowing only the converted to both sacraments. Now he jettisoned the old discipline of a pure church completely. Edward Taylor privately recorded in his "Animadversions" Stoddard's newly instituted sacramentalism, and in Cambridge, an association was formed by Increase Mather to protect other churches from being contaminated by these innovations.

The year 1700 marked the second phase of Stoddard's career—Pope of the instituted church. By this time three of his daughters had married clergy who became potential supporters, and Anthony was following in his father's footsteps. In 1694 daughter Esther, unusual for her ability and vibrant character, married the Reverend Timothy Edwards, a man of such brilliant intellect that, as an apocryphal story has it, he never studied at Harvard, but appeared on commencement day in 1694 in Cambridge to hear Stoddard's address, and qualified for his two degrees simultaneously. Tradition also has it that Esther was responsible for his own conversion, and that she herself did not join his church at Windsor Farms until their famous son Jonathan was twelve! Timothy later supported the Saybrook Platform of 1708, which emphasized the discipline of conciliar authority and denied the autonomy of individual churches, a kind of authority that Pope Stoddard advocated in Massachusetts through his Hampshire Council. The two daughters of Esther and Timothy married prominent clergymen, the Reverend Samuel Hopkins, an Evangelical missionary of West Springfield, and the Reverend Simon Backus of Newington.

The second Stoddard daughter to marry was actually the eldest, Mary. Tradition records that once the Reverend Stephen Mix had succeeded the Reverend John Woodbridge to the Wethersfield pulpit, he hastened to the Reverend Solomon Stoddard—a popular father-in-law among Harvard graduates. Stoddard approved of Stephen's ambition to forward the good work and ushered him into a room where he assembled his blushing daughters—Mary, Christian, Sarah, Rebeckah, and Hannah. When father Stoddard retired, the suitor addressed himself to the eldest, Mary. Flustered, she asked for time to consider. Young Stephen saw sense in her request, and not knowing how much time was required for her to decide, retired to her father's study to join him in a bowl of Virginia tobacco. After perhaps half an hour Stephen sent a note via one of the younger children to Mary asking for her decision, which was promptly forthcoming, indicating that the time it took to smoke a pipeful of tobacco was not sufficient time to commit oneself to marriage. What else could Mix do except return to Wethersfield and await a reply? Finally, after weeks, the missive arrived: it contained but a single affirmative reply and her signature. They were married on December 1, 1696. Such was the terse pragmatism of the Stoddard household![25]

The third Stoddard daughter who was wed by 1700, Christian, married the Reverend William Williams, by whom she gained a stepson, the Reverend William, Jr., later of Weston, as well as her own son, the Reverend Solomon, later of Lebanon. The last two Stoddard daughters would marry later: Sarah married the Reverend Samuel Whitman of Farmington in 1707 and Hannah married Christian's stepson William in 1710. Solomon Stoddard's only son in the ministry, the Reverend Anthony, married and settled in Woodbury in 1701. These men reflected Stoddard's doctrinal concern for preaching the terrors of hell to make way for the Gospel and his concern for imposing a broadened discipline in their churches, developing the exact relationship in varying ways. In Connecticut they most often supported church councils, and during the Great Awakening they most often sided with the Evangelicals.

The year 1700 also marked the beginning of a pamphlet war with the Mathers: when Stoddard's *Doctrine of the Instituted Churches* was refused publication in Boston and was published in London, Increase Mather's implicit attack on it was concurrently issued in Boston. For the first time, Stoddard balanced the discipline of the church order dependent on the sacraments with the doctrine of free access to them. In a sense, discipline and doctrine were incompatible, and contemporary sympathy for him was mixed. Some, like Presbyterian Benjamin Colman and the Brattle-Street congregation viewed Stoddard's solution as falling within Presbyterian sacerdotal ecclesiology. They came to the defense of his widened church order, but they missed his underlying Evangelicalism, evident in the lecture preached on July 3, 1701, in Boston, and his sermon delivered to the General Court on July 5, 1705. Stoddard was seen as a champion of instituted ordinances, and of elevated clerical power, of a new church discipline, the subject of his lecture to the Hampshire County Inferior Court on December 17, 1707. This message was put into practice by Governor Gurdon Saltonstall of Connecticut when he endorsed the Saybrook Platform that year. Indeed, Pope Stoddard's reign over the churches in the Valley appeared secure in 1711 when the Hampshire Association was formed by him and the Reverend William Williams.

However, the birth of the Hampshire Association marked the third phase of Stoddard's development: as an Evangelical. The purpose of associations, from Stoddard's point of view, was not an inculcation of a rigid government, or of latitudinarian rationalism, but a new breed of converted preachers promulgating revival doctrine through weekly lectures and the exchanging of pulpits. Designed partly to undo Congregational autonomy and partly to emphasize the need for a converted ministry, inadvertently, through the exchange of pulpits, it fostered itinerancy. Success was marked by the fourth harvest of new converts in 1712 and the spread of revivals throughout the Valley. This third phase, Stoddard the Evangelical, is characterized by his more Christocentric religion. Although he still retained the rhetoric of the Creator's awful distance from humanity in *Those Taught by God the Father* and *The Efficacy of The Fear of Hell*, he began to emphasize that Christ was a *Guide to the New Life*, in which all believers were united, a theme carried to the end of his ministry.

Gradually, younger people began emulating the Northampton preacher's Evangelicalism and his conversion rhetoric. He was sought as a teacher by novice ministers like Samuel Hall and Warham Williams. His sermons were solicited for publication; the Reverend Salmon Treat had the *Defects of Preachers Reproved* printed by Benjamin Franklin's brother, James, at New London.

When Jonathan Edwards was invited to preach at Northampton as his grandfather's assistant, it was apparent that Stoddard was handing down his mantle. Symbolically, the Reverend John Williams delivered the ordination sermon on February 22, 1727, and from this point Edwards became a chief support to this aged patriarch. Symbolic, too, was Stoddard's funeral oration, delivered by Benjamin Colman in July 1729, for Colman's eulogy comprehended the dynamic between discipline and doctrine tension in Stoddard's thought. At his death, however, few fully realized how thoroughly Evangelistic his message had become. In the last fifteen years of his life he would lay the groundwork of the Great Awakening by his theology of conversion, his advocacy of a variety of itinerant preaching, by his demand for a converted ministry and by his antidisciplinarian approach to organized religion. Through a network of associations this moderate revivalistic religion would be spread across western New England.

CHAPTER 2

Sacramentalist

I *The English Roots of Stoddard's Parishioners*

TO this day, the Connecticut River Valley, especially at Northampton, radiates a peculiar and unforgettable wistfulness for
the ancient roots of its traditions. In the nineteenth century this
sense was even stronger. As a local historian remarked, "There is
hardly a farm or workshop, a dwelling or church, a road or a mill,
but is connected in some way with the Connecticut River. Its waters
feel the pride of local feeling and mingle with every association."
Nature was good to Northampton. Like druids of some long-forgot-
ten race the mountains guarded its entrance from the east while
hoary Indian paths along the river beckoned the venturesome
traveler from the south. When permission was granted to two dozen
men in 1653 to settle Northampton, alias the Indian land of
Nonotuck, its allure was more than rich alluvial meadows and the
beaver fur trade: from Pynchon's settlement of Springfield in 1636 it
was clear that the remoteness of the Valley from eastern Massachusetts fostered an ethos different from that in Boston Bay.[1]

Early Northampton was a Puritan village: at the intersection of its
two main streets was meetinghouse hill, and the homelots of the
villagers were clustered around this focal point of community life. In
the meetinghouse were run the daily affairs of the settlement, while
on the Sabbath the pulpit resounded with the awesome theology of
the covenant, of preparation, election, and damnation. It was similar in geography to the English openfield villages of the midlands,
but it was unlike England in that as each new settler arrived he was
evaluated both religiously and socially and accepted or rejected as a
communicant in the sacraments of the church and as a citizen in
town meeting. Only men had the vote, and only those who were
approved by the church. The crux of the town was, literally, the
meetinghouse: religion and society were inextricably interwoven.

48

Of the original eighty-one male settlers of Northampton prior to 1661, only five were first-generation men, but these five ruled local affairs with an iron hand. The rest were younger sons, forty-three of whom had emigrated as bachelors. Their migration patterns from eastern Massachusetts and Connecticut to Northampton reveal that land hunger was only one element in their restiveness. Thirty-six had lived in Dorchester and Windsor, fourteen had resided at Springfield, and twenty had lived in Hartford. In each of these settlements the ideologies of the leading men conflicted with the strict Congregational orthodoxy of Boston Bay, as we have already seen. Since most of the settlers gained little more land in their successive migrations, anxieties other than land hunger prevailed.

One of the first-generation men was John Stebbins, the son of Rowland (b. 1592) and Sarah (Whiting) Stebbins. John was born in Bocking, Essex, in 1626, the fourth of five children. Rowland owned no taxable land in the parish, and since his marriage in 1618, he had not held any local offices. For yeomen such as Rowland, the lack of land in Essex County, England, was acutely felt, for it severely limited his resources in a period of spiraling inflation and burdensome prices for the lease of arable meadow which amounted to land strangulation as his family reached its completed size. Unlike the Pynchons of Essex county, the Stebbinses were not affected by the 1628 lay subsidy, but apparently they were disaffected with their economic prospects and emigrated from Ipswich on the *Francis* in 1634 to the new Roxbury across the Atlantic. Stebbins arrived in Roxbury four years after most of the large tracts had already been allocated, and he received only 18.75 acres. In 1639 he moved to Springfield and received 31.5 acres from Pynchon as the second division of property was being allotted. There John Jr. married Ann Munson Mundon on May 14, 1644, and before she died eleven years later she bore him five children. John Jr. became dissatisfied with the town and in 1656 migrated to Northampton, where he received forty acres and married as his second wife, Abigail, of the Bartlet family of Essex, who had migrated from Cambridge to Hartford and Northampton. John Sr., widower since 1649, joined his son in Northampton in 1665. The gain of land from settlement to settlement for the Stebbins family certainly was not spectacular, indicating that economic as well as ideological reasons persisted.[2]

The second Essex-County family to settle in Northampton were the Wrights. Their English home in Brentwood Chapelry, south weald, about nineteen miles northeast of London and adjacent to

Pynchon's home in Springfield, was in an area notorious for its nonconformist conventicles. The Wrights, like the Pynchons, were a landed family holding the manor of Brook Hall. Thomas Wright, the immigrant, son of John and Grace, was born November 19, 1610, at Brook Hall. John had been active in local affairs and responsible for works of charity. In 1586 he gave a rent charge of £2 for repairs to the parish church, and in 1602 he bequeathed a house at Halstead to the parish. Thomas Wright had five children born in England, of whom Samuel, the settler of Northampton, was the second, having been born in 1634. In England, Thomas had been assessed for the lay subsidies of 1628, but unlike Pynchon the pressure to emigrate was not as immediate. It was not until the late 1630s that leaving his homeland became a feasible alternative, as shipmoney was being levied and as persecution of Puritans reached its zenith. Thomas left Brook Hall with his wife and their five children, arriving in Watertown in the spring of 1638. At the time, Watertown's land had already been divided and to make matters worse Thomas was not accepted as a Church member or citizen, so he moved to Wethersfield, Connecticut. By 1647 Thomas was a widower, and he remarried Margaret Elson, herself a widow of the Pequot War of 1637. Thomas remained in Wethersfield until his death in 1670, but his son, Samuel, neither a church member nor a freeman of the Colony, found Northampton more suitable for a young man in search of community identity. Land in Wethersfield, too, was to remain scarce for all except the eldest sons of the first settlers, to whom land would fall by primogeniture. Thomas Jr. and not Samuel was the male heir destined to inherit his father's land, and he remained on the homestead.[3]

The group associated with John Eliot came from the area adjacent to Nazing, Essex, and began emigrating in 1631 with Eliot on the *Lyon*. One of these men, Richard Lyman, was destined to finally settle in Northampton. Richard Lyman was born on October 30, 1580, the son of Henry, a landed gentleman of Norton Mandeville, Ongar, Essex. Like Pynchon, Lyman was adversely affected by lay subsidies levied by Parliament, and although he was a man of "considerable estate," who had several servants, his revenues were threatened by taxation. In 1629, having just paid the second of two subsidies in six years and with an uncertain future as Charles I dissolved Parliament, Lyman sold two messuages, a garden, an orchard, diverse arable tracts, a meadow, and a pasture. Two years later Lyman, along with his fellow Essex men from the Nazing area, sailed from Bristol on the *Lyon* to their home in the new Roxbury. Lyman arrived with his wife, two daughters, and three sons, one of whom, John (b. 1623), was destined to settle Northampton in 1655. The Lyman family was not completely happy with the situation they found in their new home, and by 1636 they were already making plans to migrate with Thomas Hooker and his party to Hartford. Since they had arrived when much land was still available for them, land shortage does not appear to have been a major factor in their decision to remove. Rather, because their sons were not accepted as church members they would be second-class citizens. Perhaps, like Hooker, the Lymans objected to the policies being instituted in the Bay Colony restricting freemanship to church members and requiring stricter church membership policies.[4]

The group connected with Thomas Hooker in Chelmsford and Little Baddow, Essex, emigrated to Cambridge, Massachusetts, and then to Hartford, Connecticut. Of these, the Allen family was destined to settle in Northampton. Samuel Allen (b. 1588) and his three brothers, Matthew (b. *ca.* 1603), Thomas (b. 1604), and Richard (b. *ca.* 1606), lived in Chelmsford, Essex, where Thomas Hooker lived and lectured. Once Hooker was silenced, Samuel, Matthew, and Thomas decided to emigrate with the Braintree Company. Samuel arrived in Cambridge, Massachusetts, in 1632, where he married soon. The Dorchester Company, under John Warham, Hooker's colleague, attracted Samuel and he removed to Windsor, Connecticut, in 1635. Samuel died in 1648 in Windsor, and his widow married William Hurlburt, removing to Northampton with her children, including Samuel, Jr., in 1655.[5]

From the west country came settlers to Northampton, one of whom also had connections with the Dorchester Company and with the Pynchons. Joseph Parsons (b. 1613), from Torrington hundred in Devon, was a member of Warham's congregation (that had been gathered in old Plymouth) and a nephew of a prominent nonconformist, Joseph Parsons, who had been a member of John Robinson's church in Leyden. The high sheriff of Radnor, Cecil Parsons, was cousin to Joseph of Black Torrington, his paternal side being descended from Springfield, home of the Pychons. In 1612 one William Hone of London married Elizabeth Parsons, daughter of Thomas Parsons, gent., of Stortford, Essex. In 1634 the brother of Hone's father, Bartholomew, married Jane Pynchon, the sister of the first cousin of William Pynchon of Springfield. Through these interrelationships, the Pynchons and the Parsons considered each other kinsfolk. Thus, young Joseph Parsons at age twenty-three emigrated with Pynchon to settle Springfield, where he was witness to Pynchon's purchase from the Indians on July 15, 1636. Joseph married the daughter of Thomas Bliss of Hartford on November 26, 1646, and like so many young men in search of still greater opportunity to make their wilderness fortunes for their growing families, Joseph migrated to Northampton in 1655.[6]

From Lancashire County, England, came a group of emigrants apparently associated with the Reverend Richard Mather, curate of Toxteth Chapelry. These settlers resided with Mather in Dorchester, Massachusetts, before migrating further in New England. Richard Mather, who went down to Oxford in 1618 but never graduated, was there with John White and John Maverick and William Parsons. Oxford was, perhaps, a center of moderate Puritanism at the time. Richard Mather arrived in the new Dorchester in 1636, just as John Warham was migrating to Windsor, Connecticut. Mather and his Lancashire men were denied permission to form a church by Thomas Shepard, John Cotton, and Governor Winthrop, on the grounds that they could not give adequate evidence of their spiritual condition.[7]

The Lancashire men who accompanied Mather to Dorchester displayed a restiveness which may have been in part due to this religious difference of opinion. Thus, William Clark, Jr., son of a tailor of Cockersham who was baptized February 20, 1616, emigrated on the *Mary and John* in 1633 to Dorchester. He was not awarded land immediately nor did he become a church member, although he did hold the selectman post illegally for two terms, reflecting Mather's moderate Congregational laxity in enforcing Massachusetts law. He married Sarah in 1636, and by the time their ninth child was born in 1659, Northampton looked to be the last chance he had of becoming accepted as a full citizen in New England, even though it was an outpost. He moved to Northampton in 1659, never to return to Dorchester. As he predicted, he became a leader in the new town. Another Lancashire emigrant, Henry Woodward, was baptized on March 22, 1607, in the parish of North Woolton, Childwall, Lancashire, son of Thomas and Elizabeth (Tynen). Unlike the Clarks, the Woodwards were not connected with the textile industry; Henry was a physician by profession. He came on the *James* with Richard Mather in the summer of 1635, but it was not until 1639 that he was admitted to church membership. Four years later he was admitted a freeman. Henry married Elizabeth in Dorchester about 1640 and by her had four children. By 1659, with the prospect of having to establish his sons in the community in which they were not church members and could not become citizens, the Woodwards moved to Northampton. Henry Cunliffe, Jr., of Bury, Lancashire, was born on December 10, 1609. He arrived in Dorchester about 1640, and became a freeman four years later. There is no record of his having first become a church member, and this, once again, may reflect Mather's lenient attitude in not objecting to nonchurchmen becoming citizens of the Colony. He married Susanna in 1644, having one child, Susanna, born the next year. In 1659 he moved with his family to Northampton. Robert Hayward, son of Henry, was born in Childwall on September 22, 1601, and grew up with Henry Woodward, probably following his father's trade as a miller. Hayward emigrated on the *Prudence* in 1635 to Dorchester, but was not admitted to the church until 1639. He followed his friend Henry Woodward to Northampton in 1659 with a family of seven daughters and one son, none of whom was a church member.[8]

From Somersetshire, England, came emigrants who were associated with the moderate Puritanism of Richard Bernard of Batcomb. Many of these people were involved in the textile trade, for which Somerset was famous. Bernard's son, Musachiell, the clothier of the county, had settled in Weymouth, Massachusetts, in 1636. The Strongs of Chard were also tailors. John Strong (b. *ca.* 1610) was son of John, a rather prosperous merchant who left a will valued at 63 pounds, 2 shillings when he died in 1613. The widowed mother raised John and his sister, Eleanor (b. 1613), with the money bequeathed to her, and when the possibility of matrimony presented itself, she quickly took the opportunity, marrying William Cogan of South Chard, a tanner, by whom two more children were born, Eleanor and Joan. Young John and Eleanor grew up together, and as fate would have it, they married shortly after they had emigrated to New England together in 1631. One child was born to the couple in 1632/3 and they settled in Hingham temporarily until they finally settled in Taunton, Plymouth Colony, where John immediately became a freeman. Hingham was a Presbyterian haven where the church ordinances were open to all inhabitants, unlike other towns

in the Bay Colony, and Plymouth Colony did not restrict freemanship to church members, as did the Bay Colony. Therefore, in the
first two migrations that the Strongs underwent, they displayed
aversion for strict Congregational towns. Their third removal to
Northampton in 1659 was consistent with this pattern.[9]

The settlers from Northamptonshire to New England reflected
the moderate Puritan leadership characteristic of the eminent John
Dod, rector of Fawsley, a critic of strict Congregationalism, and
Samuel Stone, lecturer of Towchester, later Hooker's colleague.
Three of these settlers finally settled in Northampton, Massachusetts, for whom the town was named in their honor. The first
was John Bliss, the eldest of three sons born to Thomas (b. *ca*. 1589)
and Dorothy Wheatlye Bliss, having been preceded by three sisters, Elizabeth (bap. 1615), Mary (bap. 1617), and June (bap. 1619,
bur. 1621). His three younger brothers were Nathaniel (bap. 1622),
Thomas, Jr. (bap. 1624, bur. 1628), and Jonathan (bap. 1626). The
size of the family was typical of the age. The Bliss family was well
connected with local politicians and merchants through mother
Dorothy's father, John Wheatlye. Wheatlye, a mercer, served as
master warden of the company of mercers and as bailiff of the
borough of Daventry in 1619. The bailiff, together with the mayor
and the sheriff, was responsible for the punishment of legal offen-
ders, measuring weights, and seizing bad food. Wheatlye and his
son-in-law were admitted as freemen of Daventry, even though
Bliss lived three miles from the center of town in the parish of
Dodford. Enfranchisement in the early seventeenth century was as
much a financial as it was a political advantage, since it permitted
freedom to trade within the borough as well as to vote and to hold
office. Thomas Bliss was destined not to keep the charges of the oath
he had taken. As a smith, Bliss did not hold any land, nor did he
hold a stock of merchandise which could be taxed by a lay subsidy,
in contrast to his father-in-law, who held a considerable amount of
land, worth about 300 pounds, assessed at 20 shillings in the 1628
lay subsidy. Yet for both father-in-law and son, their financial situa-
tions were growing oppressive. For the former, taxation was destroying profits, while for the latter, increasing food prices accentuated the economic hardship connected with a fixed fee for his
trade. Exasperated by his plight, Bliss, along with other local
townsmen, confronted the man who supplied them with their basic
grain staples, Theophilus Nash of Long Buckby, a miller. Bliss was

fined 5 pounds for creating a disturbance. There was little mystery why, then, the Bliss family emigrated from Daventry to New England in 1636, settling at Hartford with Thomas Hooker and Samuel Stone. At the time, young John was sixteen years old and probably was aware of the significance of his father's decision not to settle in Massachusetts Bay: old "Decalogue" Dod of Fawsley had just issued a letter to John Cotton warning him of the opposition of moderate Puritans to the religious test for citizenship in the Bay.[10]

Like the Bliss family, the Roots of Badby were also neighbors of Daventry. Thomas Root (bap. Jan 16, 1606) was the son of John and Ann Russell, a weaver by trade and a member of the company of mercers with Thomas Bliss. Like Bliss, Thomas Root owned no land in his native parish, and the declining textile trade in the early 1630s made the possibility of financial security for his family remote. The Roots emigrated at about the same time as the Blisses, arriving in Hartford in 1636. Both Bliss and Root made certain that their landlessness and political ostracism would not plague their new careers as husbandmen, and they made certain that they were original proprietors of Hartford. After Thomas died in 1651, his son John accompanied the Roots to Northampton in 1653 among the first inhabitants. The Elmore family of Quinton, Northamptonshire, were only four and one-half miles southeast of Northampton. They, like the Blisses, were involved with local politics. Edward Jr. was of sufficient stature in his town to be made a juror of the hundred in October 1630, at the same time when Thomas Bliss's cousins, William and George, were appointed jurors of their hundred, Newbottle Grove. Edward had married in Quinton, having two sons, Richard and Edward (b. *ca.* 1625). Like the Bliss family, the Elmores were attracted to Hartford in 1636, having originally emigrated to Cambridge, Massachusetts, on the *Lyon* in 1632. Once again, the emigrant family was determined that their previous landlessness would not persist in the New World, and Edward became one of the original proprietors of Hartford along with the other settlers from Northamptonshire. With four children, and one on the way, the Elmores left Hartford for Northampton, Massachusetts, in 1655.[11]

From these four clusters of Puritan settlers came Stoddard's staunch supporters: and this is important, since each group tended to retain its moderate Puritan identity in successive stages of migration within New England, gravitating toward areas receptive to their political and religious views. Unlike strict Congregationalists, they did not advocate limiting the franchise to visible saints, and they tended, therefore, to follow Thomas Hooker in the establishment of moderate Congregationalism to the south and west of Boston. Thus, the original settlers of Warham's Dorchester, Hooker's Cambridge, and Pynchon's Roxbury, tied as they were to previously established English roots, tended to settle in Windsor, Hartford, Springfield, and finally Northampton. Although the competing motives of religion and economics were invariably interconnected for these people, and motives for internal migration within New England continued to be mixed, the Connecticut River Valley attracted those with a different attitude to the connection of religion and politics from that imposed in the eastern part of Massachusetts and in New Haven Colony. The ideals of regenerate magistracy and a freemanship of visible saints was rejected for a civil structure predicated on a far broader basis, one that could be attractive to the wilderness entrepreneur, like William and John Pynchon, as well as those Puritans who had decisive scruples and objected to the way religion was administered in the eastern region of the Bay.[12]

However, religious acceptance and a respectable role in the community still continued to be the goals of the socially accepted in old Nonotuck. In fact, very early in the town's settlement the paradox of Puritanism exploded, as desire for saving faith and jealousy of a neighbor's wealth coincided with witchcraft, and this anxiety would establish the receptivity of the town for Stoddard's later revivals. In Essex County, England, a similar dynamic had been observed in the earlier Stuart period. Fits of hysteria and other "marks of the devil" could be judged from a totally different perspective as divine signs of religious conversion. Society's perspective was often contingent with the social dynamics between the subjects to be judged and the authorities passing judgment. James Bridgman and Joseph Parsons had been residents of Springfield. Parsons's connection with the Pynchons and the Blisses secured a preeminent position for him in the Connecticut River Valley, but Bridgman had no such apparent connections. He had an obscure English past, possibly as a landless tenant-farmer of Winchester, Hampshire. In Hartford in 1640 he married, was unsuccessful in either becoming a church member or freeman, and moved to Springfield in 1643. By 1644 he was listed as the seventh-highest taxed of the twenty-four householders. The contest between Parsons and Bridgman for power ensued when in

1646, of forty-two landholders, Bridgman was fifteenth, and Parsons was thirteenth. This marks the beginning of the Bridgman-Parsons contest. As the Springfield elite were being sifted from the town's occupants, both Parsons and Bridgman were in the economic range from which the selectmen, the highest local officers, were being chosen, and in 1652 Parsons managed to get elected, while Bridgman failed. Three years later, both had migrated to Northampton where Parsons's connection with the Pynchons sealed Bridgman's fate. John Pynchon awarded Parsons rights to the fur trade in northern parts of the valley, which immediately secured for Parsons a prestigious position in the community. In December 1655 Parsons was elected selectman for the ensuing year.[13]

Almost immediately Bridgman's wife began spreading rumors that Mary Parsons was bewitched. In May 1656 Joseph Parsons charged Sarah Bridgman with slander for defaming his wife. In June, August, and September, depositions were taken by the two parties before William Holton, Thomas Bascom (commissioner for small causes), Eleazar Holyoke, and John Pynchon, who also acted as a witness against Bridgman. These depositions revealed latent hostility between two classes of people in Springfield and Northampton: those who were of the ruling elite (church members, literate, town officers, and relatively wealthy) and those who were struggling to break into the ranks of power. For instance, Symon Beamon, one-time servant to William Pynchon, and one of the latter group, stated that at a Sabbath meeting in Springfield in 1650 the Reverend George Moxon's children "were taken ill with . . . fits (which we took to be bewitched)" and Mary Parsons "and three others" were "taken ill with like fits," and "were all carried out of the meeting." This deposition revealed that Mary Parsons was not alone in being the object of jealousy in either Springfield or Northampton and that even the minister's family was threatened by slander: Moxon was also the fifth-wealthiest man in Springfield. It would be no surprise to find that the "three others" Beamon cited were related to families of prominence who had incurred jealousy of their neighbors. On October 7, 1656, Sarah Bridgman was found "without just ground" in a court at Cambridge held by Governor John Endicott, Deputy Governor Richard Bellingham, and Captain Gookin, and was required to give public apology to Mary Parsons at Northampton and Springfield within sixty days or forfeit ten pounds. The Parsons-Bridgman case is important because it revealed an intensity of competition in this frontier settlement which would erupt again in Stoddard's ministry. The early feuds between families persisted and were the basis for factions in the town when Stoddard was chosen as its minister in 1669.[14]

As social unrest tore the settlers, the town continued without a church. This in itself is significant, for in settlements where strict Congregationalism was prominent the church was gathered soon after the town was founded, for the church, not the town, was the basis of citizenship. Witchcraft was a symptom of suppressed religious, and hence political, anxiety. In 1658 Eleazar Mather was invited to preach, and on June 18, 1661, a church was covenanted by David Wilton, William Clarke, John Strong, Henry Cunliffe, Henry Woodward, Thomas Root, and Thomas Hanchett. All were part of the emerging oligarchy in the town and were linked by age, moderate Puritanism, geography of English origins, and relative social status. Except for Hanchett, all were freemen of Massachusetts. All would be Stoddard's supporters. Since all but Hanchett and Root had migrated from Dorchester, it is understandable why Eleazar Mather was chosen as their pastor. Eleazar was the son of the Reverend Richard Mather, minister of the Dorchester church of which Wilton, Clark, Woodward, and Cunliffe had been members. As we have seen, the last three had emigrated from Lancashire towns near Richard Mather's Toxteth chapelry, and Cunliffe even counted Richard Mather as his grandfather. They, like their leader, were moderate Puritans but, unexpectedly, Mather's son advocated strict Congregationalism: when the Half-Way Covenant was approved, Eleazar opposed it, while Richard defended it. Had the pillars thought that father and son were alike in their religious attitudes, they were grossly mistaken.[15]

An antagonism between minister and congregation developed with such fury and passion that when Eleazar lay on his deathbed in July 1669 his parishioners presented him with their resolution to institute Half-Way practices despite his continuing opposition:

Such amongst us, being settled inhabitants that give us ground to hope in charity that there may be some good thing in them towards the Lord tho' but in the lowest degree, understanding and believing the doctrine of faith . . . and freely professing their assent unto not (being) scandalous in life and so solemnly taking hold of the covenant, may have their children baptised and entered. Also the adult children hitherto unbaptised, of confederate believers, without themselves coming up to foresaid qualifications, may be accepted members and themselves baptised.[16]

Mather died before this petition was brought to fruition, and the congregation eagerly awaited his replacement who, hopefully, would be sympathetic to their religiosity.

II *Stoddard's Coming*

Shortly after Eleazar Mather's death, the leaders of the church and spokesmen for the Northampton oligarchy John Strong, William Holton. Thomas Hanchett, and William Clark, journeyed to the College at Cambridge to find a new minister. Solomon Stoddard had just returned from the Barbados to resume his responsibilities as librarian of Harvard. Possibly the Reverend Jonathan Mitchell, now Stoddard's colleague, recommended him to the Northampton delegation as better "qualified than any other person with whom he was acquainted." The town fathers were eager for a minister, but wary of creating another controversy. They accepted him on a trial basis, and the young minister settled in the town. On March 4, 1670, he was approved as the new shepherd of the flock. Four days later he married Hester (Warham) Mather, Eleazar's widow. This is significant, for it reveals that the novice preacher, whose religious views were untested, was given such strong assurances of success in the church after a trial of only three months, that he felt secure enough to make the town his permanent home. The approval of the town was evident in their more than adequate salary of £100 per annum with an additional £100 for a house to be paid for in two or three years, and twenty acres of land worth £100, payable in five or six years. A committee of nine of the town's oligarchy settled this transaction: John Strong, William Clark, William Holton, David Wilton, John Lyman, Joseph Parsons, Thomas Root, Sr., Robert Bartlett, and John King. All of them, as we have seen, had previous ties with moderate Congregationalism, and they would have appreciated Stoddard's family's religion as being harmonious with their own.[17]

Yet Stoddard did not accept this offer immediately. He waited two years before he was ordained as pastor and only then did he accept the call of the church. Technically, he was not a visible saint, and therefore not qualified as a church member, even though he had been chosen as a minister. On this basis he refused ordination. It was this problem of assurance that had plagued his youth. He had remained one of the unconverted until shortly before February 7, 1672, when he finally accepted the Northampton congregation's call. Only then, at his "entrance into the ministry," did he experience Christ "Effectually calling him by His grace"; only then did he admit to his flock, "you . . . are not . . . wholly strangers to my spiritual unfitness . . . for so solemn a charge."[8] It was his wife who first realized that even "with his graces of character and manner, he had really no experimental acquaintance with the Gospel." After Esther and some other townswomen began praying for his conversion:

One Sabbath as he was at the table administering the Lord's supper, he had a new and wonderful revelation of the Gospel scheme. He caught such a full and glorious view of Christ and his great love for men as shown in his redemptive work, that he was almost overpowered with emotion, and with difficulty went forward with the communion service. By reason of this peculiar experience of his he was led to think, that the place where the soul was likely to receive spiritual light and understanding was at the Lord's table,—that there, in a special manner, Christ would be present to reveal himself, in all his fullness of love to the soul of men.[19]

He finally became a full church member on April 4, 1672, and on September 11 he was ordained. At his ordination visitors from the neighboring towns of Hadley and Springfield were joined by others from the Connecticut churches of Guilford, Farmington and Windsor. The Reverend John White, pastor of the second church in Hartford, and the Reverend John Russell, pastor of the Hadley congregation, officiated with elder John Strong. Not one strict Congregationalist elder from eastern Massachusetts or New Haven Colony was present. To commemorate the event father Anthony, now one of the richest men in Boston, presented the church with a silver bowl on September 12, 1672, the trophy weighing over thirteen ounces—an expensive gift in early New England.[20]

At this point in his development Stoddard remained within the framework of established religion in the colony, which required a verbal account of religious conversion as a test for church membership. None who was unable to provide such a statement, for whatever reason, was permitted to enter into full communion. Without this qualification adult men, the only voting citizens, were excluded from citizenship. The church was the basis of the state. Since growing numbers of church members' progeny were failing to give these religious accounts to their churches, the Half-Way Covenant provided that these unconverted children could receive baptism and attend the sermon and be subject to the supervision of the minister, although they would be excluded from the Lord's Supper. It was this form of discipline that Stoddard first accepted at Northampton, a principle for which the church had been seeking endorsement since the early 1660s. Stoddard and his congregation developed an oath which Half-Way candidates were required to recite as part of their decision to enter into a "state of education":

You do here publically take hold of the Covenant of the Lord as a Grace-bestowing Covenant, subjecting yourself to the teachings and government of Jesus Christ in this church and engage according to your place and power to promote the welfare of it. And we do here publically acknowledge you a member of this church of Christ, in a state of education, promising to watch over you for the good of your soul, to take care of your instruction and government in the Lord, and to make you partaker of all such priviledges as by the rules of Christ belong to you.[21]

It was originally hoped that Half-Way members would proceed to full communion, but it was realized in Northampton that "a state of education" did not necessarily lead to conversion.

Anxiety over church membership continued in the Valley, and the Half-Way Covenant failed to sustain new piety in Northampton. Of one hundred five who "owned the covenant" in the fall of 1672, fifty-nine percent were landless sons who were being effectively prevented from entering the ranks of the ruling oligarchy by their fathers. Thirty-five were eldest sons. The ages of the sons averaged twenty-seven while the women's ages averaged twenty-six. Of all the new members in 1672 only Rebecca and John Clark, Mary Sheldon, Sarah Clapp, Judah and James Wright, and Caleb and Hepzibah Pomeroy, Thankful Taylor, Timothy Baker, Mary Salmon, and Thomas Stebbins ever became full members. Most of these were elder children, and most were from newer and non-oligarchic families except for the Wrights. Most of these new Half-Way members owned the covenant in family groups. For instance, Thomas Root, a church member since 1661, saw his wife, son, and daughter take the vows together. John Strong, another one of the original members, looked on as four children took the vows, while three others remained outside even the state of education. Similarly, William Clark, another pillar, and his wife, both members, witnessed their children John, Samuel, Rebecca, and William take the oath. Only Rebecca and John, the two elder children, would become full members. Fifty-five percent of the eligible baptized children in the town in 1672 became Half-Way members. Most who did not seek this status were younger sons and daughters. Most prominent among the Half-Way members between 1671 and 1675 were elder sons and daughters of oligarchic families. Least prominent were progeny of nonoligarchic families. It appears, then, that Half-Way status corresponded most closely with the oligarchic children's anxiety for community acceptance even if it were only partial. No such pattern existed among those who became full members without first seeking Half-Way sponsorship.

While competition existed between fathers and sons of oligarchic families, it also existed between the rulers and ruled in society in general. In the latter respect, strife between the Bridgman and Parsons families, in particular, and between church-member freemen and the nonenfranchised, in general, exploded in 1672 and lasted for three years. On April 22, 1672, Samuel Bartlett, a farmer, had married James Bridgman's daughter, Mary. Bartlett was a second generation Half-Way member whose father Robert was a moderately wealthy farmer who refused to give his son any land outright. As was the practice in Northampton, a son was merely given permission to build on his father's property, thereby preserving the nuclear aspect of the village and paternalism in the family. Mary (Bridgman) Bartlett probably felt the social pressure of her husband's second-class status, but more importantly she was ostracized by Northampton society for having had her first child by Samuel born a month before they were married. Now she was carrying her third child, John, who would be born on October 20. Town gossip probably caused Mary's father, James Bridgman, to defend his daughter by accusing Mary Parsons, the daughter of his rival oligarchic leader, Joseph Parsons, of witchcraft, and he was eagerly joined by other Half-Way members. On September 19, 1674, Mary Parsons voluntarily appeared before the Hampshire County Court to clear herself from accusations "On oath from Northampton of many persons declaring causes of jealousies and suspicion of witchcraft." Within a month Mary Bartlett died in childbirth and Bridgman charged "that she died by some unusual means, viz., by means of some evil instrument," namely, by Mary Parsons's black magic. Bridgman accused Mary of witchcraft and on January 4, 1675, at the Northampton Inferior Court, an examination of Mary's body for signs of the devil was ordered by the town's leading men, John Pynchon, Henry Clark, William Clark and David Wilton.

The examiner was, of course, the minister, Solomon Stoddard, and he performed his duty without incident, recommending that Mary Parsons be secured to trial by the Court of Assistants in Boston with a bail set at £50. Once the Assistants received Stoddard's evidences they immediately indicted Mary on suspicion of witchcraft—Stoddard had obviously found possible marks of the devil on her person. However, her trial on May 13, 1675, was speedy: she was found not guilty by a jury of twelve Bostonians. It is noteworthy that this case of witchcraft in Northampton did not elicit any public response from Stoddard. Although he apparently was enlisted in the investigation to discover the marks of Satan, he did not become a vociferous champion of witch-hunting.[22]

The Bartlett-Parsons feud was indicative of fierce competition for power between the rulers and the ruled, fostering solidarity in each of the two groups. Furthermore, as oligarchies formed, they became very protective of their leaders, who helped provide the social cement they required for their existence. Understandably, rivalries between towns were created by competition for these leading citizens. For instance, Westfield had been settled in 1670 by first-generation men—George Phelps, Samuel Loomis, and Joseph Whiting. They had secured the Reverend Edward Taylor, a strict Congregationalist opposed to the Half-Way measures, to preach in the town, but no formal church was gathered because they did not have seven "pillars." They needed only one more person of approved orthodoxy, but none in the town qualified. On July 11, 1673, Phelps, Whiting, and Loomis, "In the name and by the desire of the town," requested Stoddard to help them in establishing a "church estate" in Westfield. "Considering that the main end of New England's undertaking was the cause of God in Gospel worship," they cited Scriptural warrant in asking for one of Stoddard's parishioners: since "Solomon himself sent to Hyram in his necessity to help him with both men and materials for the building of the temple," they had agreed to "unanimously . . . give an invitation to our respected friend Lieutenant David Wilton . . . to come and settle amongst us here for the further encouraging of Mr. Taylor, the strengthening of us in our proceedings, and spending amongst us part of his serving of God in his generation." The same three men also delivered a personal "call" to David Wilton "to entreat at your hands that you would condescend in granting the object of this our invitation and call," assuring him that they "shall look upon it as a great piece of self denial in you." Without a church in Westfield, men who had not become freemen would be prevented from taking the oath since church membership was a prerequisite for the oath, so the lack of organized religion in the town had important political as well as religious consequences.[23]

Stoddard and his ruling elder, John Strong, wrote to Whiting, Phelps, and Loomis that there was "nothing to discourage" their request "but that infirmity that has attended Brother Wilton of late years" that might stand by itself as a "sufficient argument to cause us to decline your wish." "Moreover, the example of Hyram supplying Solomon with artifices and timber for the building of the temple . . . do in no way parallel the case in hand besides . . . we have already contributed to the work of Christ beyond our ability. You have with you one of the officers of our church and three brethren besides, men very desirable for the furtherance of the work in the plantation." David Wilton was valued highly by Northampton as a founder of the church, a prosperous merchant-trader, and lieutenant of the covenanted militia: his defection might have encouraged others to follow. The Westfield men sensed that the loss of Wilton as the crucial seventh pillar of their community (without whom no official town could be gathered) would indefinitely postpone the incorporation of their settlement. Quietly they went directly to Wilton to persuade him to remove to Westfield, but the lieutenant abided by the consensus of his town and refused.

The Westfield settlers had been correct, and it took six more years to find the required seven men to gather their town officially. On August 27, 1679, as the rich autumnal glow radiated from the Valley's birch and maple, Stoddard, cossacked in black with steeple crown hat and plain white neckcloth setting off his complexion ruddied by the brisk fall breeze on his cheeks, dismounted at the hitching post in front of Taylor's crude clapboard meetinghouse. Fruit of the wilderness errand had been borne to the Westfield parish at last as the Northampton minister embraced his colleague in the right hand of fellowship. Although all seemed amicable enough on the surface, Taylor let it be known in no uncertain terms in his "Foundation Day Sermon" that admission into his "city-state" of Westfield still depended on Cotton's Code. It is certain, therefore, that Stoddard's innovative practices at Northampton were known widely, if not before August 27, 1679, at least after that date, for present in the pews were the leading ministers from the length of the Valley.[24]

III   *Defender of Northampton in "the Second Puritan Conquest"*

The early 1670s were precarious for Connecticut Valley pioneers. Both royal commissioners and the French and Indian alliance threatened the safety of the colonies, especially in the north and west. Commissioner Cartwright charged Massachusetts with having impugned the rights of Englishmen by imposing Cotton's code as law. As a cudgel to threaten his opponents to remove religion as a basis of citizenship, he cited illegally settled Indian territory that would have to be returned to its aboriginal landlords. In order to thwart royal intervention, towns belatedly agreed to the formal purchase of Indian lands, but they were also shrewd in manipulating tribes against one another in order to ease the threat of massacre or retribution. In Massachusetts the militia befriended Mohawks and incited them to harass New York Algonquins while New York militia encouraged tribes to infiltrate western Massachusetts. Between September 1675 and March 1676, nine men were killed by Indians near Northampton, and the incident immediately assumed colonial proportions. On May 19, 1676, four miles north of town, one hundred fifty militia under Captain William Turner slaughtered a Nipmuck encampment of men, women, and children in their sleep. Fifteen militia died in this war, purposely misnamed after the notorious Indian chief King Philip, a war which was really "the second Puritan conquest."[25]

Although Stoddard's hands were certainly not stained with the blood of these natives, as the chief of his own tribe he supported the conquest from his pulpit and in missives to magistrates, gaining civic influence as a spokesman of the Valley.[26] Intent on protecting the boundaries of his own town from possible New York threats Stoddard and five prominent Northampton men submitted a petition to the Boston magistrates on March 28, 1676, warning them not to remove four militia companies from western Massachusetts to Boston:

We are not unsensible that your ears are daily filled with the cries of many people in this day of calamity, through all parts of the Country, & are loth to add unto your affliction, by bringing any unnecessary trouble upon you; yet we dare do no other in faithfulness unto ourselves & the Country, than present briefly our condition before you. We dare not entertain any thoughts of deserting this plantation. The Lord has wonderfully appeared of late for our preservation, & we fear it would be displeasing unto him if we should give up into the hands of our enemies, by running away, that which the Lord has so eminently delivered out of their hands, when they did so violently assault us. If we should desert a town of such considerable strength, it may so animate the enemy & discourage other plantations as may prove no small prejudice unto the Country. Besides, there seems to us a great necessity for holding this place for the relief of those forces that may be improved in following the enemy. To bring provisions either from Boston, or Hartford for the supply of an Army in these quarters is a work of no small difficulty and danger. The want of places of entertainment for an Army in these parts, may hazard the loss of many opportunities. If we may be allowed to judge, there can be no prosecuting of the war in these parts to advantage unless this & the two neighbor towns be maintained: yet we must needs say we fear it will be work too heavy for us to defend ourselves. Late experience has taught us, that unless we had been furnished with considerable numbers of men besides our own, we had in likelihood become a prey to our enemies. The enemy had a great strength in these parts, & probably does but watch for the drawing away of the army that they may renew their attempt. Our earnest request therefore to your Honrs. is that you would not suffer us to be left destitute, but allow us what number of men you judge convenient for the holding of the Town. . . .

> your humble servants
> Sol. Stoddard
> John Strong
> William Clark
> David Wilton
> John Lyman
> John King[27]

This missive, signed by the town's minister, the ruling elder, the military committee and two selectmen, was instrumental in securing a garrison of fifty soldiers to protect their triumvirate of Northampton, Hadley, and Hatfield. Westfield, under Edward Taylor, which competed for protection from both the northern triumvirate and Springfield, succeeded in gaining a smaller garrison of thirty. Stoddard had played a key role in protecting his town.[28]

Commissioner Cartwright had been at least partially correct in perceiving colonial persecution of Indians. Indeed, even Stoddard's attitude was hardly that of a missionary. He had earned the respect of his town and the Valley by urging their destruction, even advising the governor that drastic steps should be taken if the lives of settlers were to be spared:

Excellent Sir:

The town of Deerfield has suffered much formerly from the Indians, of late two of their young men are carried into captivity. This makes a great impression on the spirits of the people, & they are much discouraged. This puts me upon it to make two proposals to your excellency. The first is that they may be put into a way to hunt the Indians with dogs. Other methods have been taken, are found by experience to be chargeable, hazardous & insufficient, but if dogs were trained up to hunt Indians as they do bears: we should quickly be sensible of a great advantage thereby. The dogs would be an extreme terror to the Indians: they are not much afraid of us, they know, they can take us & leave us. If they can but get out of gun-shot they count themselves in no great danger, how many soever pursue them. They are neither afraid of being discovered or pursued; but these dogs would be such a terror to them, that after a little experience, it would prevent their coming, & men would live more safely in their houses & work more safely in the fields and woods.

. . . .

If the Indians were as other people are, & did manage their war fairly after the manner of other nations, it might be looked upon as inhumane to pursue them in such a manner. But they are to be looked upon as theives & murderers, they do acts of hostility, without proclaiming war. They don't appear openly in the field to bid us battle, they use those cruelly that fall into their hands. They act like wolves & a ·e to be dealt withall as wolves.[29]

Having acknowledged that Indians had been treated like animals, Stoddard at least partially recognized that the white man intensified the desperation of local tribes. Yet, the Evangelical sense of missionary outreach (that so uniquely characterized the Reverend John Eliot's attitude to the red man) was absent in Stoddard prior to 1710. More interested in the sacraments and the instituted church than in true Evangelicalism at this point, he and his townsmen were eager to seize almost any excuse to justify extermination of the heathen enemy.

In a forest near Northampton, a trapper, Richard Church, was scalped and four Nipmuck suspects, tracked by a militia band, were brought before Stoddard and the Reverend William Williams of Hatfield. The two judges, Joseph Hawley (Stoddard's brother-in-law) and Aaron Cooke, and the militia captain, Samuel Partridge, had one, Umpanehala, taken to the scene of the crime, where he confessed that his companions, Mahweenes and Moquoles, had shot and scalped Church; the fourth Indian, Wimpuck, confirmed this

testimony. However, the accused denied the charges. Without respect to *habeas corpus*, all four were "secured in safe custody till
further order," and in Boston, William Stoughton, the Chief Justice
of the infamous Salem witch-trials, demanded "the speedy execution of . . . those bloody villains and rebels," giving Col. John
Pynchon authority to execute them. At the trial on October 21,
1696, at which Stoddard was present, Umpanehala and Wimpuck
were named as accessories and Maweenes and Moquoles were
named principals. Not one of the witnesses, Samuel Barnard,
Ebenezer Smith, or a young Indian boy, had seen the actual murder. Martha Wait, a fifty-year-old Hadley housewife, testified that
Moquoles had threatened two weeks earlier that "he would kill a
Hadley man . . . because Hadley men threatened them when they
came in Hadley woods to hunt." Without hunting, of course, the
Nipmucks would have starved to death. Mahweenes and Moquoles,
indicted for murder, pled not guilty, but were found to the contrary
and were sentenced to death by a firing squad. Only circumstantial
evidence had led to their speedy execution.[30]

Hostilities to the Nipmucks did not end. All local tribes were
disarmed, "warned out" of the Northampton-Hadley-Hatfield area,
and ordered to go "home to Albany." The militia under Samuel
Partridge and Joseph Parsons was ordered to "shoot them down"
without provocation, since they were henceforth "rendered and ac-
counted enemies." So unwarranted did this action appear to Royal
Governor Benjamin Fletcher in Boston that he demanded a "Narrative of the whole proceeding" to determine if a mistrial had been
perpetrated, although neither Stoddard nor Williams had offered
any criticism of the judicial proceedings. One reason for the Royal
Governor's reaction to this incident was that Massachusetts Puritans
had a similar reputation for discriminating against Englishmen un-
sympathetic with Puritanism in New England. Indeed, Stoddard's
own father had been instrumental in bringing charges to bear on a
Friends' meeting in William Chamberlain's house in Boston
earlier.[31]

Both the red man and the Crown lay in ambush for those conten-
tious Puritans who had trampled the Indians' rights and the royal
charter. As the conquest of the Indians was perpetrated in hundreds
of similar incidents, the red man retaliated instinctively by massacre, by destruction of over a thousand homes, and by slaying
thousands of cattle—but to no avail. Then Charles II intensified his

seige of the Massachusetts charter which John Winthrop had absconded with so long ago. In 1678 the King ordered the General Court to despatch representatives to London to answer for colonial transgressions communicated by the royal intelligence officer, Edward Randolph, in his 1677 report on the "Present State of New England." William Stoughton and Peter Bulkeley were sent to London in the summer of 1678, met with the Lords of Trade, and heard that the King did not wish to annul the charter; he merely wanted to append "a supplemental one" designed to remove those provisions which were inconsistent with English common law, such as Cotton's Code: the religious basis of enfranchisement.[32]

Coinciding with this political intrigue were other evidences of God's controversy with New England. In the midst of the Indian wars fires raged through the dockside shops, claiming Anthony Stoddard's store among many others. Then, Puritan fortitude was tested as a smallpox epidemic swept the colony, leaving eight hundred dead in in its wake. Jeremiads resounded in pulpits across New England—surely the wilderness rainbow had lost its original hue when it had beckoned weary immigrants to a new and glorious mission. The rainbow now appeared as the celestial frown of God to an unfaithful people.

IV *Stoddard's Revolution of 1677*
and the Reforming Synod of 1679:
"The Beginnings of New England's Apostacy"

Enter Stoddard—the rough clapboard meetinghouse—the pulpit where church records were kept—where every man, woman, and child was dissected under the awful test of religious conversion. The church records—name: "Relatives," "Admitted, with Parents," "Baptized," "Personally taken the Covenant," "Admonished," "Excommunicated," "Readmitted," "Died"—in black and white, the state of a soul from heaven to hell. Every person in town, name inscribed by their pastor, then the terrifyingly empty columns next to it in the huge vellum folio.

The date, November 5, 1677; Stoddard, spiritual entrepreneur in his counting house, opened his state of souls ledger. The profit meager: of the town's 500 adults only 35 men and 41 women were communicants. Balance closed. From this day on he would abandon his account book of religion. All were equal in God's eyes. A revolution—the first in American history—had begun, without warning, in silence. For the first time a resident of the town could claim church membership as a right. For the first time the townspeople and the church were one people. For the first time in New England someone had championed religious and political equality. Thus the wellsprings of democracy in America had their beginnings.[33]

This done in silence; to the world he appeared as still the champion of the old order. Three weeks later he wrote to Increase Mather, figurehead of strict church discipline. "Loving brother," he began, if we allow deviation from church discipline, however innocent at first appearance, "it will be a means to fill [your] town, which is already full of unstable persons, with error; I look upon it a great judgment, God seems therein to lay a stumbling block before men, that such as received not the truth in love might believe a lie. Let all due means be asked for prevention." Ostensibly Stoddard spoke as one from the east but in his heart of hearts he was charting a far different course.

Although the reverend elders were uniformly anxious to end God's controversy with New England by using "all due means," Stoddard led the few who recognized that new policies were needed for a new piety. In a meeting of elders on May 28, 1679, two questions were raised: "What are the evils that have provoked the Lord to bring his judgments on New England?" and "What is to be done so these evils be reformed?" The answers were given in a petition to the General Court:

Forasmuch as the . . . General Court at their session of the 13 Oct. 1675 were moved under a deep and humbling sense of divine wrath that is broken out upon us and like to burn into a general consumption to make a strict inquisition after those provoking evils which had been the procuring cause of that displeasure and to take into their serious consideration the great business of reformation . . . for the glory of God and the salvation of this perishing people . . . upon our own utmost peril in case of unfaithfulness. . . . That the churches may concur (and) . . . discharge ourselves faithfully in all duty unto the children of the covenant, which is a principle part of the work of reformation as being the only way of the propagation of religion to the rising generation of the neglect and defect of which we are the more sadly sensible.[34]

On June 3, 1679, the court agreed to this petition and summoned a synod to meet in Boston in September "to enquire into the causes of God's displeasure."

As if to mock the exhortation of strict Congregationalists like Increase Mather who vied to preserve the orthodoxy of "one faith and
order of the Gospel," Anthony Stoddard, at the same time, was
actively supporting the Reverend John Wise as a candidate for the
pulpit in Chebacco parish near Ipswich. Wise, a friend of Solomon's
who had preached at Hatfield in 1677–1678, was a strong defender
of the freedom of individual churches to regulate policies and resisted the encroachment of Increase Mather and other strict Congregationalists.[35]

August 27, 1679: the day, as we have seen, on which Taylor
succeeded on gathering his church, a meetinghouse in which Cotton's Code of strict Congregationalism would reign supreme. Taylor
fervently held that between the saved and the damned there was no
point on the scale of being, and that no "city-state" (or rather
church-state) could long survive unless the saved were its rulers.
Stoddard, like Thomas Hooker, was less dogmatic about this axiom
of New England Puritanism, seeming to imply that by extending
communion privileges to good men, that merely good men may
make good rulers. Taylor was not at all convinced. He felt that the
true spiritual community was a "Habitation of God" founded on no
civil law but some deeper test of spiritual worthiness. This test was
Cotton's Code, the ticket of "admission to Christ's household state,"
and this in turn admitted one to "Infranchisation into a city-state."[36]

The laity, restive under the onus of clerical bickering over Cotton's Code, wished an end to the dispute. One of their spokesmen.
Deputy Ralph Wheelock of Medway, "occasioned a very warm discourse," criticizing the rulers of church and state, ministers and
magistrates alike, for having exempted themselves from the tax-
paying population. Deputy Anthony Stoddard took the podium in
the Deputies' chamber and entered a dissenting opinion. As far as
ministers were concerned, he indicated, they were entirely dependent upon their parishioners for sustenance, one which was often
very meager. Although Wheelock later recanted, latent hostility to
clerical authority had been exposed, and little was done to quell the
underlying causes of it.[37]

At the second meeting, held September 19, 1679, clerical authority again rose as an issue as "much debate about persons being
admitted to full communion" ensued, "and Mr. Stoddard, the
minister, offered to dispute against it and brought one argument.
Mr. Mather was respondent."[38] An eyewitness penned the following
account of Stoddard's first confrontation with Increase:

Some of the elders in the Synod had drawn up a conclusion "That persons should make a Relation of the work of God's spirit upon their hearts, in order to coming into full communion." Some others of the elders objected against it, and after some discourse it was agreed to have a dispute on that question, "Whether those professors of religion as are of good conversation, are not to be admitted to full communion, provided they be able to examine themselves, and discern the Lord's body." Mr. Increase Mather held the Negative; I have labored to make good the affirmative. The result was that they blotted out the cause of making a relation of the work of God's spirit, and put in the room of it, "The making of a profession of their faith and repentance," and so I voted with the rest . . . that It is requisite that persons be admitted unto communion in the Lord's Supper, without making a personal and publick profession of their faith and repentance.[39]

Fortunately, both Stoddard's "Nine Arguments against Examinations concerning a Work of Grace before Admission to the Lord's Supper" and Increase Mather's refutation have been preserved. Together, these two essays initiated the Stoddard-Mather controversy, which was to extend into the next century, symbolizing the elders' polarization over church discipline and doctrine similar to the Hooker-Cotton controversy of 1636.

The structure of Stoddard's "Nine Arguments" reflected Ramist form. Howev r, in place of the Scriptural text Stoddard presented his own thesis nd defined the three key terms which were basic to his exposition: "Profession of faith," "godly conversation," and "knowledge to examine and discern the Lord's body." After these definitions he proceeded to list nine arguments in defense of the thesis, and then inserted secondary arguments and Scriptural texts. The "Arguments" presented a radical redefinition of Christian initiation, and when Increase Mather sought to refute these "Arguments," he first had to rephrase Stoddard's theses, redefine the terms Stoddard had used, and refute each of Stoddard's arguments by restating them in accordance with strict Congregationalist terminology. The thesis Stoddard proposed to defend was:

All such as do make a solemn Profession of their [faith and] Repentance, and are of a godly Conversation, having knowledge to Examine themselves, and discerning the Lord's Body are to be admitted to the Lord's Supper.

Stoddard did not define "profession" as had John Cotton in 1634. It was not an evidence of spiritual regeneration. Rather, in keeping with the moderate Congregationalism of the Reverend John White, Stoddard defined it as "assent unto, and acknowledgment of the doctrine of faith and repentance [as the only doctrine according to the hope of salvation] together with a promise of obedience to all the commandments of God." Similarly, he defined "godly conversation" as that whereby a person walks in all the commandments of God, not living in the practice of any known sin or omission of any duty" (p. 1).

Stoddard believed that it was the individual's responsibility and not the minister's "to discern the Lord's body":

What is knowledge to examine themselves and discern the Lord's body? Ans. 1. Knowledge to examine a man's self is knowledge of things that he ought to examine himself about, viz. faith, repentance, love.

"Knowledge to discern the Lord's Body" was Stoddard's shorthand for experience of God's grace. It was not predicated on the assent of understanding but on sincere repentance and humility before the awesome Sovereign, genuine love to God and, finally, true faith.

At this initial stage in his theology, Stoddard dwelled on the first of these aspects of "godly conversation" rather more than the others:

Now obedience. What nature of them is and competence to distinguish false grace from true. [Ans.] Knowledge to discern the Lord's Body is a knowledge of the nature, necessity and use of the Lord's Supper. Dr. Ames, *De Conscientia*, [book] 4, [thesis] 7.

Stoddard, at this time, implicitly rejected the conversion experience as the central datum of covenant theology. The "competence to distinguish false grace from true" did not rest in the minister's ability to examine a person's recollection of what the conversion experience was like; rather, the issue revolved around the proper use of sacraments: they should be available to all who were baptized in the church. In reality it was reformulation of the priesthood of all believers: every man must be able to examine his own conscience.

This new sacramental obedience required every man to be his own casuist, and Stoddard relied on William Ames, Puritan casuist *par excellence*, to supply the technique of the accusing conscience: "He that lives in sin shall die; I live in sin, therefore I shall die." Conversely, the approving conscience argued, "Whosoever believes in Christ shall not die but live; I believe in Christ, therefore I shall not die but live." Stoddard like Ames relied on casuistry as an integral part of practical divinity accessible to laymen, enabling them in searching "the glory of God, the edifying of our neighbor and the help of our necessary actions." Right actions were as strongly motivated as they were good, since they proceeded from a conscience enlightened by the Word.[40] For Stoddard, Ames's most important application of casuistry was to the doctrine of preparation, since Ames claimed that it was the duty of the individual to evaluate his fitness to participate in the ordinances:

What kind of preparation is required to the holy use of the Supper? . . .
A. 1. The preparation to be made . . . requires first a discerning of the Lord's body, secondly treat of ourselves, thirdly a worthy exposition.
A. 2. This discerning starts in a right understanding and judgment concerning the nature, use and necessity of the sacrament. Now, because these things cannot be understood but out of the foundations of the Christian religion, concerning sin and the misery that follows it, concerning Christ and his benefits, and also concerning our duty in thankfulness and obedience to God, therefore, the knowledge of the principle grounds of religion necessary to salvation is necessary also to this sacrament.
A. 3. The examination of ourselves consists in a serious trial whether we be so disposed that we may with fruit use this sacrament which now we discern to be divine. The rule of this sacrament is the Work of God as it respects the institution of this sacrament. . . .
A. 4. A worthy disposition both not consisting in perfection . . . but in a suitableness of our affections to so holy an action which suitableness may consist with great imperfection . . . we receive the sacrament as the seal of Grace and God's promises.[41]

At this point in Stoddard's theology the chasm between the state of nature and the state of grace was not so wide as to prevent the obedient and righteous to carefully cross the uncertain suspension bridge of preparation to the other side. For Ames and Cotton, however, preparation and conversion were radically separate, making it impossible to use any measure of preparation as a "seal of grace." A "worthy exposition" to them referred to evidence of conversion, not of preparation. This marked Stoddard's decisive break with strict Congregationalism, rending the Puritan notion of visible sainthood from any rationalist moorings and emphasizing the crux of divine glory and human piety in an act of private self-introspection. Accordingly, it was impossible to distinguish between "two sorts of adult [church] members, one that might and one that might not come to the Supper" because exclusion presumed that religious experience could be evaluated and election could be rationally perceived (p. 8). By radically redefining what was meant by ability to examine oneself for spiritual fitness, Stoddard superficially appeared to agree with both the 1662 synod that required such an examination prior to communion and Increase Mather and other strict Congregationalists. However, Mather attempted to reveal this tactic to his fellow conferees by rephrasing Stoddard's first argument. Ability to discern the Lord's Body, he confided to his colleagues, was really "being able doctrinally to discern the Lord's Body," but this was "without any examination concerning a work of grace." Of course, Stoddard had not defined the examination to consist of only a rational assent; indeed, this was only the first step in the process of preparation. So, Mather completely ignored the reassertion of divine sovereignty and asserted that Stoddard meant "that every one that is in judgment of charity a believer, is immediately to be admitted to the Lord's Supper without any examination whether a believer or no!" In fact, Stoddard indicated that the second phase of preparation was not rational assent but experimental immersion in the Spirit in communion: the envelopment of man's free will by the omnipotent all-sovereign will was not a doctrinal but a sensational reality which the heart could experience. Or, to change the metaphor, the ordinance was a food which vivified religious emotions (similar to the Greek Patristic tradition's identification of the Eucharist as the medicine of immortality). It was important that it be available, especially to the weak in spirit, to nourish them; "Is it not injurious to deny the ordinances to those Jesus hath promised a blessing unto in the use of it? May we not see fit to hinder them in the use of spiritual comfort and the increase of faith when we deny them the means that God hath appointed thereunto. How can we censure them for their failing when we deny them that which is a means of preservation from failing?" (p. 1).[42]

Stoddard the sacramentalist and Mather the disciplinarian based their arguments on opposing interpretations of Scripture. Mather viewed the two Testaments as being radically separate, with the ordinances of the new dispensation requiring greater purity; Stoddard viewed the Testaments as continuous in the history of redemption and the ordinances being more capacious in their requirements of admission. This was revealed in Stoddard's second argument when he indicated that since "profession and godly conversation were sufficient in adult persons in order to communion in all ordinances in the Jewish church," they were "sufficient with the addition of knowledge to examine themselves to discern the Lord's Body in order to such communion in the Gospel church" (p.4). Mather recognized that his opponent was playing the Ramist game of redefining the "middle term" of an argument, and he realized that in order to expose his opponent he would have to unveil the new "middle term" in its worst light. He indicated that what Stoddard referred to as "knowledge to examine themselves to discern the Lord's Body" was really a "declaration of a work of grace" and that while this had not been called for in the Jewish temple "under the dispensation of the Gospel more holiness is required of professors than under the old Testament." Mather claimed John Cotton as his authority, revealing one source of the strict Congregational heritage.[43] While Mather used typology to show that the two Testaments were radically separate and hence required different application of the ordinances, Stoddard relied on their continuity to show that Jewish rites had their true counterparts in Christian ceremonies and that the Passover, for instance, as a common meal, could be used as a precedent for communion extended as a sacrament for all. However, Stoddard not only used typology to support a more broadened view of the ordinances, he also used it to explicate the nature of the church, which revealed his Prestyberial discipline. Presbyterialism was a position midway between Congregationalism (which stressed the particular autonomy of each church) and Presbyterianism (which viewed each church receiving its power from a highly structured interchurch hierarchy). A Presbyterialist emphasized a more inclusive form of church membership and concentrated church control into the hands of church officers. Unlike Presbyterian ministers, Presbyterial ministers viewed ordination as unique with each church they served. Thus, Stoddard explained that "The church of the Jews was not [really] called national but all of the nation," that is, it was not really Presbyterianism but between Congregational autonomy and Presbyterian hierarchy: "if the whole English nation were in church fellowship it would not be a national church but several Congregational churches" (pp. 4–5). Stoddard was careful to defend the minor proposition upon which his Ramist argument hinged, "Because there was nothing more than profession and holy conversation required of the adult children of the Jews. . . .

They did profess the doctrine taught by Moses, I Cor. 2; compare Acts 8:16" (p. 5).

The third argument was designed to redefine visible sainthood by calling infants born into the church covenant as one variety of saint and those who had given a "personal profession" as the other. Stoddard cited Richard Mather's *Defence* of the 1662 synod and John Norton's *Responsio . . . ad Apollonio*, both of which supported the contention that membership into the church mystical entitled one to membership into the church militant and visible. Stoddard was careful to select those writings of his predecessors which supported his own broadened view of membership (pp. 5–6). Mather in his confutation of Stoddard's argument made it clear that he disallowed the "orthodox in judgment and not scandalous in life" to be automatically "qualified for church membership."[44]

The fourth argument clarified this Presbyterial point of view by claiming that "Those who do sincerely make that profession which the church is built upon," that is, "the profession of the faith of Christ," "are to be admitted to the Lord's Supper" (p. 6). Once again, the middle term camouflaged his meaning. As Mather pointed out, "profession" meant "rational assent," not an "examination concerning a work of grace." Stoddard's redefinition permitted him to cite strict Congregationalist writings, like John Davenport's *Power of Congregational Churches* (1672), John Cotton's *Holiness of Church Members*, and John Allin and Thomas Shepard's *A Defense of the Answer* (1648). In each of these works, however, "profession" was used in its strict Congregationalist sense. Mather, knowing this, attempted to rephrase Stoddard's argument to make this patent to the synod that "profession of that faith upon which the church is built" was not identical to "examination concerning a work of grace."[45]

The fifth argument that "Such persons as were received to full communion by the Apostles are to be received by us to full-communion" was referred to that passage in Acts 16:14–15, where Lydia was baptized by Paul for "her visible receiving of his doctrine" (p. 7). The example of Lydia had a long tradition within moderate Congregationalist circles extending back to Richard Sibbes and Thomas Hooker, who had claimed that the beginnings of grace were indiscernible at times and that preparation for salvation could be a lengthy process. Mather objected to Stoddard's appropriation of Lydia's conversion as the example to guide the Congregationalist

application of the ordinances, implying that Lydia's case was unusual: "The Apostles did require true faith and repentance to be in
those whom they admitted unto full communion, therefore without
doubt, when need did so require, they examined those whom they
admitted. . . ."[46] In answer to this objection Stoddard acknowledged that church membership was a "way of credit and profit" but
regardless of whether "it's more easy to get into the church" today,
"It is not our concernment to keep all hypocrites out of the church,"
and furthermore "relations [of conversion] are not any ordinance of
God . . . " (p. 8).

Directly following his citation from Lydia's baptism and admission
into the church at Corinth, Stoddard argued the point in his sixth
proposition that "Such as are fit to be baptised are fit likewise for the
Lord's Supper" and that "baptism is a sacrament for strengthening . . . of a faith, as well as the Lord's Supper" (p. 8). Yet, at this
time Stoddard did not view either ordinance as a device to convert
the unregenerate: the purpose of the sacraments "is not to beget
faith but to draw forth faith already wrought in the head" (p. 9).
Therefore, Stoddard was orthodox in his theology of preparation to
the extent that he viewed the ordinances as seals of "faith already
wrought in the heart," viewing it profane "for such to be baptised as
are visible unbelievers. Baptism doth suppose holiness and the very
end of it is to strengthen faith (Rom 4:11)" (p. 9). Of course, Mather
could not object to the position that the ordinances were seals of
grace, so he merely reiterated his previous criticism of Stoddard's
definition of "profession."[47] At this point Stoddard was merely re-
shaping the institution of church admissions and not intentionally
altering its quality. As such he was still far from the doctrine of
instituted churches he would espouse in 1700.

This was made evident in the next argument, which dealt with
"Scripture qualifications" of being admitted to communion: "holy
profession (I Cor. 1:2) holy conversation (Jas. 2:18) and knowledge to
examine themselves. . . . " Here Stoddard made it clear that reason
and revelation were of different orders. Revelation preceeded reason, and therefore revelation was in good Ramist form, its own proof
to which reason was superfluous: "By reason of their hope here we
are to understand the ground of that doctrine their hope is built
upon" (p. 10). The ground to which Stoddard referred was the individual's experience of the holy, a datum of awareness which was its
own proof. Mather in his confutation did not acknowledge the ap-

peal to an *a priori* ground of "spiritual conversation," but, rather, he stressed the rational explication of knowledge "concerning a work of grace." Stoddard's seventh argument revealed his evangelistic anti-intellectualism, while Mather's confutation revealed just the opposite, a thoroughgoing intellectualism. This gap in theological method would only widen with time.[48]

Stoddard's eighth argument revealed his consciousness of the origins of his sacramental theory. Like John Humphrey and William Prynne, who viewed exclusion from sacraments as warranted only as a disciplinary measure, Stoddard indicated that "If those thus qualified do not deserve to be laid under censure, they are to be admitted to full-communion . . . because the denial of full-communion is a censure" (p. 11). Mather, aware of the English debates, answered that exclusion from full-communion was not a censure, because the Half-Way Synod had created two classes of membership. Failure to admit Half-Way members to the Eucharist was no censure because "A church-censure is when a man is cut off from such priviledges as once he did partake in or had a right unto. Whereas the persons in question [i.e., Half-Way members] never did partake of the Lord's Supper nor ever had a right thereunto." Mather hoped to side-step the pitfall of the English debates by indicating how strict Congregational polity solved the problem.[49]

The ninth argument exposed Stoddard emboldened as a champion of a church polity. Confirmation, he claimed, was the Apostolical institution of admitting persons to communion, and its basis was knowledge of "the principles of faith" (p. 12). He aimed his argument at those who would disallow those Half-Way members to communion because they had not the necessary qualifications: "Such as are born and baptised members of the church . . . and do not scandalize their profession" are qualified, he protested. In no way was "The growth of faith . . . necessary for the regular participation in that ordinance. They that have the least measure need it and they that have the least measure are capable of sanctifying God's name in it . . ." (pp. 13–14). Mather, infuriated by Stoddard's use of strict Congregationalist authorities to substantiate the argument, could not help but refer to the beginnings of strict Congregationalist principles in Holland by Ainsworth, Ames, and Peter.[50]

However much a rebel Stoddard appeared to Increase Mather and other strict Congregationalists, he was still very far from ad-

vocating opening communion to all, even the unregenerate. Instead, he was actually exposing the theory behind a recently instituted practice in Northampton which permitted baptized children
to take communion with their parents. No longer, at least in his
church, would Half-Way members be considered second-class citizens. His method in presenting the theory demonstrates how
Ramist logic, which depended on the *a priori* "middle term," could
be used effectively within the Puritan brotherhood against opposing
views. Once words such as "profession" were redefined it was
difficult for an Increase Mather to counter the propositions Stoddard
offered. The "Arguments" present the rudiments of an articulate,
emotive sacramentalism: Stoddard had begun to undercut an excessive discipline-oriented intellectualism which depended on a rational understanding of conversion. In a sense, he was reversing the
institutionalization of purity so effectively imposed on Massachusetts Bay polity by John Cotton, and with this challenge it
appeared to some, like Increase Mather, that he was threatening the
very order of religion and society.

With an almost boundless anxiety, Mather retreated to his Boston
study and tried one last-ditch attempt to stave off the frontier
parson's assault by completely misrepresenting the sentiments
expressed at the synod:

That both churches and elders be most watchfully and strictly circumspect
in admission unto full communion in the Lord's Supper, [so that] none be
admitted but upon satisfactory account given unto the church of their
knowledge faith and experience as a sufficient ground . . . to hope
they . . . are able to examine themselves and to discern the Lord's Body
according to direction (I Cor. 11:28, 29) . . . And that the table of the Lord
be kept pure and not be polluted and profance by unworthy communicants.[51]

The majority of the New England ministers at the synod stood
behind Stoddard and reiterated the jeremiad that "we have in too
many respects been forgetting the errand upon which the Lord sent
us hither." Those evils which "have provoked the Lord to bring his
judgments on New England" were immoderate apparel and
hairstyles, neglect of worship, Sabbath-breaking, "sinful drinking,"
"mixed dancing," "unlawful gaming," and "naked breasts," not
quite what one expects of these staid Puritan ancestors! Stoddard
and the other clergy wanted more people placed under the watchful

eye of the church even if strict Congregational purity was rejected, so they issued their conclusion on October 15, 1679 that

> It is requisite that persons be not admitted unto communion in the Lord's Supper without making a personal and public profession of their faith and repentance, either orally or in some other way, so as shall be just satisfaction of the church. . . . (I Cor. 11:28, 29)[52]

Stoddard emerged victorious in this scrimmage. His antiintellectualistic Calvinism which viewed God and religious experience as not subject to reason alone further undermined the rationalistic thrust of the Cambridge Platform, and when the synod affirmed that God was essentially unfathomable, capricious, and known only to the hearts of the faithful, the disciplinarian basis of New England theology began to crumble.

As though announcing victory, Stoddard ceased to distinguish between full and Half-Way members in the fall of 1679, thereby silently allowing all the children of the covenant into communion. As he did this a wave of heightened religious sensitivity swept his parish, and the first awakening at Northampton was recorded as eight men and fourteen women were admitted to fellowship. Apparently his theory worked in practice. If his opponents were aware of this "harvest" they would have been galled all the more. Indeed, Increase Mather, for instance, "preached a very potent sermon on the danger of not being reformed by these things" to the General Court, and despite his failure to have Stoddard's conclusions deleted from the Synod's published proceedings he continued to bemoan the "anger and displeasure of God" being visited on "this poor people" who had been duped by a country bumpkin.[53] Similarly, the Reverend John Russell of Hadley not only wrote a lengthy refutation of Stoddard's "Nine Propositions" but also informed Mather of the daily activities of the renegade to the north:

> Our good brother Stoddard hath been strenuously promoting his position concerning that right which persons sound in the doctrine of faith, & of (as he calls it) a holy Conversation, have to full communion. It now stands them in hand, who were of the Synod in 62, to look to the maintaining of that defense which they prepared in their 4th proposition for the securing of the churches from pollutions by unprepared ones encroaching upon full communion in the Lord's Supper & voting. I take the great care of that matter (if any things be doable in it, which I utterly despair of) to be upon yourself.

But if any thing be let us see it. When the objection was that the owning such for members would corrupt the churches; the answer then was it was [not] that breadth in admitting to membership that would corrupt, but such a breadth in admitting to full communion; but now the say is the admitting to full communion will not pollute the church: provided discipline be maintained, tis that that must maintain the church in its purity. But alas! upon the admission of these to full communion what discipline shall we have or can we expect. Surely none thats like to preserve the church or help them that would keep it pure. I do every day sorrowfully increase in satisfaction that the doctrine of those propositions in the Synod 62 doth tend in the end of the work (how good soever the end of the workers was) to shake & undermine the fundamental doctrine & practise of the Congregational way, viz. that visible Saints are only matter of a church.[54]

Harangues among the ministers continued to generate widespread anticlericalism among the populace. In Boston, Stoddard's father continued to defend the ministerial lot from potential detractors, and when, in 1680, the question of whether tithes should be involuntarily assessed on the citizenry (the Anglican practice which had been opposed by Congregationalists since John Cotton), Anthony Stoddard supported a compromise measure. Together with old-guard John Richards, Thomas Danforth, and Lawrence Hammond (Prerogative men who supported the charter), Anthony Stoddard answered the Court's question that the "most necessary [thing] to the advancement of learning" in the colony as "a great need of more allowance to be made to sundry of the Lord's servants. . . . Every minister [should] be allowed not less than £100 per annum." If this were too much for the people to bear, the General Court was to be empowered to levy tithes on incomes. In effect, Stoddard's father together with the old guard were supporting a more Erastian type of church government suggestive of the direction that Solomon's own thought was now taking.[55]

V   The Safety of Appearing (1685)

A truce of sorts was apparently called by Stoddard and Mather after the synod, but the Northampton pastor applied his Evangelical techniques with even greater gusto, as his church experienced its second awakening in 1683 with fourteen men and thirteen women being admitted. Since the results of the synod had only paved the way for an overt promulgation of Stoddardean revivalism to the world, in the fall of 1685 Stoddard completed *The Safety of Ap-*

pearing at the Day of Judgment in the Righteousness of Christ. In order to secure "greater acceptance" of it he unsuccessfully attempted to persuade Mather and Samuel Willard, both Boston ministers, to write "a few words" praising it, explaining to Mather that "I am still fearful that that work is still to do which you told me you thought was almost done." The recent harvests at Northampton appeared to reveal "strange and amazing providences" "that God has some great work in hand." This "Small treatise" which Stoddard sent in manuscript to Mather on October 17 has been ranked by Perry Miller, "along with a few books of Cotton Mather and John Wise's *Vindication* as one of the bridges by which New England passed from the seventeenth to the eighteenth century." Miller labeled it as "the only speculative treatise since the founders and before Edwards that makes any constructive contributions to New England theology." In its own day it received wide distribution, and even though Mather and Willard opposed its publication, it was printed by a prominent Boston publisher. Its preeminent place in the Great Awakening is illustrated by the fact that in the year Stoddard died, 1729, a new edition was reissued with the valedictory praises of Benjamin Colman, leader of the Brattle Street Church in Boston, that it "outshines all the rest" of Stoddard's works. Another edition, in 1742, during the Great Awakening, illustrated its Evangelical importance as did its reissue prior to the second Great Awakening in 1804.[56]

Less a manifesto of dissent than a call for a more thoroughly Calvinistic view of salvation, it began by asserting the awesome, incomprehensible sovereignty of the divine, quite unlike the Benevolent Being of the Mathers and of Willard, whose actions in history and creation were the objects of rational scrutiny. Indeed, whereas the first generation who followed Cotton's rational approach to religion decided on a test for religious experience, Stoddard found the whole approach utterly abhorrent. To him, the mystery and inscrutability of "an absolute free agent either to bestow mercy or to deny it" placed the divine outside of human accountability. (p. 13). Reason alone could not probe the holy: "men know not how to deny their own reason; they don't carry a sense upon their hearts of the imperfections and deceits of their own reason; they know not what dim-sighted things they are" (p. 3). Stoddard's antiintellectualism undermined the contractual aspects of federal theology that Samuel Willard and others were laboring to maintain.

Reasonable covenants could make God more palatable to men, they felt. "We conceive of God's decrees in a rational way," Willard explained, "because else we could entertain no conceptions at all about this glorious mystery." Stoddard disagreed. Ruthlessly stripping any false hope in human ability, he denied that God, like nature's well-oiled machine, was subject to rational comprehension. Conviction in the Savior was grounded in revelation, not on reason. Because the covenant was offered unconditionally to the elect, it was impossible for man to determine who was one of the elect. Although one was probably damned, one must strive to quicken the seeds of grace.[57]

Stoddard did not have access to Locke's theory of a unified "understanding," nor did he need it. He spoke from experience—not from philosophical erudition. In *The Safety of Appearing*, he asserted that the unifying agency of religion was the spiritual organ connecting the emotions and judgment. (Later he would assert it was also the political cement of the country.) "Once men are convinced of this ground of safety that faith is wrought in them by the mighty power of God, all that ministers can urge upon them will not take place; the choicest evidences will not sink into them till God opens their hearts" (p. 7, 1729 ed.). Although using the language of faculty psychology, it implicitly rejected the view of man's feelings and perceptions as independent and discrete. Instead, human awareness was unified by the organ of the conscience, the heart, which conjoined the Augustinian parts of the soul, knowledge and love (or, will). Stoddard believed that God's grace was a mystery to be contemplated but not to be comprehended: man could experience and "be greatly affected with the Gospel for a time," even though "it cannot assure the man of the truth of it" (p. 188).

Elaborating on the nine-part structure of the 1679 "Arguments" *The Safety of Appearing* focused on the glory of God and the helplessness of man, reflected by the rubric on the title page:

Phil. 3:8.9. Yea doubtless, and I do count things but loss for the excellency of the knowledge of Jesus Christ my Lord, for whom I have suffered the loss of all things, and do count them but dung that I may win Christ and be found in him not having mine own righteousness which is of the law: but that which is through the faith of Christ, the righteousness which is of godly faith. (t-p.)

Stoddard's orientation, like his 1679 defense, was evident in his dialectic of reason and revelation:

The light of nature may discover to us that many pretended ways of acceptance are delusions, for it is contrary unto reason to imagine [that] God will take up with such things, but to determine what is the way is clearly beyond the most raised understanding of man without divine revelation. (p. 4)

Hearkening to the recent travails of war and pestilence he exhorted his congregation to a new spirituality: "The Lord has watched over you in the time of days when you lay open to the fury of the heathen and that has given you special token of his presence with you in his ordinances" (Sig A4v). Stoddard's sacramentalism at this time did not extend to "the heathen" Indians of the Valley, for he regarded them as having "lost the knowledge of the way salvation" (p. 2). Later this view would change. *The Safety of Appearing* was not without its internal inconsistences, and although Stoddard implicitly rejected faculty psychology, he viewed preparation in two stages, which may have confused readers because in the first stage, which was limited to the external call, man's rational capacity was instrumental in enlightening the soul with knowledge. However, the external call was intimately connected to the effectual call which was apprehension of the whole man:

God deals with men as with rational creatures and prevails upon their hearts in a way suitable to those natures, though he puts forth acts of power yet not of violence upon the will. But he gains the consent of that by the discovering [of] those reasons that are of sufficient weight to sway it. Indeed, the understanding and the will in man, being faculties of the same soul and really one and the same thing, the same act of God that puts light into the understanding does also suitably incline the will by convincing us and making us believe those truths that are the grounds of them. We believe and love, believe and repent, believe and fear, believe and submit, believe and venture on Christ. (p. 6)

While Stoddard called man's capacities his "faculties" he implied their conjunction of interpenetrating capacities. Thus he could say that the whole man was a blend of all his faculties, and all his faculties tasted "the choicest evidences" of "the mighty power of God" when "God opens their hearts as he opened the heart of Lydia" (p. 6).

Religious conversion, according to Stoddard, involved the total personality, which was personified in the Savior's "mediatorly" role. The New Testament did not abrogate the Old since "Christ's righteousness is the righteousness of the Law" (p. 23). "It answers the demand the law makes of us and therefore it is safe appearing in it"

(p. 24). Stoddard distinguished between the covenant of works, "an everlasting rule of righteousness wherein God requires perfect obedience" (p. 29) from the covenant with Adam, as "a particular covenant whereby he was constituted a legal head or representative of his posterity to act in our behalf . . . to be the figure of him that is to come. . . (Rom. 5:15). He was the figure of Christ inasmuch as he was made a public person as Christ was" (p. 35). While the covenant with Adam has never been fulfilled, the covenant of works has been fulfilled by Christ (p. 36). Thus, "the covenant of works did admit of a mediator (p. 39) who stands between God and man"—Jesus Christ (p. 40). Stoddard indicated that the same wholeness of personality so basic to man was inherent in Christ: "There are three things requisite unto the mediatorly office of Christ—the fitness of his person, the consent of the father and his own consent." This integrity of one's conscience was integral to the efficacity of the covenant of redemption which was predicated on the mutual consent of the Father and the Son (p. 45).

The second argument of *The Safety of Appearing* revealed Stoddard's use of typology. A type can be defined as "any person, action or thing appointed by God to signify or represent some Gospel truth. The types of the Old Testament were instituted by God to shadow forth Christ Jesus" (p. 64). As was common with his age, Stoddard used the suffering servant of Isaiah 53 as typological evidence that "it was foretold that Christ should die for our sins" (p. 61). Several other Old Testament sacrifices were also types of Christ (Lev. 1:4, 5:5, Gen. 22:13, 8:21) "because Christ is often called a sacrifice (Eph. 5:2) and said to offer up himself (Heb. 9:26). Hence he is also called 'the Lamb slain from the foundation of the world' (Rev. 13:8) . . . the offerings of Christ were the accomplishment of what was typed of old (Heb. 13:12, 13)." Typology, Stoddard believed, proved that The Lord's Supper, and its type, the Paschal Supper, had a mysterious efficacy:

1. Because the deliverance out of Egypt was a type of our spiritual and eternal deliverance. Exod. 20:2 . . . .
they were delivered out of Egypt that they might be brought into Canaan which was a type of heaven.
2. Jesus Christ is called our Passover I Cor. 5:7.
3. Christ's blood is called the blood of sprinkling Heb. 12:24.
4. They were enjoined not to break a bone of the Paschal Lamb Exod. 12:46 . . . (and) the soldiers did not break the legs of Christ (John 19:36). (p. 67)

Thus, Hebrew sacramentalism foreshadowed the efficacy of Christ's blood, which "held forth the purification of the soul . . . (Heb. 19:13–14)" (p. 68), and the "nourishing Virtue of Christ" as "Spiritual meat . . . and . . . spiritual drink" (p. 69).

Furthermore, central to this reinvestiture of the sacraments with a new aesthetic, the taste of divine beauty was something to be cultivated. God's glory was to be seen, for instance, in "the white garments of the priests and the beautiful garments of the high priest" foreshadowed, just as "comliness in the sight of God [which] does arise from the sight of Christ (Zech. 3:4)" (p. 70). The general lack of concreteness of Stoddard's imagery of the divine was important to his psychology of religion, which provided a place for emotion. For Stoddard, the heart does not reason, it feels. In the third argument he indicated that when one's "heart reasons that God had so much love to sinners as to send his son to die that they might be reconciled to Him for his own glory" (p. 71), this demonstrated that the unilluminated soul could subvert the most profound truth of all. The Father's divine glory was consistent with the Son's exalted humanity. (p. 86)

The fourth argument, illustrative of the Christology of the Great Awakening in that it diluted the humanity of the Savior, identified Jesus with the triune God. As though echoing the ancient Monarchian theology of the second and third centuries, Stoddard's rhetoric enveloped the carpenter of Nazareth in a cloud so that the person of Jesus seemed to dissolve in "an infinite ocean of grace in the heart of God, whereby he can bestow the greatest gifts upon his creatures. . . . This is plain from that absolute liberty which the Scripture does ascribe unto God in all his acts" (p. 85 [1729] ed). The paradox of infinite grace and absolute liberty neatly brackets the divine drama, with man helplessly caught in the middle.

Stoddard's harsh Calvinism stressed the glory, the unaccountability and the mystery of God, and the fifth argument made it clear that only God could "give life (Heb. 10:2–3)" (p. 93). The absolute freedom of the divine will mysteriously bound man and his savior with faith. Man could rely on the new covenant. Although man was initially passive in receiving this faith, once having it he became an active agent in his own redemption. The sixth argument deftly twisted the dialectic showing how God's sovereignty encompassed the divine plan; although man appeared to be an active, free agent in mortal eyes, "the calls of the Gospel . . . many times propounded in a way of invitation" really "have the force of commands"

(p. 107). Man was constrained to follow them whether or not he realized it.

Since man's perceptions were inextricably conjoined in "the heart," spiritual renewal proceeded from this center of the personality, and the seventh argument indicated that the spirit assumed the role of converting agent, almost subsuming the role of the mediator. Once the "spirit convinces men" of the truth, man's heart experiences "a new light" (p. 112). "It is a work of the spirit to satisfy the heart" (p. 117). The spirit could be received, Stoddard noted, either "through the Word" (i.e., preaching) or "through the demonstration of the principles" (123) in the ordinances, hinting at a balance between Word and sacrament that would mark the next phase of his development.

The eighth argument developed his theory of preparation, which echoed Thomas Hooker's: "from God's bestowing the beginnings of salvation on believers here in this world" "there are some degrees of salvation which God bestows" and these beginnings start from "an inchoation already . . . through sanctification and inward comfort" (p. 128). Stoddard explained that "I take sanctification for that work of God's spirit whereby he does more and more purge away the remainders of sin and carry on the work of holiness in the hearts of his people and this is the fruit of faith in Christ. (Acts 26:18)" (p. 131). The regenerating heart was the locus of religious affections (through which every believer has experience of a great change in himself) which "are acted by . . . higher principles than self love" (p. 131). In this selfless love, Stoddard believed that sometimes the people of God "do enjoy actual communion with God in this world" when he discloses "his own glorious nature to them" either by "the acting of grace" on "the heart" "to see his power and glory as they have seen him in the sanctuary (Ps. 63:3)" (p. 136), or "by revealing . . . Christ and Gospel-grace to the soul" which answers "all objections of the heart" (p. 136). Furthermore, "promises of particular mercies" or God's quickening the "heart to holiness wherein they have some sense of sweetness that is in the promises" were additional ways Stoddard viewed man's approach to the holy as being efficacious. In any case, however, reason was totally inadequate to frame the encounter of the regenerate with their creator and redeemer, and, perhaps consciously echoing Henry More's Christian Platonism, Stoddard asserted that the saints "do not need a candle to see the sun" (p. 138).

The ninth and last argument stipulated that "it is safe appearing before God in that righteousness the efficacy where of unto salvation we are taught in the sacraments in the New Testament" (p. 141). Both baptism and communion were seals of faith, presuming the righteousness of the believer (pp. 142–44). Yet, this did not imply that the ordinances did not have a strengthening role. However weak one's faith, the ordinances could vivify it and make it stronger. As yet, however, Stoddard did not wish to open the ordinances to the unregenerate, unbaptised members of the community of Northampton, and in hopes of protecting the message he was conveying he addressed himself to "The pride of man's heart" when "self love" becomes the ruling passion (p. 172): "as with a traitor that gets into a castle because he sees no other way of preservation, so awakened sinners, though they have many misgivings of heart that all their righteousness of heart will not do, . . . look to this as the most probable course." The casuistical intent of *The Safety of Appearing*, was revealed by the admonition that "terrors of conscience . . . scared" sinners "into religion" because they "are afraid to see the plague of their own hearts" (p. 185). Stoddard was using the Amesian casuistry, exhorting that, where faith is real, the approving conscience is active and "the spirit works a principle of faith and draws it into act, sanctifies the reason and understanding and discovers the glorious excellency of God whereby the heart is assured" (p. 223). Furthermore, "All that have inward light and teaching become unto Christ. Tis true there is an illumination that is not effectual to work faith . . . but there is an inward light that is always attended with faith" (p. 227). Inner Light was the "principle put into every man in his first creation to seek his own happiness" and that once imbued with a glimmer of this light "it is against nature . . . to stay away from Christ" (p. 228). Thus, the workings of the spirit conform to nature, albeit mysteriously; this was Stoddard's way of making the deity both incomprehensible and yet not totally irrational. Once drawn "out of darkness into light man's heart is affected" by three religious emotions: "hopes of pardon and glory, . . . love . . . and fear" (p. 229). The three basic emotions were stimulated by the traditional persons of the trinity: love of the spirit, hope of the son's pardon and glory, and fear of the father's wrath. Even in 1685 the trinitarian persons were becoming abstract, a tendency that was to continue into the Great Awakening as the images of love and light, heart and sun coalesced around the glorious nature of

Christ, who subsumed the role of the other two persons of the trinity.

Finally, the ninth argument argued "from the sacraments of the New Testament" that "it is safe appearing before God in that righteousness the efficacy whereof unto salvation we are taught . . . God . . . is by sensible signs teaching of us this truth . . . [that] Baptism . . . is a shadow of some spiritual thing[:] salvation through the sufferings of Christ" (p. 141–44). Stoddard relied on the ancient ransom theory of the atonement when he indicated that "Christ's death was the payment of our debt" (p. 145).

Stoddard closed *The Safety of Appearing* in traditional sermonic form by offering four uses of the doctrine and eight specific directions to daily application, reinforcing his newly developed and thoroughgoing sacramentalism. The uses were designed to reprove the falsely righteous, to assist individuals in self examination, to awaken sinners and to help saints persevere (pp. 159, 203, 261, 309). The directions included better attendance of the ordinances, attaining a clearer understanding of salvation, not being superstitious or discontent, following the examples of saints, hearing and applying the Word, and securing "a more spiritual acquaintance with God" (pp. 335, 341, 342, 346, 350). But it was in the first direction that Stoddard evinced his more than implicit break with Massachusetts Puritanism. "God is setting up the offer of . . . grace before you in his Word and in the . . . Lord's Supper," but, he exhorted, "God no where requires a faith of assurance in those that partake of the ordinance," because it was "a special help to those that are in the dark with a good conscience" (p. 338). Curiously, the 1729 edition omitted the last phrase. Reminiscent of his early *tripos* poem at Harvard, Stoddard exhorted that it is better to be damned "for attending with the hope that one's faith might be stirred up than be damned" for not participating. He assured his Northampton flock "that there is no bar in any mens way" (285, 1729 ed.), because "God fits some men to discover men's uprightness unto them and to shew them how to get it. Have recourse to such as may comfort you with the comfort whereby they themselves are comforted of God" (p. 340; p. 286, 1729 ed.). Yet, despite his offering the ordinances to all those "believers" wishing it, Stoddard still had not taken the step to call it a converting sacrament.

The Safety of Appearing was not without its internal inconsistencies, but its general thrust was away from the incipient eighteenth-century rationalistic Calvinism which was exemplified in the theology of Mather and Willard. Probably a composite of sermons preached between 1679 and 1685, it reflected a pragmatic emphasis: the nine theses (which form the basic argument) occupy less than half of the book while the uses and directions comprise the rest. Over half of his message was devoted to the practical art of living to God. This Stoddardean pragmatism revealed him as a true frontiersman.

Alerted that things were not as calm as they appeared in the Valley, and probably spurred on by this first major publication of 1687, Edward Taylor wrote to Stoddard in February 1688 that he heard a "report that comes very hot to us upon some occasions afoot in your church" that they were about to "cast of relations and to bring all above fourteen years of age that live morally, and having catechistical knowledge of the principles of religion, to the Lord's Supper. . . . " Taylor offered the well-worn arguments that open communion, so long feared but not yet applied, would defile the true nature of the ordinances as seals. Did he want, Taylor entreated, future generations to "date the beginnings of New England's apostasy in Mr. Stoddard's motions?" Trying to convince Taylor that he was sincere and justified in his beliefs, in June 1688 Stoddard tried to explain how he had arrived at his position:

But I shall give you this brief account of the reason of what I did. I have been abundantly satisfied these many years, that we did not attend the will of God in this matter; and that our neglect therein is the occasion of the great profaneness and corruption that hath overspread the land, and therefore thought it both necessary for myself, that I might be found doing the will of God, and necessary for the country, that we might not go on further to forsake God. If in this matter I should be under any mistake, I should be glad of better light. But I judge that it is the cause of God, and am therefore under pressures of spirit in all regular ways to promote it. If I cannot carry it on in a way of peace, and according to a rule, I am willing to submit to the rule of God; but shall look upon it as a frown on the land.[58]

"A frown on the land"—how this contrasted with the heady joys of earlier days when strict and moderate Congregationalists—Cotton and Hooker, Shepard and Warham—had been united in a common expectancy that their mission to the wilderness would bear the fruit of the Second Coming. Apocalyptic millenarianism had faltered with the shifting piety in New England to the point where fear of divine wrath now nearly had replaced millenarian hope.[59]

Still, Taylor was sincerely affectionate in not wishing to offend his brother in Northampton, and he felt that if he refuted the 1679 "Arguments" perhaps this would convince him of his errors. How little Taylor understood of the momentum Stoddard had gained by 1688 after the publication of *The Safety of Appearing*, a momentum which was lost on his other opponents as well! Thus, Taylor procured a copy of the "Nine Arguments" and began his refutation, but even as he took pen to hand his Northampton brother was taking a step bolder than any other in his thirty-seven years.[60]

VI   *The Sermon on Paul's Epistle to the Galatians (1690)*

Although Governor Sir Edmund Andros had begun his administration with a firm but fair hand, many New Englanders resented his intrusion into their politics. Increase Mather had sailed to London to persuade the King to restore the old charter. Many were probably surprised when the Glorious Revolution of 1688 did little to improve matters. When James II was deposed and William of Orange became regent, things ironically looked bleaker than ever for Mather's mission. William revealed his intention of imposing a new charter in which religion would have no impact on Bay Colony enfranchisement laws. Perhaps Stoddard in his western outpost sensed the political realities of the trans-Atlantic struggle, but in any case, astutely judged that the time was ripe for a sweeping change in the order of church and society. Anthony Stoddard's death in 1688 symbolized the passing of the first-generation settlers. Indeed, the period 1688–1691 was the beginning of a transition of power for Northampton's oligarchy as pestilence swept the west. Finally in 1696 the two elderly deacons, William Holden and Jonathan Hunt, were replaced simultaneously on their deaths in September by ambitious younger men, Nathaniel Phelps and John Clark.

On October 5, 1690, Stoddard preached a sermon on Paul's Epistle to the Galatians (3:1). As Edward Taylor noted, the sermon taught "that the Lord's Supper was a converting ordinance . . . and urged till on an occasion of the ruling elder's absence by reason of sickness and many if not almost all the ancient members of the church were dead then he calls this church to a new convenanting and among other articles presented gains a major part to this article to bring all to bring all to the Lord's Supper that had knowledge of the principles of religion and not scandalous by open sinful living."[61] Although it is rare that one sermon can be used to mark a major turning point in a minister's career, Stoddard's message reverberated across Massachusetts in murmurings and whispers, as the orthodox renewed their steadfast intent of preserving ecclesiastical purity that Increase Mather was striving to secure through a restoration of the old charter. Until this point Stoddard had genuinely resisted the final step toward opening the church in Northampton to all the good-living people of the town regardless of their previous church estate, but now he cast the die. All the respectable adults in the town were to be given ostensibly a common religious and social footing. The broader significance of Stoddard's Presbyterial polity was that it anticipated by a year and a half the new charter issued by King William, which rejected church membership as a prerequisite for citizenship.

Essential to understanding the inspiration of the Galatians sermon is his "Arguments for the Proposition . . . " in which he consciously followed the English Protestant converting ordinance doctrine which traced its lineage back through John Humphry, Geoffrey Timson, and William Prynne to Thomas Erastus. Unlike his earlier pragmatically inspired exhortations, Stoddard now revealed how his own education affected his shaping mind. Apparently under his Harvard tutors, Jonathan Mitchell and John Norton, he had mulled over the works of theologians, and had extracted the essence that most appropriately fitted the practical circumstances which confronted him. Like a true pragmatist, he now was applying his eclectic solutions in his laboratory at Northampton. Carefully, Stoddard selected the text of his manifesto sermon to reflect the situation of the churches in New England as he perceived them. Paul had written the letter to the Galatians because they had maintained that all who entered the church were bound to observe all the requirements of Mosaic law. Paul argued that faith alone justified man and that the works of the law were powerless to lead to salvation (Gal. 1–3). The Galatian Judaizers attacked Paul's doctrine of Christian liberty and Paul's own Apostolic authority, but the Apostle staunchly defended his authority and his position that the Savior frees man from the law (Gal. 3:10–14). Stoddard implied by his use of this epistle that he, like Paul, was being falsely accused by those who wanted ordinances predicated on the observance of legalistic requirements. The strict, legalistic Puritans, "foolish Galatians," limited the Lord's Supper to the few.

In Ramist fashion Stoddard opened with the inexorable logic of his text:

Text. Gal. 3:1 Oh! Foolish Galatians! Who hath bewitched you . . . ?
1. He upbraids them with their folly
2. . . . he puts a smart question . . . , "Who hath bewitched you?"
3. He mentions their fault . . . . They did not obey the truth
4. The aggravation of the fault . . . . They had means to make them believe the truth.
1. Their eyes beheld Christ in the sacred representation
2. That Christ was crucified among them
   1 At Jerusalem . . . he was really put to death
   2 At Rome . . . Christ may be said to be crucified by the power of the Romans
   3 At Galatia . . . in the preaching of the Word and especially in the Administration of the Lord's Supper.

Although Stoddard used Ramist logic to break open his text, he was still operating within the medieval exegetical fourfold tradition that viewed every event in Scripture and nature as conveying four kinds of truths, including the literal and three symbolic interpretations—the allegorical, the tropological and the anagogical. For instance, in the Galatians text, Pilate crucified a rebel Jew—this was the literal sense. Yet, the person borne on the cross was more than mere man, it was the symbol of humanity destroyed by the evil power of the state—this was the allegorical sense. The appearance of Christ when he was revealed "to the people in both preaching and sacraments" at Galatia was the moral pedagogy or tropological message to have everyman live according to the Gospel.

Finally, the anagogical meaning, the one used by Stoddard as the doctrine for his sermon, was summarized succinctly:

Doct: The Lord's Supper is appointed by Jesus Christ for the begetting of grace as well as for the strengthening of grace.
Argument 1. It is appointed to be administered to many that are not really saints.
Argument 2. The Lord's Supper hath in its a tendency to begetting of faith.
   1. Therein is an offer of Christ.
   2. Therein is a remembrance of the death of Christ.

3. Therein is a confirmation of the truth of the covenant of grace.
Argument 4. If the Lord's Supper be not appointed for the begetting of grace . . . they that have no grace have no occassion to seek the increase of grace. . . .
Argument 5. . . . God in other ordinances is taking care for the conversion of sinners as well as the edification of Saints.

In one blow Stoddard toppled the whole theory that sacraments were seals of an already existing state. Instead, he reconsidered them as means to an end, as devices designed to encourage religious awakening. The Lord's Supper was not merely a preservative from sin, it was a means to salvation, an integral part of the *ordo salutus*. It was erroneous to limit the Lord's Supper to none but visible saints. Indeed, no matter how strict one was in admitting saints to communion, many false witnesses regularly gained admission (p. 2).

Stoddard, like John Cameron, hedged the problem of irresistible grace. From the human point of view, the divine offer was in reality a command, "that it's a duty to come and that it's dangerous to stay away . . ." (p. 3). Freedom from the law and liberty in Christ was a responsibility as well as a privilege: "Some refrain from the Lord's Supper out of fear that they are unworthy and even member saints have periods of doubt; yet to desist unless one is certain would make 'sacrament days . . . ' days of torment and disquietment to the people of God and that which was ordained for their comfort would be for their affliction" (p. 4). Communion, like all other ordinances, was capable of turning "men from darkness into light and from the power of Satan unto God. . . . ." Stoddard's light/dark imagery utilized fourfold symbolism again: traditionally Christ was believed to have identified Himself on the allegorical level with the sun: "I am come a light into the world that whosoever believeth in me should not abide in darkness" (John 12:46). On the tropological level, however, solar-light imagery described souls responsive to grace and conversely "everyone that doeth evil hateth the light . . . " (John 3:17). Finally, the anagogic level revealed Christ, the light of the Sun, in his glorious union with the Father in eternity, shared by the righteous, who shall "shine forth as the sun in the Kingdom of their Father" (Matt. 13:43). If other contemporaries looked to the fragmentary symbolism of God as the Sun and everlasting light (Ps. 84:11; Ps. 104:2; Isa. 60:19–20). Stoddard relied on the Gospel to provide a reinvigorated and unified Christological language in which all points of reference converged on the mediator.

Similarly, the minister's role in the divine drama of redemption was reinvigorated as an apostolic mission. "Our ministry," Stoddard exhorted, is "the ministry of reconciliation." The two primary theological *foci* he emphasized were the Word and ten ordinances. In the application of both, Stoddard conceived that God operated directly on the hearts of mankind. Above all, the religious experience was emotional, requiring all the power of language to "draw forth the many actings of grace." To this end Stoddard applied the fourfold imagery to kindle the "principle of life" in his auditors' hearts, "to turn the hearts of the fathers to the children and the disobedient to the wisdom of the just" (pp. 4–5). Stoddard raised four objections to his own doctrine in an effort to counter arguments from his opponents, such as Edward Taylor and Increase Mather:

Objection

1. . . . baptism [is] a sacrament of regeneration [but] the Lord's Supper [is] a sacrament of nourishment Answer. Baptism is a sign of regeneration . . . but yet it is not always a means of regeneration . . . . and many adult persons have been regenerated before they were baptised as Cornelius, Lydia . . . .

2. the bread and wine in the Lord's Supper are food . . . only to nourish those that have a principle of life

Answer 1 . . . if any men were vicious and so separated from communion . . . they lost their sacramental nature

2 . . . sinners are invited to come unto Christ as the bread of life and the water of life (John 6:35)

3. If such as are not converted do come to the Lord's will become guilty of great sin

Answer 1. Saints may be guilty . . . in an unholy manner . . .

2. Men may not neglect their duty . . . and must go as far as they can in a way of obedience.

3. There is ground to hope God will give them grace at the time

4 . . . it is best to let all wicked men come to the supper

Ans. It is appointed to be a means of conversion only to all visible believers that are not scandalous and can discern the Lord's Body (pp. 6–7)

Finally Stoddard offered four uses of his doctrine, which demonstrated his Evangelical intentions.

Uses. 1. Of awakening them that have come often to the Lords Supper and are yet not converted

2. Of advise to the Church not to be backward to admit orderly professions to the Lord's Supper though you may fear they are not savingly converted

3. Tho no man can have any sincere desires to be converted till he is converted, yet many of you from a conviction of your danger in your present condition may be earnestly desirous to be converted.

4. Exhortation to . . . unconverted persons . . . to get into a state of grace . . . Here is encouragement to you to cry to God for his blessing . . . (Matt. 20:30) Here is conviction of the dreadful anger of God for sin (Matt. 26:26) Here is a spectral opportunity to . . . examine whether they be converted or no . . . . (I Cor. 11:28) Here is a new engagement to be the Lord's . . . . Here is conviction that there is no salvation in any other way. Here is much encouragement to believe on Jesus Christ. (pp. 8/9)

For Stoddard, the sacramentalist, the duty of the minister was to give his parishioners every opportunity to seize grace, while the duty of the people was to strive constantly after it: Christian liberty implied both a privilege and a duty to attend the sacraments. This was still very far, however, from true Evangelicalism.

Edward Taylor, in the midst of refuting Stoddard's mild 1679 "propositions," was taken aback and immediately turned to his own Foundation-Day sermon, inserting specific arguments against Stoddard's new ideas. Similarly, in his *Sacramental Meditations*, Taylor portrayed communion as a "sweet supper" "Filled with all grace," but it was reserved for the saints alone:

> But lest this Covenant of Grace should ere
> Be held by doubting Saints all violate
> By their infirmities as Adams were
> By one transgression and be so vacate
> It's Seal is food and's often to be used
> To seal new pardons freshening faith, misused.
> Then make me, Lord, at thy sweet supper spy
> Thy graces all well flourishing in me.
> And seal me pardon up and ratify
> Thy covenant with me, thus gracious be.
> My faculties all decked with grace shall Chime
> Thy praise, with Angels and my grace shall shine.[62]

These were private criticisms, not divulged to the public, but in Boston the ecclesiastical reaction to Stoddard's Galatians sermon

was indirect but more overt. Polemics penetrated tracts in a haunt-
ingly pervasive way, and the Cambridge Association was formed by
the Mathers in 1690 to develop a united front against Stoddardeanism and deliberated "in fear and trembling lest Solomon Stoddard should speak, but it was prevented from attacking him lest it
publically jeopardize the pretense of New England Unity." Unlike
his father, Increase, in England, Cotton was less restrained in defending the orthodoxy, but even he did not venture open attacks on
Stoddard. Instead, he had *A Companion for Communicants* issued
in Boston in 1690, reiterating the well-worn "Devout methods of
preparing and approaching the Blessed ordinance." Alluding to
Stoddard, he cautioned against "a sort of man who tells us that a
base profession of dogmatical historical faith (which . . . they find it
hard enough to describe) together with submission to the Government of the Visible church will entitle a man to the Sacraments."
Instead, Mather mandated that a "probable and credible profession
of saving faith (and no less than that)" was the requirement for
admission. Probably referring to Stoddard's 1690 sermon on Galatians Cotton Mather explained that the Eucharist "is not Ex In-
stituto, a converting ordinance . . . , this ordinance has never by
accident been sanctified for the first conversion of them that had
never been brought home to God before." Exasperated, he looked
to the valley and exclaimed, "Indeed, this dogma is a new thing; the
assertions run counter to the common sense of the church in all ages
and have an army to man against them."[63]

When Increase returned to Boston, father and son sought to dis-
credit Stoddard openly in a biography of Stoddard's former Harvard
tutor, Jonathan Mitchell. In the preface, Increase denied the value
of membership requirements for New England churches, even denied that public profession should be required, conceding that it
was enough for a church to "know for as man can judge that person
whom they admit to the Lord's Supper are fit and have a right to be
there." Having made this major concession, Increase then noted
that the "real apostacy . . . and degeneracy from the reformation"
was the notion of the Supper as a converting ordinance which
transform the church into the world. Alluding to Stoddard's intellectual mentor, Increase shrewdly noticed, "You know that your Pastor
Mitchell had a latitude in his judgment as to the subject of baptism . . . but as to admission to the sacrament I know no more that
was more conscientiously careful to keep unqualified persons from

partaking than was he." Indeed, as though Increase had read Stoddard's "Arguments for the Proposition," which explained his sources of converting ordinance theology, Mather indicated that "above all their notion is to be rejected . . . who assert that the sacrament is a converting ordinance . . . their heterodoxy has been . . . refuted not only in Congregational writers, such as Mr. John Beverly against Timson but also by . . . Presbyterians . . . , Mr. Gelespy in his *Aarons Rod*, Dr. Drake in the *Answer* to Mr. Humphry and Mr. Vines in his *Treatise of the Lord's Supper*." As Cotton Mather's *Magnalia Christi Americana* was taking shape, he, like his father, injected a partisan tone critical of Northampton's alledged apostasy.

Stoddard, however, continued unabashed as struggle for power in his town erupted in another witchcraft case. In the spring of 1691 Mary Randall, a young daughter of a newly arrived and socially aspiring family, experienced fits of violence similar to those of Sarah Good and Sarah Osborn in Salem the following year. Charged with witchcraft by the Springfield court in September 1691, Stoddard was unable to find marks of the devil on her person so no trial was ever instituted; she was merely released in her father's custody. It was the last case of witchcraft to come before Hampshire County. Was the hysteria Mary exhibited a misinterpreted sign of a religious conversion experience, as Stoddard preached in his best style from Galatians? Perhaps, for we do know that a third religious awakening rippled through old Nonotuck five years later. It is sociologically important that this third collective response to Stoddard's preaching occurred as the first-generation oligarchy was in the process of abdicating its power to younger sons and that social as well as religious aspiration and sensitivity of the youth were heightened.[64]

VII The Tryal of Assurance (1698)

As far as the Mathers were concerned, Stoddard's concealed apostasy was only a more remote aspect of the problem of authority facing them in their own pulpits. Between 1697 and 1699 vociferous opponents of strict Congregationalism had been discovered in Brattle Street, Cambridge, and in Charlestown. Both symbolized the changing religious climate of New England. In the former location, a group of Harvard-educated merchants, Thomas Brattle and his brother and John Leverett, offered the pulpit of their church to Benjamin Colman, an avowed critic of Congregationalism. In Charlestown Simon Bradstreet offered innovative policies to his

parishioners which were very far from the strict Cottonian Code
imposed by that church's first minister, Zachariah Symmes. These
events happened to occur as Increase Mather was preparing initial
drafts of his *Magnalia Christi Americana*, the epic of Christ's works
in America. As the title suggested, the epic format demanded that
each *dramatis persona* must fit his role in the divine errand, so
Increase completely ignored any diversity of opinion regarding the
foundation of Massachusetts' franchise and Cotton's Code. According
to him, both Massachusetts and Connecticut had been established
on identical principles, and John Cotton and Thomas Hooker were
in complete agreement on every point of doctrine and ecclesiology.
In like fashion he had just written the section on Jonathan Mitchell,
Stoddard's Harvard tutor, and Stoddard was furious with Mather's
treatment of him as a supporter of Cotton's Code.[65]

In order to set the record straight that not all had been as uncon-
tested as the Mathers had recently depicted, Stoddard delivered a
brief attack on maintaining the old code of strict polity without
revision. Offering an exhortation from II Peter 1:10, "Brethren, give
diligence to make your election sure," Stoddard launched into John
21:17, "Simon, Son of Jonas, lovest thou me?" Speaking as though
he were a strict Congregationalist, Stoddard offered the doctrine
that "If a man does not certainly know that he has performed an act
of saving grace, he cannot be certain of his sincerity from his walk"
(pp. 1–2). It was immediately clear that the light/life imagery used in
the Galatians sermon was primary to the rhetoric of this message: "If
a thing shine like a fire in the night yet you cannot know it to be fire
from thence unless you see in it some property of fire; If a thing acts
as if it had life, you cannot know from thence that it has life unless
you know some action to be a vital action, You cannot know that a
man does miracles unless you know some one action to be miracu-
lous" (p. 4). But, just how does one know the essence of an action or
a thing? Rather than being preoccupied with psychology, Stoddard
made it clear he was concerned with the essence of being, with
ontology, just as Plato was in the *Dialogue of Theaetetus*. Knowledge is not opinion, but rather it is participation in essence and
reality, being and truth.[57] For Stoddard there was no substitute for
the experience of being. This permitted him to draw three corol-
laries:

1. An holy life is a certain way of a holy heart . . .
2. They that walk in a way of unholiness are not sincere . . .

3. Many men seem to themselves to walk in a way of unholiness yet don't certainly know that even they did perform an act of saving grace. (pp. 5–6)

Just as opinion was not truth, appearance did not constitute reality. The ontological dimension of salvation was that the new being, the regenerate person, depends on divine grace, not on one's actions, and three arguments were given to show why it was false to judge holiness by adherence to moral law:

Arg. 1. It is the action of grace that makes and shews the walk to be holy . . . not the orderliness of men's walk . . . nor the affectionatives of mens hearts in religion . . . nor good carriage . . . nor a good behavior.
    2. . . .
    3. If the holiness of a man's action can't be discerned severally it can't be discerned in conjunction.
    4. If there be no act of grace there be no sincerity.
    5. The multiplication of more acts as are common to saints and sinners don't show him to be sincere. (pp. 7–10)

These warnings were issued against legalisms Stoddard perceived in his colleagues' hypocrisy of knowing who was converted and who was not. It is false to look to outward actions to discover one's spiritual condition, Stoddard reasoned, for the inner spirit is not the object of rational introspection.

This led naturally to the uses of this doctrine. One was designed to help those who "are unsatisfied about their sincerity though they have a pretty good conversation. . . ." Another was to help those who could not be certain of a man's sincerity from his conversation "because if they don't see the action of grace they cannot be assured," because "the inward actings of grace are invisible to others" and "men cannot by words or actions make the actings of grace so visible to others that they can distinguish them" (pp. 11–14). As if this were not a radical enough doctrine of the absolute otherness of religious experience, Stoddard issued his "warnings" that "some men will be confident that they are in good estate though they do not know that even they believed in Christ" (p. 14). Finally, Stoddard pleaded, "don't let grace be in an arbitrary condition, let it flourish" (p. 17). *The Tryal of Assurance* promulgated Stoddard's theological arguments to a restive Boston audience. In less than a year the Brattle Street congregation secured Benjamin Colman, newly ordained by a London Presbytery, and they published a "manifesto" of their opposition to strict Congregational practices. In this melee it appeared that Stoddard and the Brattle group were mounting a two-pronged attack on the orthodoxy, albeit in an uncoordinated fashion. John Higginson and Nicholas Noyes, two strict Congregational clergymen, leveled their criticisms at Colman and associates "in the controversial power of church order and discipline" which they had set "set up" by themselves. "Sirs," they exclaimed, "how could you foresake the dear churches some of you belonged to [and] the practice of the churches of New England in such and so many instances" as ordination by a London Presbytery and open ordinances? Cotton Mather echoed the xenophobic lament that they invited an "ill party thro' all the country . . . [and] throw all into confusion. . . ."[66]

CHAPTER 3

Pope of the Instituted Church

I A New Order of Society

BY 1700 the opposition of the orthodox Congregationalists, led by the Mathers, to moderates in both the Connecticut River Valley and in eastern Massachusetts seemed to adumbrate an intracolonial religious war. Cotton Mather wrote his *Magnalia Christi Americana*, a polemic for the supposed monolithic platform of Congregationalism in the first sixty years of the Bay Colony's holy experiment, but he was aware that dissent had stemmed from his own progenitor Richard Mather through the careers of his Harvard tutors Norton and Mitchell. The Anglo-American debates which had been initiated in 1637 by Richard Bernard, the minister of Batcomb, Somersetshire, whose son had emigrated to Weymouth but returned home, demonstrate how the first generation's attempt to define a monolithic platform based on the early church had divided New England Congregationalists. Moderates like Thomas Hooker and John Warham, who founded Connecticut Colony, rejected the Winthrop-Cotton model of religion as the basis of the state. The knowledgable lay-Puritan, William Pynchon, who founded his own trading settlement at Springfield, had his own minister, the Reverend George Moxon, implement worship according to Pynchon's ideas, which ultimately cost both their freedom to live in the colony. Pynchon rejected the premise upon which Cotton's Code rested, that only the experientially pure in heart were fit to vote and hold office, and Pynchon was not alone. The Cambridge Platform of 1648 had so polarized the strict and moderate factions within Congregationalism that at the end of the century the battle was still being waged; the Brattle Street Church was founded by the desire "of the people for a larger freedom in church discipline and doctrine. Namely 1) enlargement of baptism, 2) greater control

103

of the Congregation in choosing a pastor and directing church government, 3) omitting a relation of conversion for church membership, and 4) freedom to conduct worship without regard to the plain
style of the early Puritans."[1] Thomas Brattle initiated the formation
of this church when he transferred his Boston property, "Brattle
Close," to Thomas Clark, on January 10, 1698. A year and a half
later, the society had expanded and included Boston liberals Capt.
Benjamin Davis, John Mico, Thomas Cooper, John Colman, John
Leverett, Ebenezer Pemberton, and Simon Bradstreet. On July 19,
1699, they persuaded Benjamin Colman, then in England, to be
their pastor. Two weeks later Colman sought ordination by the
London Presbytery, fearing that he would not be ordained in Boston. This, of course, violated the Congregational principle that a
minister must be ordained by the church he was to serve, with the
approval of the Bay elders. On November 1, 1699, Colman was in
Boston and the church drafted "A Manifesto," which was a thinly
veiled challenge to the standing order, although it paid lip service to
the Westminster Confessional. It advocated the Anglican practice of
reading Scripture, offered "Baptism to those who only profess their
faith in Christ and . . . any child offered to us by any professed
Christian,"[2] and redefined visible saints as those who merely professed the faith. It opened selection of the pastor to all baptized
adults instead of the male members, as was the usual practice, and
it did not mention the need for a church covenant. Membership
in a particular church implied membership in a national church.

  Brattle's "Manifesto" slammed another wedge into the façade of
Massachusetts orthodoxy, immediately provoking Cotton Mather's
anguish:

A Company of head-strong men in the town, the chief of whom, are full of
malignity to the holy ways of our churches, have built in this town another
meeting-house, To delude many better-meaning men in their own company, and the churches in the neighborhood, they post a vote, in the
foundation of their proceedings, that they would not vary from the practice
of these churches, except in one particular. But a young man [referring to
Benjamin Colman], born and bred here, and hence gone for *England* is now
returned hither at their invitation, equipped with *ordination* to qualify him
for all that is intended. On his returning and arriving here, these fallacious
people, desert their vote and without the advice or knowledge of the ministers in the vicinity they have published, under the title of a *Manifesto*,
certain Articles, that utterly subvert our churches and invite an ill party

thro' all the churches, to throw all into confusion of the first opportunities. This drives the ministers that would be faithful unto the Lord Jesus Christ, and his interests in the churches, into a necessity of appearing for their defense. No little part of these actions must unavoidably fall to my share. I have already written a large monitory letter to these *Innovators*, which tho' most lovingly penned, yet enrages their violent and impetuous lusts, to carry on the *Apostasy*.[3]

Society also reflected a contest for power in 1700. Since the founding of Northampton in 1661, its oligarchy had controlled the town with an iron hand, preventing any but those with the proper qualifications from gaining admission to it. For instance, while the average estate of all inhabitants was worth £229, the average for the eighteen rulers was £534. All were church members, freemen, and selectmen, and from their ranks were chosen the deputies, the militia officers, and the ruling elders and deacons. Local power for the first generation could be traced back into the dim reaches of the English countryside; but in the new world intermarriage determined the networks of interlocking alliances. First-generation fathers were reluctant to concede their power in the form of land or wealth as long as they were alive, because political rank was intimately connected to landed position. Longevity aggravated this disproportionate control of towns by the few since nearly seventy percent of Northampton men lived beyond sixty. In order to preserve their nuclear families men with above-average estates, like Enos Kingsley, threatened their sons with disinheritance should they leave town, even after their deaths. It was a rare occurrence when men like George Alexander, William Clark, or John Strong actually granted land-titles to sons before their death. Since the system of partible inheritance was the only one used in Northampton, all sons were eligible to receive their share in their father's estate. Perhaps because of this paternal hold on Northampton land, thirty second-generation sons were awarded town lands, but only after they had been married. This points to another problem in Northampton and other Valley towns. Since inheritance was delayed, marriage was postponed, over sixty percent marrying over the age of twenty-four. Because they were dependent on either the town or their fathers for land, sons remained in Northampton, and by 1700 it had become a closed society. Between 1700 and 1729 only nine new families moved into town.

In 1700, the symbol for Northampton's consensual community
was its still-preserved open-field system of farming and husbandry,
but all of the old oligarchy except John King was dead. Since 1677
the oligarchy had fought to retain the nuclear quality of its
community by tightly packing homelots, ordering that no new
homes should be built unless they adjoined other homelots. The
family structure in Northampton combined the separate nuclear
household related through kindred networks in the community.
Marriage into families of even nearby towns was uncommon. Between 1670 and 1700, as the town's population increased from 500 to
1,000, one hundred heads of household emigrated while twenty-
eight moved into town. Most of those leaving were second-generation sons in search of land. Late maturity due to paternal pressures
probably contributed to the phenomenon that in Northampton, despite a doubling of population in three decades, on the average, five
children were born to all second-generation wives, at least two less
than in Plymouth or Andover families for the same period. These
patterns persisted into the third generation as the age at marriage
for men stabilized at nearly twenty-seven while for women it increased by nearly two years to twenty-four. On the average, third-
generation family size was reduced by one child. Paternalism and
reluctance of fathers to delegate power in the community, together
with succeeding generations' willingness to abide by delayed inheritance and community responsibility, led to a closed, intermarried,
society in Northampton. Adolescence was extended into one's twen-
ties while anxiety to develop sexually, socially, and spiritually increased.

Given the social situation, what do Stoddard's three revivals prior
to 1700 tell us about the impact of religion on social structure? An
analysis of all new communicants during the revival years of 1679,
1683, and 1696 reveals that many of the males had fathers who could
be expected to live long before any inheritance would be forthcoming. The ages of men averaged twenty-four, suggesting that interest
in religion was related to social status and strict paternalism. A
similar pattern is observable in the women. Religion, it would appear, offered a welcome release from these social pressures. Stoddard intuitively realized the social dimension of his religious revivalism, and his next publication would adumbrate his own views
on discipline.

The question still remains: was Stoddard a party to the Brattle

Society's struggle, and did they support him? Although Stoddard's *The Doctrine of Instituted Churches* was probably inspired by the Brattle-Mather controversy in the winter of 1699/1700, William Brattle seems to answer the latter question in the negative on November 18, 1700:

A great deal of trouble has been among us by reason of Mr. Stoddard's book, & [Increase Mather's] the *Order of the Gospel* etc. But I thank God (as to my own part) of [I] find weightier things to exercise my thoughts about. I hope I shall forever be cautious how I let my Religion spend into itself in those trifling controversies: Trifling (I mean) comparatively.[4]

Although Stoddard was sympathetic to the Brattle Church's opposition to the Mathers, and although he possibly took his cue from his friends Leverett, Colman, and Pemberton when he published his own 1700 manifesto, Stoddard did not incline to the latitudinarianism that the Brattle Society espoused. Stoddard was, by this time, a consistent sacramentalist, and his pragmatic view of the evolution of religious tradition had no place for the formalism, the esthetics, or the rationalism of the latitudinarian way. Stoddard wanted a national church, but he rejected both the Mathers' uncompromising Congregationalism on the one hand, and the Brattle Society's incipient Anglicanism on the other. However, the Brattle Society saw in Stoddard a forceful ally that could rally western support against the Mathers, and therefore they often came to his support when it was to their advantage in furthering the cause of Presbyterian discipline, not necessarily Evangelical doctrine. The Mathers, on the other hand, viewed this alliance of unlike twins apart from the issues, since it represented an eastern and western bloc to their power.

II   The Doctrine of Instituted Churches *(1700)*

The Doctrine of Instituted Churches, published by Ralph Smith "at the Bible under the Piazza of the Royal Exchange in Cornhill," London, in the spring of 1700, was Stoddard's first and only book on church government. It was hardly a product of his youth since he was now fifty-seven; therefore, it must be seen as his studied rejection of strict Congregationalism, as well as the Brattle group's latitudinarianism. Stoddard did not go back to the founders of the colony as Cotton Mather did in the *Magnalia*. Instead, he criticized

the Reformation's emphasis on discipline over doctrine, rejected
Calvin's authoritarian church-state of Geneva, and called for a return to Old-Testament institutions. For Stoddard, the New-Testament church was not institutionally normative. Those early years of
primitive Christianity were ones of experimentation, and if, indeed,
they had practiced a form of Congregationalism, it was because of a
political situation in which they had no control of government. The
situation in New England was entirely different, according to the
Northampton minister, because the government was in control of
the faithful. The emphasis on keeping the unfaithful from the ordinances which had characterized the early church's fight to retain its
identity was not applicable. The history of redemption, indeed,
stemmed from creation, not the Apostolic days. A return to the true
Christian church was, for Stoddard, a return to those typological
parallels in the Jewish synagogue. The "type" of the synagogue
prefigured the "antitype" of the church, just as Old-Testament ordinances prefigured those instituted by Christ. Stoddard's 1700
treatise was not merely a rejection of Congregational polity or
latitudinarian theology, it was a rejection of the magisterial Reformation. Stoddard saw a new hope for redeeming the spiritual gardens in the New England wilderness through Old-Testament institutions.

Keeping in mind this major thrust of *The Doctrine of Instituted
Churches*, one can better appreciate how it was not merely response
to Increase Mather's *The Order of the Gospel*. For years scholars
have argued over which was written first. Stoddard's was published
in London between March and July 1700, and Mather's was published in March in Boston. One tradition holds that Stoddard wrote
in reply to Mather, while another hypothesizes that the Boston
printer refused for reasons of his own to publish *The Doctrine,* so
Stoddard was forced to send it to London. In the meanwhile Mather
secured a manuscript copy of it and wrote his reply. A third possibility is that both documents circulated in manuscript and were
rewritten, incorporating language common to both, but whatever
the case, neither was merely a reply to the other. Stoddard was
responding to both the Mathers and the Brattle Society, Mather to
both the Brattle Society and Stoddard.[5]

The ten-chapter work argued that a return to early church government, the Gospel Order, was a futile attempt. The "Nature of an
Instituted Church and the Ordinance to be attended therein" had

caused "great animosities, discords, and persecutions" so that "multitudes of people are left at a loss whether there be any certain ruler to guide us or any certainty to be attended in these things" (1). Human institutions must change with the passing of time, Stoddard implied, and the contemporary problem stemmed from those who rested their case solely on tradition. The structures of Christianity must change as do all human institutions. Yet, strict Puritans, for instance, "have been exceeding tenacious of the traditions and ancient images of the church," through "a veneration for antiquity and . . . the sayings of ancient factions as [being] canonical," and basing "their church order on the New Testament [while] ignoring the Old Testament" (2). Tradition alone could supply no categorical answers such as "looking on all Old Testament rules . . . as out of date." Typology was a key which permitted a balanced scriptural exegesis, since it took into account the continuity of Old-Testament type and New-Testament antitype as symbols of the change in institutional history. For instance, circumcision was a type which prefigured baptism: all who were admitted to circumcision also should be admitted to the New-Testament ordinance. The same held true for the Passover and the Lord's Supper. The three categories of rules that applied to Christian life were:

1) Those which were of a "general, Moral" nature, similar in both the Old and New Testaments; 2) those types of the Old Testament Institutions, such as salvation, the nature of the church, ordinances and the law; 3) those antitypes pertaining to New Testament Institutions, such as church officers, the sacraments, and the sabbath. (3–4)

Chapter two, on "The Nature of Instituted Churches," indicated how far apart Stoddardean church government was from the Cambridge Platform. The latter had dichotomized the church into mystical and militant with the latter including a body of visible saints joined together in covenant to conduct public worship. Stoddard rejected the dichotomy and added a third category, the "instituted church," a "society of saints joined together according to the appointment of Christ for the constant carrying on of his public worship" (5). In Congregational polity, each "particular" church was complete in and of itself and membership in one church did not imply membership in another. Each was separately convenanted and ministers were separately ordained to each. Furthermore,

membership was a privilege conferred on those whose spiritual experiences were deemed satisfactory. Stoddard objected to the "re-
striction" of an instituted church "to those . . . who after the strict-
est examination give considerable evidence that they are saints" (6).
Rather, he defined "visible saints" as those who "make a serious
profession of their religion together with those that descend from
them till rejected by God" (6). The third chapter went on to deny
explicitly the basis of federal theology, the covenant:

> . . . some have thought that the form of a Congregational Church is a
> Church covenant, explicit or implicit, wherein they bind themselves to
> walk according to the order of the Gospel. . . . It is pleaded that nothing
> else can bind a free people to one another but an Ecclesiastical Covenant
> but there is somewhat else that binds a free people in the same town to
> mutual subjection to the government of the town, . . . these are bound by
> God and the rule of the Gospel, not by a Covenant. (7)

Only the national covenant existed in Old-Testament time: never
was there a synagogue covenant, and, therefore, there was no warrant, no "precept" nor "precedent" for church covenants, nor was
"there any need of it," if one could judge from the dissention over
church covenants in the early history of New England institutions.
Although it was just that every Christian should join in fellowship,
"there is no evidence that every member should covenant particularly with [one] church" (8).

Opposing the rationalism of strict Congregationalists, Stoddard
maintained that the church was founded on the arbitrary command
of God, not on the rational compact of men. The church covenant
did not bind men, since it was the "law of the land and the law of
God" that binds them (8). In the wilderness of western Massachusetts, where the enforcement of civil law was often difficult,
Stoddard indicated that the enforcer of church law was not man but
God, the supreme arbitrary lawmaker:

> Grant this particular covenant and we shall be to seek what church many
> children do belong to, if the father is in covenant with one church, the
> mother with another, the child was baptized in a third and still lives in a
> fourth. This doctrine of the particular covenant is wholly unscriptural, is the
> reason that many among us are shut out of the church, to whom church
> privileges do belong. (8)

In a short fourth chapter a certain amount of Congregational autonomy was left to the local "churches to choose their own officers, i.e., elders and deacons, [like] all free societies" (10) by majority vote. Stoddard's democratization of church elections did not, however, extend to women or servants or children who were wards of the state: "they that are not free are not to partake of the liberty" (10).

Having outlined the authority of the laity, the fifth chapter exposed the reverend elders' power:

> The teaching officer is appointed by Christ to baptize and administer the Lord's Supper, and therefore he is made the judge by God, what persons those ordinances are to be administered to, and it is not the work either of the brethren or ruling elders, any ways to intermeddle in that affair or limit him. We never read that the Apostles did advise with the church whether they should baptize such as offered themselves. As the administration of those ordinances is committed to them, so the judging concerning those who they are to be administered unto. . . . (12)

The elders were viewed as being scripturally parallel with the Apostles, a high view of clerical prerogatives, and even Cotton Mather felt that Stoddard had overstated the case, "For one minister alone envisioning him weilding a mitre in his western see." To assume this "power unto himself is to make himself a congregational pope."[6]

Not only were ministers the sole "rulers of the church," their authority to censure, to baptize and admit members was not bounded by the parish (23). Just as local churches were part of the national church, ordination of a minister was also into the national church. It was not necessary to be a pastor to a particular church to be a validly ordained minister:

> every man that is a pastor of a particular church stands in a more general relation as minister of Christ; Some that are not pastors to particular congregations are yet ministers of Christ; and every man that is pastor to a particular church is a minister of Christ, and by virtue of that relation he may do acts of office to the members of other churches occasionally, assemble with his own, and towards the other churches being desired when he can conveniently be spared from his own, and towards particular persons that are members of no church. (11)

Again, the frontier situation had led Stoddard to this conclusion. Itinerant ministers were needed on a frontier constantly moving westward, and the Massachusetts parish system threatened this expansion with artificial constraints. Indeed, even itinerant ministers should be able to baptise and admit settlers to the Lord's Supper (11). Once again, it was practical consideration that had led Stoddard to question the value of retaining rigid institutional structure.

The ordination of church officers, treated in chapter six, indicated how Stoddard viewed authority devolving on an Evangelical ministry. While the authority of the lay deacon was "confined to one congregation," the authority of the reverend elders extended "not only . . . over their particular church but also over others since" God "committed to national and provincial churches the care of particular congregations" (14). In order to control itinerant ministers, it was stipulated that "In a provincial church . . . ministers ought to be ordained by such elders as are appointed by the public ecclesiastical authority of the land. In such countries where the church is not in order, it is meet that ministers be ordained by some suitable persons deputed by the neighboring elders, but in case of necessity ministers may be ordained by some brethren appointed by the church to that service" (14).

Chapter seven outlined six parts of worship: prayer, music, preaching, baptism, communion, and ecclesiastical censure. The use of set forms of prayer (that had been advocated by Brattle and Colman) were forbidden because "he that hath not the gift of prayer is not fit to be a minister . . ." (15). The only music allowable was the singing of Psalms. Plain preaching was to be emphasized rather than, as the Brattle group advocated, reading the Word. Baptism was considered the fourth part of worship. It was a means to salvation administered by the ordained preachers to any righteous person, that is, "such adult persons as make such a profession of their Christian faith as is morally sincere are to be baptized. . ." (18). On this requirement of moral sincerity hinged admission to the Lord's Supper, and repeating his earlier statements, Stoddard permitted "all such professors of the Christian faith, as are of blameless conversation and have knowledge to examine themselves and discern the Lord's Body are to be admitted" (18). In fact, all those qualified "are commanded by God to participate," and the church "is bound to receive them" (19–20). Stoddard had advocated these qualifications for church membership at the 1679 synod and for the succeeding twenty years he had tested his theory in his own parish. The sacramental sentiments expressed in the 1700 tract were not a product of the controversy with the Mathers, or feelings for the Brattle group, but were seasoned thoughts which had slowly matured over two decades. Thus, when he criticized the use of the sacraments as disciplinary devices, he was responding not only to the Mathers, but also to the heritage of strict Congregationalism that traced its lineage to John Cotton, Hugh Peter, William Ames, and William Bradshaw:

There can be no just cause assigned, why such men should be debarred from coming to the Lord's Supper, they are not to be debarred for not giving the highest evidence of sincerity. There never was any such law in the church of God, that any should be debarred from church privileges because they did not give the highest evidence of sincerity, not for want of the exercise of Faith; it is unreasonable to believe men to be visible saints from their infancy till they be forty or fifty years of age, and yet not capable of coming to the Lord's Supper, for want of the exercise of faith; they are not to be denied because of the weakness of grace, they that have the least grace need to have it nourished and cherished. (20)

Echoing Thomas Hooker and John Warham, Stoddard's spiritual progenitors who saw value in sacraments used as means to conversion, Stoddard declared,

If the Lord's Supper be only for the strengthening of saints, then they who are not saints, do profane the ordinance, when they do partake, and it is not lawful for them to partake, and then they that do not know themselves to be saints, don't know that it is lawful for them to partake, and so far as any man hath scruples about his saintship, he must proportionately have scruples about the lawfulness of his participation, and so Sacrament Days which would be days of comfort, will become days of torment.(22)

The sixth part of worship, ecclesiastical censures, rested in the exclusive authority of the teaching elder. By separating censures from the sacraments, it was clear that they were not to be confused. Ordinances were not censures, they were another part of worship, so the authority that devolved directly from Christ to "a pastor to be a ruler" which confers "the power of binding and losing" was a censure, not to be confused with church admission (23). Discipline was sharply separated from doctrine, which was symbolized by the seventh act of worship, benediction, "the blessing of the congregation . . ." (23–24).

The eighth chapter "of churches consist[ing] of Diverse Congregations" was designed to alter the structure of the Massachusetts parish system. One of the basic tenets of the Cambridge Platform was the autonomous authority of each gathered church, but Stoddard rejected the geographical and administrative isolation that New England federal theology fostered. "A church consisting of diverse congregations is a society of diverse congregational churches joining together according to God's appointment for the constant carrying on of the public worship of God . . ." (25). Five arguments were marshaled to prove validity of "National Churches":

First, from the light of nature, . . . man was made for the worship of God that man is fitted for society, and the great end why he is so is . . . that kingdoms and countries should join together in promoting and advancing the worship of God [as] one people [having] power to regulate and govern the several parts of that body.(25) *2dly*, from God's appointing the nation of the Jews to be one church Acts 7:38 . . . partly because the Christian churches of the Jews were subordinate to the National church of the Jews, they were members of the National Church and did attend Jewish ordinances; and therefore, by institution, Christian churches are not absolute but subordinate to a National Church. . . . (25–6)
3rdly, from the public covenant that is between God and the people of Israel wherein he engages public prosperity unto them upon condition of their obedience (26)
4ly, from the promises that God hath made of making Gentile nations to be his people. . . . And it is expressly foretold by Christ that whole nations should receive the Gospel and become churches. Matth 21:43 (26)
5. Because the supreme ecclesiastical authority doth not live in particular congregations; if there be no national church then every particular congregation is absolute and independent and not responsible to any higher power; this is too lordly a principle, it is too ambitious a thing for every small congregation to arrogate such an uncontrollable power, and to be accountable to none on earth; this is neither a probable way for the peace of churches nor for the safety of church members . . . . the primitive churches were under the governing of the Apostles. (26)

Stoddard had witnessed for two decades the seemingly endless bickering between himself, Edward Taylor, and the Mathers. He knew his supporters in the Valley outweighed his opposition and it was also becoming obvious that the Mathers' power was being eroded by ministers like John Wise, Simon Bradstreet, and the Brattle Group. Shrewdly, he espoused a national basis for federal theology which undercut the Cambridge Platform, but he was also politically astute enough to understand that constituencies were building blocks of power in Massachusetts. So, he advocated that the county be the subunit of the province, and that collectively the county's ministers exercise government over the local congregations, "yet with subordination to that authority that is over the whole" (28). Stoddard made it clear he was not promoting his own candidacy for Pope of the colony, as "one supreme officer to be a type of Christ who would have control over the national church," as if to allay fears that the epithet given him by the Mathers were, in fact, true. Furthermore, there should be no "national place of worship," such as a bishop's see (28).

Yet the question remained, how could such an ecclesiastical government with congregations administered by classical or county subdivisions, and these subdivisions administered by the province, actually be implemented in Massachusetts? The answer was the synod. Acknowledging in chapter nine that varieties of governments existed in national churches, "that type which is governed by the synod alone seems most consonant with the Word." A national synod which "is the highest ecclesiastical authority upon earth," receives its authority from "1) the public covenant . . . between God and his people, 2) his institutions in the Old Testament," and "3) the rules laid down for the church to walk by in the New Testament" (29). In each of these three foundations of synodical authority Stoddard demolished autonomy: the public covenant superseded the particular church covenant, the inclusive institutions in the Old Testament superseded John Cotton's Code of sacramental purity and the exclusive control of synods by the reverend elders effectively superseded the role of the laity in church government.

Finally, in chapter ten "the Power of Synods" was restricted to three spheres: 1) "to teach the people," 2) "to inflict ecclesiastical censures or to take them off," and 3) "to oversee the calling of persons to the ministry" (34). These three functions of the highest ecclesiastical authority dealt with discipline. They were administrative charges. Stoddard reserved matters of doctrine for the individual's own conscience. No man was "bound to receive the doctrines or practice the rules held forth by the synod" because synods were "not infallible and, therefore, no rule or doctrine is to be received from them" (32).

Stoddard ended his manifesto in a revolutionary rhetoric based on Luther's ideal of individual introspection. Doctrine was not a code

of discipline to be delivered by an ecclesiastical council. Doctrine
was man's reflection on his own faith: "by an implied faith we are
bound to prove all things" (32). Theological empiricism placed each
man at the helm of his own spiritual voyage. It cut through the webs
of Congregational bickering and shattered the supposed authority of
the 1649 Cambridge Platform, the 1662 Half-Way Covenant, and
even the results of the 1679 Reforming Synod.

Two aspects of Stoddard's 1700 manifesto reveal its departure
from previous writings. First, it represented a return to a stricter
doctrinal Calvinism than that of Bay orthodoxy. Secondly, it asserted that God's ways are inscrutable and that experience is the
only basis of doctrine. Like Calvin, Stoddard severely limited the
powers of natural reason, and refused to allow man to judge the
spiritual condition of his fellows. Like Calvin, Stoddard exhorted
each man to take up the sword of the Spirit and the helmet of
salvation—the whole armor of God. Like Calvin, Stoddard experienced unrest and disorder and was plagued with the problem of
making doctrine work.

In his first period of development as a sacramentalist he had
merely attempted to substitute one order for another, the sacraments for Cotton's Code. In the second period of development, as
pope of the instituted church, he had become aware that sacraments
alone could not serve as the keystone upon which to hang spiritual
life, and so he introduced the preaching of the Word as a coequal
agent, placed discipline in the hands of councils, and left doctrine to
the individual conscience. With this one stroke of genius he reinvested religion with a bibliocentrism and vigor reminiscent of the
founding fathers before disciplinary strife destroyed the original
fervor.

Immediately, Increase Mather attacked both Stoddard and the
Brattle group in *The Order of the Gospel*, asserting all the traditional tenets of strict Congregationalism, examination of candidates
for church membership, the truth of particular church covenants,
the election of church officers only by full members, and the necessity to keep the ordinances pure. Yet, even Increase had intimations
that the popularity of his beliefs was waning. "Is there no one that
will stand up . . . ?" he beseeched his readers. "It is not my own
course, but yours, which I have undertaken and plead for."[7] Once
again Mather tried to put Stoddard on the defensive by drawing
questions pointedly from the Cambridge Platform. He specifically

addressed the first five to Stoddard and 6, 9, 12, 13 and 16 to both the Brattle-Street group and Stoddard:

1. Whether particular churches ought to consist of saints and true believers on Christ?
2. Whether there ought not be a tryal of persons concerning their qualifications or fitness for church communion before they are admitted thereunto?
3. Whether are not the brethren, and not the elders of the church only to judge concerning the qualifications and fitness of those who are admitted to communion?
4. Whether it is necessary that persons at their admission into the church should make a public rendition of the time and manner of their conversion?
5. Has the church covenant as commonly practised in the churches of N.E. any scripture foundation?
6. Is public reading of the scripture without any interpretation part of the work incumbent on a minister of the Gospel?
9. Ought all that contribute towards the maintenance have the privilege of voting for the pastor of a church?
12. Does the essence of a ministers call, consist in his being ordained, with imposition of hands by other ministers?
13. May a man be ordained a pastor except to a particular church, and in the presence of that church?
16. Is it a duty for Christians in their prayers to use the very words of that which is commonly called the Lord's Prayer?[8]

A basic doubt plagued the Mathers that *The Order of the Gospel* would not be sufficient to quell Stoddard and the Brattle faction. In an effort to gain support from outlying communities, Cotton Mather visited Salem and Ipswich and solicited the help of John Higginson and William Hubbard to coauthor *A Treatise on the Order of the Gospel,* which praised Increase's book as "a . . . most highly needful and useful and seasonable . . . elaborate and well-composed work, "and reiterated its support for the unchanging truths of "what was done sixty years ago . . . in the churches of New England" (p. 4). Higginson and Hubbard warned that those "who are given to change . . . ought to be denounced publically," for change was the source of the most wicked crime—heresy. John Higginson and his colleague Nicholas Noyes of Salem promulgated on December 30, 1700, another response to Stoddard and the Brattle group, arguing against the abandonment of the public relation of conversion, enlarging baptism, relaxing particular church covenants, and the limited role of the laity in church government.[9] About the same time, Higginson, together with Nicholas Noyes, William Hubbard,

Zechariah Symmes, Jr., of Haverhill, Samuel Cheever of
Marblehead, Jeremiah Shepard of Lynn, Joseph Gerrish of
Wenham, and Edward Payson of Rowley published a prefatory "At-
testation" in Cotton Mather's "A Defence of Evangelical Churches,"
warning that the Salem Association opposed Stoddard:

Among the endeavors to unhinge our churches, whereof we have cause to
complain, a special *Mark* belongs to those of a late treatise, entitled *The
Doctrine of Instituted Churches*. And we judge it needful that a testimony
should be born against the unhappy *novelties* therein assaulting the State of
our churches; and that the rising generation be warned against the declension from the *Order of the Gospel in the Churches*, which tis the tendency
of such writings to betray them into.[10]

Not allowing attacks on the Brattle group to go unchallenged,
Benjamin Colman quickly penned a witty and somewhat satiric
Gospel Order Revived. The unfathomable anxiety Stoddard and the
Brattle group kindled in the Mathers' minds was in part responsible
for the enormous anxiety expended on the *Magnalia*, the first at-
tempt to document a monolithic Puritan discipline in New England.
In 1700 it was clear that the Mathers and their party had support in
Boston, Marblehead, Salem, Rowley, Ipswich, Wenham, and
Haverhill, but it was also clear that they were on the losing side in
terms of numbers.

When Cotton and Increase published *A Collection of Some of the
Many Offensive Matters Contained in a Pamphlet Entitled The
Order of the Gospel Revived* in 1701, they merely brought to the
public their private fears of some subterranean plot against the colony. Since Increase was the acting president of Harvard and since
his arguments for stricter church discipline incurred popular dis-
trust of his position he crystallized a sentiment long latent in the
colony. When he had accepted the presidency *pro tempore* in 1685
it was understood that he would continue as minister to the church
in Boston. While he was in England from 1688 to 1692 securing the
provincial charter for the Bay Colony, the control of the college had
fallen to his two tutors, John Leverett and William Brattle. They
promoted "the reading of Episcopal authors as the best books to
form our minds in religious matters, and preserve us from the narrow principles that kept us at a distance from the church of England," while Mather, in 1697, recognized the changes in the college
and "thunder'd out anathemas upon all that went to the Church of
England as apostasy from the primitive faith."[11] In vain the Mathers
attempted to obtain a new charter for Harvard which would have

protected the orthodoxy by requiring a doctrinal test for all who wished to teach there. By 1700 Increase's hold over the presidency was daily diminishing, and although he was requested by the General Court to reside in Cambridge to be closer to his college, he refused, as he had in 1693, 1695, and 1698. Finally, in 1701 the Court ordered him to change residency from Boston to Cambridge, and when he once again refused, they appointed Samuel Willard, the placid and unoriginal minister of the Third (Old South) Church, as vice-president, a decision that taunted Increase because the vice-president was not required to live on campus. As we shall see, Solomon Stoddard approved Mather's ousting, and supported John Leverett of the Brattle group for president.[12]

III   The Necessity of Acknowledgement of Offences *(1701)*

On July 3, 1701, with Mather's expulsion from the Harvard presidency imminent, Stoddard preached the annual lecture in Boston, this time avoiding the argument of his 1700 manifesto. In this sermon his object was the people, and he used Evangelical rhetoric to awaken them to "their offences" to God. Unlike the strict Congregational jeremiad that looked Janus-like back to the purity of the early church and forward to the purity of the millennium church of the saints, Stoddard's "Hosead" of 1701 was directed to the present. In Hosea 5:15 God threatened "I will go and return to my place till they acknowledge their offenses," (3) and Stoddard exhorted his countrymen that God had left them (4) and would not return until they made a national atonement:

Doctrine: God will not be reconciled to his professing people till they acknowledge their offences. (5)
"What offences must they acknowledge?"
Answer: The offences of the land . . . that the people and country are guilty of. (6)

Unlike strict Congregational jeremiads that laid the blame at the doorsteps of the meetinghouse, Stoddard charged that each citizen, most of whom were outside the meetinghouse doors, was at fault, that "such prevailing sins as do not fall under the cognizance of authority, whenever a people do manifest a corrupt departed heart, an heart gone away from God, they break covenant and are guilty. . . . The land becomes guilty thereby" (7). The covenant referred to was not the one federal theology had designated, that of a particular church, but the public covenant described in *The Doctrine of Instituted Churches.* It was not the local church that was covenanted; rather, it was the nation. This rhetoric revealed Stoddard's new image of the covenanted people—a new, common bond of brotherhood predicated on the Jewish idea of nationality: New Israel, New England, were the antitypes to the Motherland Israel and England.

According to Stoddard, "such sins . . . have got such a head that authority cannot suppress them." "People are got beyond the restraints of authority" and "rise up against their rulers" (7). In other words, punishment by civil law or ecclesiastical censure was an impotent cure for the spiritual illness of New England. In fact, one reason why the sins had not been "duly witnessed against" was because the rules themselves were guilty. Since "A people is considered [as] a body politic, they are *jointly* in covenant with God, and the sins of the rulers makes the land guilty" (8). Who were these rulers? The governor, the court of assistants, and the president of the college. Stoddard charged them with the duty of acknowledging their spiritual duty to keep the nation in its holy covenant. The "body of the people" also had a responsibility to "acknowledge their offence" "with grief and shame" (11–12). Without public atonement, "hard dealings" from God were certain and "no hope of Reformation" was in sight (13). Stoddard ended the lecture with four "uses" or practical advice. Admitting "it is a hard thing for a corrupt people to be reconciled to God," Stoddard attributed part of the difficulty to the current rationalism, "carnal reasonings," pride, and the love of sin (15–17). The way to set things aright was not through more rationalization or censure but through religious awakening. Furthermore, failure to reform would merely perpetuate this "awful judgment" of the Almighty (20). Failure to reform meant certain economic ruin—"the means of . . . trading and husbandry" hung in the balance (22). "Year after year, for a long time, several [disciplinary] means have been used to prevent God's judgments: fasts have been proclaimed, laws have been made, men have renewed [church] covenants, and yet we are an afflicted people" (23). After these reproofs, Stoddard urged the audience to "examine whether we in this country do acknowledge our offences?" (24). Not the offenses of other men, but one's own, not "the common infirmities of mankind, [but] our own iniquities," not "some particular gross act of sin" but our own "ways of sin," not owning offenses with an excuse, but owning them plainly, not "owning old sins" but owning "such as present temptations lead in" (24–29).

The final "use" of exhortation" accused the people of opening a "great wound in the country" in their lack of reformation. A great many things are permitted by civil authority that are sinful to God. Looking around the pulpit, Stoddard challenged the fashions of the day with vanity. Of course wigs were lawful in the eyes of the courts, but weren't they sinfully vain? Of course taverngoing was within one's legal limits, but didn't it lead to sinful excesses? (30–32). In his closing remarks, Stoddard indicated that civil laws can't make a nation holy. The whole course of history from the beginning of Massachusetts was predicated on the intimate coordination of church and state. As more and more fell outside the churches, civil righteousness came to mean that if one obeyed the laws of the state, nothing further was required. Things that "are not in their nature evils" could be contrary to true religion, Stoddard cautioned. Moreover, those outside the churches should be aware of the advantages of getting "holy dispositions and an heart willing to do your duty." Look around, he warned, could you "like these things in other persons?" (31). "It is a sign that you know you are guilty when you don't like it that men should say those things of you that you do [of them]" (33). "It is a poor way to justify yourselves from much arguments as you despise in other cases" (33). Playing the nation's casuist, Stoddard displayed his true Evangelical intent when he left his audience with the thought that "It is good to mind what your heart says in the most solemn times" (34).

Apparently, the immediate result of Stoddard's lecture was to help crystalize opposition to Mather's presidency at Harvard, and on September 6, 1701, Mather was formally ejected. The side effects were even more telling, for, indirectly, Stoddard was responsible for the founding of Yale in the fall of 1701. Ironically, Increase Mather made the first overtures for a second college after his dismissal, but his intent was to preserve in the south what had been lost in the north: the old orthodoxy. When, in the early autumn of 1701 the trustees of Yale founded the college, it was obvious that they were men who opposed the latitudinarianism that was across the Charles River, but they were not necessarily opposed to Stoddard's Evangelicalism. Included in the group were James Pierpont, of New Haven; James Noyes, of Stonington; Israel Channing, of Stratford; Abraham Pierson, of Killingworth (Clinton); Thomas Buckingham, of Saybrook; Samuel Mather, of Windsor; Samuel Andrew, of Milford; Timothy Woodbridge, of Hartford; Noadiah Russell, of Middleton; and Joseph Webb, of Fairfield. In fact, Elisha

Williams, who took over the rectorship at a critical moment and reinvigorated the religious thrust of a Yale education, was "a native of the Connecticut River Valley, no doubt bringing with him that region's Evangelical tradition—fostered principally by Solomon Stoddard—and imparted it to the students, many of whom, during his tenure, were also from that area." Harvard took the opposite path under John Leverett, secularizing education through the Arminian doctrine of supernatural rationalism. Stoddard's later support, as we shall see, came from Yale, where his Evangelical message was promulgated in that institution's educational charter.[13]

Lest the Stoddard-Mather-Brattle dispute remain all gloom without levity, in that quaint fishing village of Marblehead, where wits were invigorated by the salty east wind, journalist Josiah Cotton preserved a cantering rhythm:

> Relations are Rattle with Brattle and Brattle,
> Lord Brother Mayn't command,
> But Mather and Mather had rather had rather
> The good old way should stand.
> Saints Cotton and Hooker, oh look down and look'ere
> Where's Platform, way, and the Keys?
> Oh Torrey write story of Brattle Church Tory
> To have things as they please.
> Our merchants *cum* Mico do stand *sacro vico*
> Our churches turn genteel;
> Our Parsons grow big with Wealth, Wine and Wid,
> their heads are covered with meal.[14]

IV God's Frown in the Death of Useful Men (1703)

However much Stoddard sought to stimulate a mass revival in the Bay Colony, it remained, in his view, more responsive to the wiles of Satan and the English pound than to the Gospel—witness Queen Anne's war, the epidemics in Boston, and the continuing Indian conflicts. The death of John Pynchon of Springfield was another case in point. Long prominent in the Connecticut River Valley, Pynchon had been one of its leading citizens, a wealthy trader, a colonel in the militia and a selectman. His death on January 17, 1703, at the age of seventy-eight, symbolized the passing of the second generation. Stoddard was sixty himself, so it provoked him to a certain urgency in his own mission. As a tribute to his friend, Stoddard chose Isaiah 3:1-3: "The Lord, the Lord of hosts doth take away from

Jerusalem and from Judah the mighty men and the man of war, the judge, and the prophet . . . , the captain of fifty and the honorable man and the eloquent orator."

Although the ostensible purpose of the funeral sermon was to praise Pynchon's accomplishments, its real intent was exposed by Stoddard's Evangelical rhetoric, calling attention to God's anger against the sins of the professing people. He noted how "Prosperity at present" could all but vanish "in a little time" as it had been "with the people of Judah." "And accordingly God is threatening of them with dreadful judgments (1), with famine and drought (2, 3), with removal of useful men" (2). The passing of power to a new generation was occurring in Northampton (see Appendix 7) as well as in the colonial legislature and in the college on the Charles, and this change portended "a public calamity" unless the people atoned for their sins (3).

A rhetoric of religious awakening was used which would become characteristic of the New Lights some twenty years later; society was viewed as a brotherly union or commonwealth predicated on the celestial bond of "Love," the religious cement of the universe. Indeed, among the primary qualities which the Northampton minister identified in "useful men" was their gift to "discover Love" "Because such men have a great interest in the affection of others." This then is the obverse of the Congregational jeremiad of divine wrath: positive affections manifest in the "great mercy when God raises up serviceable men among his people (13). "And when He does this, He greatly favors a people for this makes way for the outward prosperity of a people that they may live quietly and peaceably and this makes way for their spiritual prosperity that they may be a religious godly and well-carriaged people" (14). Stoddard made it clear that his doctrine was not predicated on moral or intellectual development:

Several young ones in the country have liberal education . . . but this will not make the country happy if they have not a spent to do service . . . . (16) Learned education is an help both to civility and piety, but it cannot effect either . . . . Men that are brought up at the feet of Gemaliel have need (as Paul) to see a light from Heaven. (17)

Quite apart from liberal thinkers at Harvard, such as Charles Chauncy, Stoddard opposed any optimistic moralism. "Humanum est errare" (To err is human), he counseled; "when shall we find men without infirmities?" (18). Consistent with his view of an or-

dered and orderly society, Stoddard reiterated the maxims of the
great chain of being, in which each individual had a foreordained
station to fill in the hierarchy of existence: "He that may do God and
his country good service in a lower station, may be altogether unfit
for a higher station" (20). Order presumed harmony among the
people of the commonwealth, and Stoddard made it clear that
"Useful and Serviceable" men "should not be despised" and
criticized by their inferiors. Indeed, since God was "removing serviceable men" such as Danforth and Stoughton and Pynchon, "the
sorrowful effects" of the loss of these men would be prevalent "a
long while" (22). The divine displeasure was also evident "in conjunction with other sorrow" such as "trouble from enemies" and
diseases. Once again Stoddard directed his appeal to the rulers, "To
such of you as are in power."

1. You must have a great care that you do not condemn the righteous or
justify the wicked (25)
2. That you be good examples to the people (26)
3. That you do nothing to promote any man of viscious conversation
Labor to promote Holy men.
Psalm 101.6 Mine eyes shall be upon the faithful of the land. (27)

V   The Way for a People to Live (1703)

Five months after John Pynchon's death, Stoddard was invited by
the Massachusetts legislature to deliver the election sermon. On
May 26, 1703, the newly notorious Northampton prophet publicly
announced the failure of Cambridge educators and Boston lawmakers in their religious missions. Ever since John Calvin had linked
teaching with a special form of ministry, university educators in
Protestant countries had borne a certain religious duty.[15] As the
presidency of Harvard continued to remain unfilled, Stoddard
urged that "I know there are difficulties in the way of settling the
college, but it were better for the country to wade through them at
first opportunity, than to expose ourselves to those calamities that
may come upon us for want of a good settlement (13). While direction of the college in Cambridge remained uncertain, the rulers in
Boston were also failing in their godly mission to the people. Society, Stoddard explained, was an orderly whole. The great chain of
being locked each person into a specific role with specific obligations
to both inferiors and superiors: "each one must observe his proper

station" (5). Each legislator, for instance, was neatly compartmentalized in his duties. Representatives were expected to resist meddling in the affairs of the governor or his council: "It is not the duty of one ruler to fulfill the offices of another, but everyone is bound to attend the work of his office" (5). The second thrust of the sermon was to reinforce the people's security in a balanced government and their duty to the governor. In Massachusetts at the time the Royal governor and council were pitted against the popularly elected lower house. The propaganda of either side might give one the impression that the other side controlled the power, but, in fact, each had its own political weapons—the Court in its numbers, the governor, Joseph Dudley, in patronage. Stoddard found himself on the governor's side, promoting John Leverett for the presidency of Harvard, for he was anxious to argue that contrary to reports from the Court's supporters, balance of power existed in Massachusetts' government.[16] In order to emphasize the theme that "the people must not over-rule the rulers" Stoddard chose Exodus 20:12, "Honor thy father and thy mother," and broadened it to refer to all one's superiors, a familiar Puritan exegesis.

The third thrust of the sermon was its argument for unity. Stoddard shifted from the classical metaphor of the great chain to the Pauline metaphor of the church as the Body of Christ. He did this in two phases. First, he compared a body of unregenerate men to "a natural body wherein there are diverse organs appointed to particular services" (5). With great subtlety he shifted from the natural to the regenerate body of Paul's imagery. The rhetorical device displayed his evangelical intent. It was as though during the course of actually preaching the sermon the people were converted by the Northampton preacher. This nature/grace dialectic resonates throughout the sermon: "the duty of rulers" was "to work . . . faithfully" and "to be a good example" while the duty of the people was "to submit to their government" (6). Looking to the Royal governor, the preacher cautioned "that it is a great matter of concernment to a land to have godly men to be rulers in the commonwealth and in the church" (8). Stoddard did not want to return to the old Winthrop-Cotton Code of regenerate magistracy—his goal was to reestablish the accessibility of Christian initiation and religious fellowship as a bond for the nation. To this end he charged the governor to "Advance and promote religion," suppress sinful practices, "and see that men may do that which is just between man and

man" (9–10). "If rulers be careless in promoting religion and morality, God will punish the land" (11). Referring to a maxim of a
foremost Elizabethan Puritan, William Perkins, Stoddard charged
that it was not enough for rulers to promote religion; they must be
godly themselves: "Rulers are called gods, and it is [a] pity they that
are like him in power are not like him in holiness" (14). A fourth
message of Stoddard's sermon was directed to the ways in which he
felt the legislature discriminated against western Massachusetts.
During the Indian wars there was always the fear that colonial
troops would be withdrawn from the settlements along the
Connecticut River Valley to protect eastern Massachusetts. Furthermore, Stoddard referred to "unnecessary burdens" such as taxes
and militia duty which had been imposed on Hampshire County
men.

The final point Stoddard made was directed to the ministers of the
colony to "Labor after the saving conversion of men." The true
meaning of conversion, he explained, had been lost over the years.
"Some take baptism for regeneration; some think [with John Cotton]
that men may be regenerate without any antecedent preparation."
This was false, he explained, for "restraining grace is not sufficient in
order to eternal life; yea, there must be a good measure of inward
piety in order to the reforming of the land: if there be not, a people
may reform in a pang, but they will return to their vomit again" (17).
As he knew from personal experience, the path to saving conversion
could be long and demanding. Although he advocated the sacraments as means of "spiritual edification" he understood the dangers
of using them as a panacea for conversion. In order to protect "the
efficacy of the ordinances" he warned against the "additions of men's
invention" such as Anglican rites and ceremonies which were
threatening to infiltrate New England through Tory sympathizers
and the newly formed Society for the Propagation of the Gospel.
Perhaps this warning was intended to strengthen colonial religious
solidarity against a feared assault by the S.P.G. on New England,
and in parting, the people and the rulers were again exhorted to
carry to others "according to your duty: It is a great mercy when
God does prepare the hearts of rulers and ruled to do their duty to
one another . . . by giving them consciences [and] by making them
drink in good principles . . . (25). A nature/grace dialectic oscillated
throughout the sermon and was reflected in the final exhortation:
"We should attend the light of nature," "search the scriptures,"
"and beg the teachings of the Spirit of God" (25).

Few, however, openly sided with the Northampton Pope's instituted church and its converting ordinances. Sometimes, in the privacy of their churches, they upheld Stoddard's principles. Gurdon Saltonstall, for instance, promulgated the need for converting ordinances and and instituted church on December 26, 1703, to his New London congregation. It was a theme he often retiterated and it helps explain the background to Connecticut's religious course after he became governor in 1707. Saltonstall was a man who lived the issues, and his long friendship with Stoddard and the congeniality of their beliefs set the course of Connecticut church government when he became the chief executive of the colony. (See sec. VII below.) Sometimes, however, privacy provided the opportunity for silent criticism of aspects of their friend's ideas. Samuel Mather, for instance, chose not to criticise Stoddard's converting ordinances openly before his Windsor flock so he penned a precis of private objections which remained unpublished. Perhaps these friends in their wisdom realized that had public endorsements or critiques been offered at this time they would have generated division among their ranks which would have further destroyed ministerial unity and would have drawn public attention to the issues and aspirations on both sides of the Stoddard-Mather debates.[17]

VI   Danger of Speedy Degeneracy (1705)

Ironically, Increase Mather had been instrumental in uniting Presbyterians and Congregationalists under the Heads of Agreement when he was in London in 1691. This agreement, which allowed for ministerial alliances while preserving Congregational autonomy, was the basis for a movement of tighter ministerial control in Massachusetts churches between 1704 and 1740. At the June 1704 annual Ministerial Convention, a proposal was drafted by twenty-six ministers including the Bostonians Samuel Willard and Cotton Mather and Brattle-Street men Ebenezer Pemberton and Benjamin Colman. Stoddard and Increase did not sign this letter urging that ministerial associations be strengthened. The major emphasis of this movement, which probably explains why Stoddard was not an endorser of it, was its strengthening of the autonomy of the individual church covenant. In the *Instituted Churches*, the basis of popular unity was the national church and the public covenant. Therefore, when Stoddard was invited to deliver the annual lecture to the Governor and Court on July 5, 1705, he used the opportunity to criticize the petty squabbles among churches, choosing as his text

Judges 11.11.v: "the children of Israel did evil in the sight of the
Lord and served Baalim." The religiosity of the first generation "of
the Israelites that entered into the land" was commendable, he
noted, "and though they had infirmities, yet they walked before
God in much integrity." Probably alluding to John Cotton, Stoddard
reflected that "Joshua lived but seventeen years after the entrance
into Canaan and within a while the rest" of the first generation
"were carried to their graves. . . . After them arose a generation of
another spirit." "The criminals" were all "the children of Israel, not
one of the tribes, but it was a general defection." "The crime" was
that "they did evil in the sight of the Lord" (3–4). Although some
churches had experienced division and dissention, these were only
isolated symptoms of a general malady of spiritual corruption (5). At
the heart of the problem was "that when godly men die . . . there
rises up an unconverted generation" (6). The urgency to promote
Evangelical religion among the people was to save them from destruction. Instead of using a rhetoric of hope as had the first generation preachers who looked expectantly for the millennium in the
immediate future, Stoddard reverted to the second generation Congregationalist rhetoric of terror. God punishes the wicked and saves
the righteous, and it is necessary to have examples of holy men to
pattern one's life after: "Where there be plenty of holy men in a
land . . . men will be provoking one another to an holy emulation,
but where there be a few good men there will be a scarcity of good
examples" and the path to a publicly covenanted people is much
more tenuous (8). No matter how efficacious the Eucharist was supposed to be in helping men to conversion, cautioned the wary
Evangelist, "sweet liquor put into a corrupt vessel will be tainted"
(10). Revelation infuses reason with light: "Spiritual light received in
conversion strengthens the reason of men and makes the law of
nature more legible" (11). It infuses the government with higher
purpose of its collective responsibility. The point at which this
speedy degeneracy began to overtake the land was when the original impulse of the visible saints to "converse about their callings"
began to falter (15). Worship no longer was an end in and of itself
and many began attending lectures so that they could "visit their
friends" afterward. This was reflected as family religion deteriorated
and as the Scriptures fell into disuse (16–18). As the churches failed
in catechizing the youth and in entering them into membership,
evils befell society (19–20). In point of fact, the number of criminal

cases had increased dramatically over the preceding decade. According to his analysis, ills of society were the result of divine "vengeance on his people," whose ways are departed from their fathers. Even though some are "children of very worthy men [and] carry on a . . . form of religion," Stoddard made it clear that this was not enough (21). Half-Way membership was not a substitute for full communion. If the warning were not heeded "the design of planting the land" with the gardens of Christ would be frustrated: "the design of our fathers in planting this country was that their posterity might fear and serve the Lord." They would not have left England

meerly for their own quietness, but they were afraid that their children would be corrupted there. But what advantage will the plenty of this land be if we should grow a corrupt people here? . . . The planters of the country might even repent that ever they came over into the land: the design will be very much lost. (24)

The original errand into the wilderness to plant gardens of Christ was a design nearly destroyed. Although he, as spiritual physician, had used the ordinances as devices to restore life to this dying people, Stoddard painfully admitted, "we may conclude that the ordinances have not much efficacy among them" (28).

VII   The Inexcusableness of Neglecting the Worship of God

One month after Stoddard had delivered the annual lecture, a group of nine ministers, including Colman, Willard, Pemberton, and Cotton Mather, convened in Cambridge on the first Monday of August and framed a draft which became the Massachusetts Proposals of 1705. The influence of Increase Mather was evident from its heavy borrowing from the 1691 London Heads of Agreement. Two major revisions of church government were made by the Proposals. First, ministers were required to be licensed by an association of pastors before they could be ordained. This device could be used to safeguard the orthodoxy of candidates. Secondly, church councils were given the power to "consult, advise and determine all affairs that shall be proper matter for the consideration of an ecclesiastical council within their respective limits, except always, the cases are such as the associated pastors judge more convenient to fall under the cognizance of some other council." At this time in Massachusetts there were already five ministerial associations and the Proposals supported their discrete authority. There was to be no national church and each congregation was independently convenanted. In contrast, Stoddard had advocated one national synod to preside over these countywide councils, which embodied one national covenanted church. Each parish, according to Stoddard, was under the discipline of its countywide council and all parishes partook of the same public covenant.[18]

In Connecticut the situation was different. There, Yale College trustees were instrumental in gaining support for Stoddard's millenarian dream of a colonywide public covenant and genuine national religious unity. When Gurdon Saltonstall was elected to the governor's chair in December 1707, he immediately supported the movement which culminated in a colonial synod at Saybrook in May 1708. Out of this synod developed the Saybrook Platform, which endorsed the Savoy revision of the Westminster Confession, approved the Heads of Agreement clause permitting local variations of church government, and delineated fifteen articles based on the Massachusetts Proposals concerning the relative power of synods and local congregations. In this final point the Saybrook Platform approximated Stoddard's view of individual churches subsumed by county councils. However, it stopped short of a national synod and a national church: the ecclesiastical court of highest appeal was the council. In October 1708, the Platform was ratified by the Connecticut legislature, highlighting the difference in government between the two colonies: the new charter in Massachusetts had destroyed clerical power, while the King appointed a governor who could veto bills of the upper house; in Connecticut the governor and the upper house were selected by the enfranchised citizens, and church government had been actually developed by the legislature. Furthermore, Connecticut had been founded on the principles of moderate Congregationalism, which allowed nonchurch members to be enfranchised lawmakers. Gradually these men had taken initiative in defining ecclesiastical policies to their liking. The Saybrook Platform merely institutionalized moderate Congregationalism as Stoddard had amended it.[19]

Stoddard realized this historical situation and delivered a sermon to the Inferior Court at Northampton on December 17, 1707, simultaneously with Gurdon Saltonstall's election. This sermon marked the beginning of a trend in his sermon style. The doctrine is devoted to the Stoddardean principle that all righteous-living men regardless of whether they have saving grace or not are bound by duty to attend worship. Worship consisted of hearing the word and partaking of sacraments, and in this sermon equal emphasis was given to both instead of stressing the sacraments as means of regeneration. Furthermore, in tone one notices a return to a millenarian outlook, more expectant of the Second Coming than fearful of the terrors of the unconverted state. Earlier Stoddard had vacillated between a rhetoric of fear and hope; now this shift to hope marked his entry into the last phase of his career.

In only three periods of church history, Stoddard maintained, did religion flourish enough to employ the strict Congregational ideal of regenerate communion—in the ages of Luther and the German Reformation, the English Reformation under Edward VI that spawned the Marian exiles, "And those holy men who first planted this land [and] carried on the work of Reformation to an higher pitch" (iii). However, in each of these periods of reform, the prophet warned, "Those that have been eminent reformers of the church of God have seldom or never been so happy as to effect a perfect reformation" (ii). Primary among the faults of the founding fathers of Massachusetts was their "not accepting non-scandalous persons to their communion and in not acknowledging a public government in the church" (3). It was false to continue to build on this sandy foundation, and, in fact, the leaders of Massachusetts "have no sufficient reason to take practices upon trust" merely because they were "the practices of our fathers" (iv).

Foremost among these accepted practices was the rite of Christian initiation. Recalling the passage from Exodus 12:47–48 ("All the congregation of Israel shall keep it"), Stoddard exhorted his audience to form an inclusive *national* covenant once again (2). The doctrine he proposed in this Evangelical sermon was "that sanctifying grace is not necessary unto the lawful attending of any duty of worship. . . . The whole congregation, whether godly or not, was to keep the passover. . . . If men be not holy yet it is lawful for them to attend any duty of worship. And as men may not excuse themselves from moral duties from the want of grace, so they may not excuse themselves from any duty of worship . . . prayer, . . . hearing the Word [and] preaching the Word" (4–5). Stoddard flatly asserted, from his own personal experience, no doubt, that "it is lawful for men in a natural condition to preach the Word" (6). All the usual

typological arguments from the inclusive nature of Jewish ceremonies were given (7) with the major difference that now Stoddard
related circumcision and baptism, passover and communion, offering of sacrifice and tithes, "officiating in the work of the priesthood"
and the ministry as "part of the eternal covenant" (17). Instead of
trying to inculcate fear for not attending to religious duties, he now
argued that "the use of this doctrine is of warning that you be not
afraid to attend the duties of worship because destitute of sanctifying
grace" (18).

So much for the new emphasis on hearing the Word—the rest of
the sermon now reverted to Stoddard's preoccupation with the
Lord's Supper as a converting ordinance applied in twelve uses. The
only significant thing about these uses was that in the ninth Stoddard attributed his theory of converting ordinances to Mark Frederick Wendelin (1584–1652), the anti-Lutheran rector of Zerbst, and
Gisbert Voetius (d. 1676), the Utrecht professor. This provides certain evidence for the German Reformed Pietist sources of Stoddard's sacramental theology. The result was a shift from rationalism
to mystic contemplation of the divine, from self-centered concerns
to love of God, elevating the role of affection. Secondly, like the
Pietists, Stoddard had begun to emphasize a Christocentric attitude
to conversion. Adoration of divine attributes shifted to
private meditation on the Eucharist as "the memorial of Christ's
death," a Zwinglian doctrine as modified by the German Pietists,
based on I Cor. 11:26 (26). This contrasted with earlier Puritans,
William Ames, for instance, who viewed conversion as regeneration
of the will, not the illumination of "affective understanding." Stoddard considered this view of the Lord's Supper fully in line with the
types of the Paschal Supper in the Old Testament, and that both
ordinances signified "Evangelical doctrines" not ecclesiastical censures: "this appointment that unclean persons might not come to the
passover did not signify that those who were spiritually unclean
should not have communion with God . . . but [rather] be excluded
out of the Kingdom of God" (28). The impact of German Pietists on
Stoddard's thought crystalized the direction of his mature revivalistic style.

Finally, this sermon gives us a glimpse of the actual situation in
Northampton. It had been "about forty years past" when Eleazar
Mather was minister that there was a multitude in town who were

unbaptized but "that neglect was taken into examination, and now there is an alteration in that particular" (26). In spite of this, Stoddard claimed that "there be four to one that do neglect the Lord's Supper, as if it did not belong to them . . ." (26). His figures were accurate. As of September 11, 1706, there were only forty-six men and fifty women church members in a total adult population of slightly over six hundred in Northampton. Prior to 1708, therefore, when he still had not opened communion to the unregenerate, church membership continued to lag behind the rise in population despite his eradication of any distinction between full and Half-Way members.

Increase Mather wasted no time in launching into debate with Stoddard and hurriedly had *A Dissertation* against him published by Benjamin Green. Although Increase admitted from experience that it was probably futile to change his mind, he felt that by "this collision the truth will gain." Once again all the well worn arguments against encouragement of *Unsanctified persons (while such) to Approach the Holy Table of the Lord*.[20] Adding more fuel to the fire Stoddard supported William Leverett, Increase Mather's other enemy, as president of Harvard and wrote to Benjamin Colman expressing his position. The colloquial style of the letter and its friendly tone suggest that Stoddard and the Brattle Street Society had common interests in promoting Leverett to the presidency:

Revd and Dear Sr.
I received you letter, moving me and my neighbors to solicit the Gen'll Court to settle Mr. Leverett in the college; had your letter come in season, you might have expected a readiness in me to have made a return according to your desire, but it come not at hand till the matter was issued to the desires of others who seek the welfare of the land accomplished, therefore, I was not in very much haste to find answer, concluding that you would fix upon the right reason of it and not apprehend your letter to be neglected, but although I have not had an hand in Mr. Leverett's settlement, yet I do rejoice in the present welfare of the college and desire God to continue Mr. Leverett to be a great blessing in the place, give him my service when you see him and Mrs. Coleman, Mr. Wadsworth and Mr. Pemberton. I am your humble Servant,
Sol. Stoddard
N—Hampton
Feb: 7th 1707/8[21]

Together the Brattle Society in Cambridge and the Stoddard supporters in Connecticut and western Massachusetts were effectively eroding the once supreme power of the Mather-Cotton dynasty.

The relationship between Stoddard and Colman was predicated on Stoddard's idea of the instituted church which he had just jettisoned. In Colman's Boston lecture on June 10, 1708, on *The Piety and Duty of Rulers to Comfort and Encourage The Ministry of Christ* he exposed his quasi-Evangelical streak, which would persist into the Great Awakening; however, unknown to himself he had just permanently broken with his Northampton friends by placing more emphasis on discipline than doctrine, on the instituted church than conversion, on ritual than Evangelicalism. While Colman reduced the divine sovereignty of the creator to the object of Newtonian physics, Stoddard reinvested the Pauline nature/grace dialectic with an urgency unmitigated by eighteenth-century cosmology.

The Inexcusableness of Neglecting the Worship of God was a public confession of failure. It marked the final crossroads in Stoddard's career. Until this point he had preached the converting nature of Christian communion, but he had to admit that even in his own church it had failed miserably. More than three quarters of his church were still outside the Lord's Supper. A symbolic confirmation of Stoddard's decision to jettison his theory of converting ordinances came from his son-in-law William Williams. Born in Newton as the third son of wealthy Captain Isaac and Martha (Parker) Williams, he was related to a lineage of Puritan forebears including Deacon William Parker of Roxbury, his maternal grandfather, and Robert Williams of Roxbury, his paternal grandfather who, like Anthony Stoddard, had weathered the Antinomian Controversy. William graduated Harvard in 1683 with his cousin John Williams who accepted the call to Deerfield, and Samuel Danforth who became the minister at Taunton. William soon married the granddaughter of John Cotton, but after her death in 1698 he married Christian Stoddard, Solomon's daughter, in 1699. William contributed greatly to Stoddard's influence through his own family network in the valley. By Elizabeth he had William, later minister of Weston, Massachusetts, and Elisha, minister of Newington (1722–26), rector of Yale, and a tutor of Stoddard's grandson Jonathan Edwards. By Christian he had Solomon, the minister of Lebanon, Connecticut, who answered Edward's defense of qualifications for admission to communion, and Israel, loyalist merchant of Hatfield and gallant soldier in the French and Indian Wars who opposed cousin Edwards.[22] William Williams had not been an early vocal supporter of Stoddard. He had settled in Hatfield after Anthony Stoddard had succeeded in persuading John Wise to leave Hatfield and to head the Chebacco parish near Ipswich after only a short trial period of preaching. In Hatfield, William remained mute to the outside world for two decades, but in 1707 he broke this spell of silence.

Williams published *The Danger of Not Reforming Known Evils* as his own manifesto of agreement with Stoddard's shift from sacramentalism to the discipline of the instituted church: "the evils of this country are for the most part in such things as are known, yea such as have been acknowledged" so recently by the Northampton minister. Williams referred to the discipline of converting ordinances in instituted churches and charged that the people were not making fullest use of them: "You pretend a zeal for Christ's Institutions," Williams argued, "and commend your forefathers that ventured their blood to rescue the ordinances from popish corruptions; and yet when you may attend it in Gospel purity, you turn your backs on it." Williams agreed with Stoddard that the people still had a "readiness" to savor their spiritual estrangement "as a sweet morsel under their tongues" despite their efforts: what was needed was a new piety, and to this end both now turned their energies.[23]

This change in tactics went back to the crux of Puritan homilitic theory: balance between teaching and persuasion, reason and emotions. Ever since Peter Ramus had disjoined the process of argumentation and placed it with logic, rhetoric was reserved only for reason, not for emotion. This evisceration of Puritan preaching was reflected in faculty psychology, which viewed reason and emotions as separate entities. Neo-Ciceronians like Gerard Vossius, whom Stoddard studied at Harvard, urged the preacher and orator that to insure practical results more must be done than merely instruction of the understanding. The preacher must win the acceptance of the will and excite the religious affections.

The understanding, the will, and the affections were the ancient faculties of the soul as Aristotle had described them, and Puritans had used these categories in preaching. The first part of a sermon was devoted to instructing the audience in the exegesis of a biblical text from which was drawn a doctrine. The second part was devoted to convincing the audience through a series of questions and answers that the doctrine was sound. The third part was devoted to exciting the emotions in the uses and application of the doctrine to daily life. As we have seen, the structure of the sermon form in the hands of Stoddard began to reduce this three-part division into two equal halves; the first condensed instruction and conviction while the second expanded the emotive application and uses. This shift in emphasis is the measure of the emergence of Stoddard The Evangelist:

Corresponding Puritan Thought Forms

Sermon Structure	Human Faculties	Morphology of Conversion	Homiletic Goals
Opening of Text- Doctrine	Understanding	Knowledge	Instruction
Reasons	Will	Conviction	Persuasion (Casuistry)
Application and Uses	Affections	Legal fear Humiliation	Exciting the Emotions

Stoddard gradually eroded the place of knowledge in the conversion process and this was reflected by his own homiletic technique. As one can see from the fifty-eight sermons preached between the fall of 1719 and the spring of 1720, the text was chosen only after the application and uses had been decided upon. Scripture had become secondary to the application and uses just as instruction was inferior to exciting the emotions. This radical inversion of the Puritan sermonic form is another contribution of Stoddard's emerging Evangelical religion. It implied that the religious affections are more primary to the conversion process than the rationally apprehended Word of God. This implicit Stoddardean antiintellectualism is reflected in his rejection of the learned for the converted ministry, which was the starting point for later radicals such as John Davenport who entirely dismissed the value of education for preaching the Word.

VIII The Falseness of the Hopes of Many Professors *(1708)*

Five months later Stoddard once again was invited to deliver a lecture at Boston. On these trips he would usually visit Samuel Sewall, the prominent merchant and colonial magistrate. This time he chose as the text the Sermon on the Mount (Matt. 7:26), which reflected his increasing Evangelical style of preaching. The doctrine he drew was "that many professors build their hopes of salvation upon a sandy foundation." Here again he reiterated the theme of hope rather than fear. "You must distinguish between the foundation of faith and of hope: . . . Faith is an accepting of the offer of salvation by Christ but Hope is the expectation of salvation" (2). On the one hand hope was founded on "A knowledge that we have accepted the offer of the Gospel" while on the other hand it comes from "A knowledge that we have the other qualification that Salvation is promised unto" such as "love to God," "Mortifying the deeds of the flesh," "walking in the law of God" and "all God's commandments" and "being righteous" (4–5). Stoddard warned that when one judges himself to be an heir to salvation merely because he sits "under good teaching and sit[s] at the table of the Lord" this was a false ground of hope (9). Hope was inward religious experience. Outward signs do not confirm inward spiritual conditions and accordingly "there [was] a great deal of chaff on the floor of the Gospel church" (9).

It was further true, Stoddard warned in his first use of the doctrine, "that many professors will not do well at last"—they will not be saved. The state of being regenerate was either all or nothing; "twenty probabilities will not prove you to be an heir of salvation." Throughout the sermon Stoddard used the term "knowledge" to refer to religious experience. He also introduced the term "religious affections" to refer to a perception less certain than "knowledge"; "Men when they are dying . . . may be under delusion, especially if they have religious affections; they are sorry for their sins, and content if God spares them to live more carefully" (20). He closed the sermon with a third use of the doctrine, "Of warning that you don't build your hopes upon a sandy foundation," arguing that faith is an active state to be nurtured and grown (23).

IX   An Appeal to the Learned (1709)

An Appeal was the swansong of Stoddard as Pope of the instituted church. Directed to Mather's *Dissertation*, it registered derision for discipline devoid of adequate doctrine, of mixing false emotion in "passionate lamentations with his arguments; if his arguments had been stronger, they would have been a vindication of those complaints; and he had done his business effectually, if there had been more reason and less affection . . ." (ii). Affection had its place but only with adequate doctrine: Stoddard tersely confessed, "I am no enthusiast" (iii).

Instead of being a presentation of his own arguments, *An Appeal* was really a refutation, point by point, of Mather's *Dissertation*. Yet, it was more than a mere rebuttal, since it built a case for interpreting two crucial passages of Scripture: Matthew 21:11–12 and I Corinthians 11:27–29. The first passage in which the king's guest was turned away from a feast because he was not properly attired was interpreted by critics of Stoddard to refer to the way communicants should be turned away from the Lord's Supper if they did not wear the cloak of faith. Stoddard rejected this exegesis and said that the passage referred to the more general case of spiritual pardon by the Lord (3–4). The second passage on the Lord's Supper specifically permitted even the scandalous to be admitted if their intentions were good (19). In Christian initiation it was all too easy to prescribe a rigid, legalistic formula for communicants. Thus, Psalm 6:16, which contained David's spiritual experience, should not be used as a normative model for others (20). Stoddard's view of religious experience was capacious. For this reason "The Lord's Supper is instituted to be a means of regeneration, it is not appointed for the converting of men to the Christian religion, for only such as are converted may partake of it; but is is not only for the strengthening of saints, but a means also to work saving regeneration" (22). Stoddard charged Mather with having made "an idol of the Lord's Supper; crying it up above all the ordinances . . . as if it were peculiar to Saints as heavenly glory, and to be attended with more reverence than all the other ordinances" (96). This was the heart of *An Appeal* because Stoddard was now shifting his own emphasis more toward preaching the Word as a means to Evangelical religion. Although this tract was one of the least original pieces Stoddard ever penned, partly because it was nearly pure polemic, it did reveal his own shifting piety to a more thoroughly Gospel-oriented Evangelicalism. In *An Appeal* Stoddard passed from Pope to preacher.

While no direct reply to Stoddard's rebuttal was forthcoming, an anonymous tract which was probably written by Increase and/or Cotton Mather was published in Boston in 1709 as *An Appeal, of Some of the Unlearned*. It praised Increase as a leader of the pious "from his youth to seventy" and chided Stoddard as a "Man of very little reading." This was the cul-de-sac of the Stoddard-Mather debate, a petty, quibbling, sulking piece not worthy of an author's name on the title page. In the end, the anonymous author could only admit "that all the ministers in New-England could not persuade him out of his opinions."[24]

In western Massachusetts, Edward Taylor offered a more reasoned but still impassioned reply to Stoddard in "The Appeal Tried," which was written in the winter of 1709/10. In it he cited Mather's arguments against Stoddard, Stoddard's replies, and finally his own rebuttals, central to which was his argument that discipline not doctrine was the heart of true religion. Taylor offered little but additional fuel to the feud and ended the tract with the uninspired conclusion that "That ordinance is no converting ordinance that requires love for Christ by all that partake in it but such is the Lord's Supper. That ordinance that expects visible saints from it though they be in as saints is no converting ordinance."[25]

X   *Results of the Stoddard-Mather Debates*

As is evident from the manner in which the debates degenerated into temper-ridden aspersions on the abilities of opponents, the chief results of the pamphlet war were twofold; to gradually solidify opposing parties and to gradually polarize Evangelists and disciplinarians, Stoddardeans and the orthodox rationalists. In the east a hegemony of sorts with the Mathers as its spokesmen persisted while Stoddard in the west realized that his chief appeal was to his moderate Congregationalist and Presbyterial neighbors to the south. As though a truce had been called, the Mathers went their way and the Stoddardeans were left alone henceforth till Stoddard's death. A kind of anaesthesia enervated the hot feelings of the past years, and even Cotton Mather reported that "variance and contention" seemed to disappear as each minister sought his own *modus vivendi*. Stoddard had achieved notoriety and a certain success in defending his doctrines from the Mathers, while the Mathers realized the death of their supremacy of discipline. In his emboldened determination to speak his mind on what he considered the most important issues of the day, Stoddard had perpetrated the first successful revolution in American thought. He had done this not out of blind adherence to the past, but out of the pulsating pragmatism of the frontier experience. Uncloistered, his vision clearly pointed to a new method of doing theology and preaching the Word.

CHAPTER 4

Evangelical

I A Pauline Renaissance in New England

SINCE the publication of the *Instituted Churches* in 1700 Stoddard had labored to organize the ministers of Hampshire County, and his influence also extended to Connecticut where, in 1703, Timothy Woodbridge of Hartford County, the trustees of Yale College, and a Fairfield County group led a similar movement. In May 1707, after Gurdon Saltonstall was installed as Governor of Connecticut, a call was issued for ministers to assemble in each county town to assert "a firm establishment amongst ourselves, a good and regular issue in cases subject to ecclesiastical discipline, glory to Christ our head, and edification to the members. . . ." The contest between Congregationalist and Presbyterialist in Connecticut did not undo the desire for ministerial unity and the issue of church government was mediated, allowing dissenting churches to "worship and discipline in their own way" by conciliatory clauses. In October 1708 the Saybrook Platform had been submitted to the Connecticut Assembly, which immediately endorsed it. Elated, the churches quickly moved its ratification.[1] However, in Massachusetts the conciliar movement met defeat. In 1704 a letter had been circulated among the ministers urging establishment of area associations and a general council to coordinate them, obviously based on the suggestions Stoddard made in the *Instituted Churches*. The feud between Stoddard and Mather prevented the rapprochement that was possible in Connecticut, and the Massachusetts Proposals of 1705, urging ministerial associations, failed to gain the support of the General Assembly or the churches. Ironically, the Stoddard-Mather factionalism aided the antiassociationist and the anticonciliarist causes. Stoddard persisted, as was his way, continuing to work for an informal association in Hampshire

141

County with his similarly staunch son-in-law, William Williams of Hatfield. In 1712 the association was a very informal network of the churches of Deerfield, Hatfield, Springfield, Hadley, Enfield, and Northampton. Unlike the situation in Connecticut it was not an officially recognized consociation but rather it was composed of churches who presumably had voted to become part of a "classical" organization similar to that which Stoddard had advocated in the *Instituted Church*. The Hampshire Association's first act occurred in 1712 when a weekly lecture was established allowing for the exchange of pulpits. This symbolized Stoddard's own changing piety. No longer was the hope of a Great Awakening concentrated in the right use of sacraments. Rather, it was a rekindled Evangelicalism that held forth the hope to New England and now this could be implemented through a council devoted to this end.[2]

Pauline Evangelicalism emphasized the dichotomy of the states of nature and grace, preparation and conversion. No longer was any hope offered for those in a state of sacramental preparation, for true conversion was of a radically different order. The Council's ministers, Daniel Brewer of Springfield, Isaac Chauncy of Hadley, Nathaniel Collins of Enfield, John Williams of Deerfield, and William Williams of Hatfield, all reflected this Pauline message in their sermons. All were Harvard graduates. Brewer and the two Williamses attended Harvard with Gurdon Saltonstall, the future Presbyterial governor of Connecticut. Chauncy and Collins attended Harvard in the mid-1690s, when the power of the Brattle Society was waxing. They were linked by friends and, as their sermons revealed later, by a common theological outlook. All had sought churches in the Connecticut River Valley, despite family ties with the Bay. Furthermore, Stoddard's more general influence in the Connecticut River Valley was enhanced by the marriages of his twelve sons and daughters. Esther, his stepdaughter, married the Reverend John Williams of Deerfield. Mary married the Reverend Stephen Mix, the pastor of Wethersfield; Esther married the Reverend Timothy Edwards, the father of Jonathan Edwards and minister of East Windsor. Christian married William Williams, the minister of Hatfield and Stoddard's protegé. Anthony was minister in Woodbury for sixty years. Sarah married the Reverend Samuel Whitman of Farmington. John, known as colonel of the regiment, was a member of the general court and the governor's council as chief justice and judge. Rebecca married Joseph Hawley—sometime preacher and schoolmaster of Northampton—and Hannah married the Reverend William Williams of Weston. These ministerial connections throughout western Massachusetts enhanced Stoddard's ability to develop the solidarity among associations. Stoddard's growing influence and notoriety in the Valley was neatly depicted by an apocryphal story. Once, when riding on horseback from Northampton to Hatfield, he passed a shady glen called Dewey's Hole. In a darkened thicket he was ambushed by a party of French and Indians. Unflinchingly he stared at his would-be assassins while a Frenchman aimed his musket at his heart. One of the Indians interceded before the man could cock the hammer, and exclaimed, "That was Englishman's God." Stoddard was permitted to continue on his journey to his daughter and son-in-law in Hatfield.[3]

Stoddard's influence in the Valley continued to grow as his own theological and ecclesiological outlook was becoming more Evangelistic, and it is wrong to assess his contacts with Presbyterialist ministers in Connecticut at this time as reflecting his own theological and ecclesiological position. Nor is it valid to see in his association with the Brattle Society in Cambridge an exact reflection of his own views. In the period between 1707 and 1712 Stoddard emerged as the first consistent American Evangelist, promulgating a Pauline renaissance in New England. His shift from sacramentalist to Pope had been neither steady nor complete, but his shift to Evangelical was total by 1712; and this is reflected by the changing needs of his own community of Northampton. The dispersion of settlement is reflected by the fragmentation of the original land into smaller and smaller parcels as population approached two thousand by 1712. Outlying groups of settlers forced a rearrangement of the community, and the result was that several families threatened to coalesce into new settlements. The decline in community was paralleled by the rise of the family: the basic social unit became a new focalpoint of society and religion.

The federalist ideal of first- and second-generation New England Puritanism had elevated the particular church covenant to a prominence that nearly usurped the role of mediator between God and man. As we have seen, Stoddard rejected the particular church covenant for this reason, and developed his own sacramental theory to aid regeneration. In order to facilitate the doctrine of sacramental efficacy, Stoddard the Pope promoted the discipline of instituted

churches. As this became a burden rather than a blessing, he returned to doctrine—the dynamic Christ-centered religion that had
characterized militant Puritanism under Edward VI. As an
Evangelical, Stoddard's object was not to continue with the Mathers
to dispute the nature and morphology of the conversion experience
and how to institutionalize it, but rather to preach the ceaseless
mystery of faith. His object was not to return to the purity of the
ancient church, but to seek that community that had been gathered
around the Scripture since the days of the Old Testament.[4] Stoddard's last phase as an Evangelical was accompanied by a shift in the
rhetoric of his sermons. Earlier he had appealed to a sacramental
system of works in which works were only as good as the spiritual
motion they manifested. Observable signs of sanctification were the
basis of covenant conditions. In the writings after 1712 the figure of
Christ in Stoddard's thought ceased to be peripheral. No longer was
participation in Christ restricted to visible saints' communion.
Rather, Paul's Christ-mysticism became the center of the Evangelical experience.

II   Those Taught by God (1712)

Stoddard promolgated his Evangelicalism in "A Sermon preached
at [the] Boston lecture, July 3d, 1712": *Those Taught by God the
Father to Know God the Son are Blessed.* In it he indicated it was
not the sacraments but "Divine teachings [that] render persons
blessed" (1). Taking as his text Matt. 16:17 (Blessed art thou Simon
Bar-Jona, for flesh and blood hath not revealed it unto thee, but my
father which is in heaven) two significations were dichotomized in
Ramist fashion: "Negatively the meaning is it was not only revealed
by flesh and blood" and "Positively [it is] not to be understood of the
conviction by miracles, for many saw Christ's miracles that were not
happy but of the conviction by the Spirit of God" (3). Since true faith
was based not on communion or in belief in miracles, it must be
based in the Word of God and hence the "Doctrine: Those men are
blessed to whom the divinity of Jesus of Nazareth is revealed not by
flesh and blood but by the Father that is in heaven" (4). Against
those already incipient tendencies in New England theology that
were to lead to antitrinitarian doctrines that Christ was not God but
higher in the chain of being than mere men, it was argued from
typology that "The divinity of the Messiah is abundantly taught in
the Old Testament" (Ps. 2:7, 110:1, Is. 9:6; Jer. 23:6; Mic. 5:2; Zach.

13:7) as well as in the New (John 9:37). If he felt that his earlier theory of converting ordinances had contributed to an erosion of the distinction between saint and sinner, between the mediator and mere man, he now wished it known that he had advocated nothing of the sort: "There be a number of men to whom" the divinity of Christ "is revealed by the Father that is in heaven, and those are blessed men" (5). Indeed, he argued, many men really "don't know who are blessed." "If riches and dignities or morality or baptism or church fellowship would make men blessed we might be able to pronounce many men so. But if it depends on the Father revealing Christ to men, then we are under an uncertainty. It is difficult for some good men to know it concerning themselves, but much more difficult to know it concerning others" (17). This was the first "use" in the Boston lecture against hypocrisy. Referring to the problem of the Winthrop-Cotton Code of the test for regeneration, it was argued that although "We may have grounds of strong persuasion concerning some, . . . we must not pretend to an infallible knowledge. . . ." Three "considerations" were offered to explain this point. First, "if men profess the divinity of Jesus Christ we don't know that it hath been revealed to them by the Father" (17). Secondly, "If men tell that they had a very affecting discovery of Christ, we don't know that it is any more than a common illumination" (18). Thirdly, "If they tell us that immediately upon that discovery they came to Christ we can't tell but that they were mistaken" (19). The second "use" Stoddard offered was "Of examination," "Whether you have been taught the divinity of Jesus by the Father that is in heaven" (20). Even though, he argued, "You make a profession of the divinity of Jesus . . . , this doesn't make you blessed" unless it "is revealed by the Father" (21). The third "use" "Of warning" exhorted the Boston magistrates "Be not at rest till the divinity of Jesus be revealed to you" for without it "you will surely perish" (28–29). The final point urged the audience to action: "You might be looking *backward,* and take notice of your transgressions, looking inward and take notice of the plague on your hearts, looking forward and take notice of the grave and the bottomless pit" (32). Yet action in itself produced nothing. "You may say men are passive in receiving the revelation, not active in working it. You abstain from vicious ways; you read; you come to meeting; you pray: God is a free agent; you cannot force him; there is no compelling God to make this revelation to you" (33). Yet despite the uncertainty of striving, hope remained "If men were seeking more earnestly, they would have more success" (32). *Those Taught by God the Father* represents Stoddard's final phase of Christ-centered, Pauline preaching.

III The Efficacy of the Fear of Hell *(1713)*

December 3, 1713, marked the beginning of a revival that spread from Northampton south as "more than ordinary pouring out of the spirit of God" was recorded by Stoddard when he preached to the Inferior Court. *The Efficacy of the Fear of Hell* is actually a collection of eight sermons, the last five of which were collectively entitled the *Benefit of the Gospel*, and those were presumably preached while the Northampton Church was undergoing its religious awakening in the fall of 1712. This awakening occurred simultaneously with Hampshire Association's lecture series. In other churches in the Council and beyond similar awakenings occurred, with flocks of new converts being admitted. These sermons, then, are the first to document the variety of Evangelical preaching that led people into Connecticut Valley meetinghouses in the pre–Great Awakening period.

Stoddard chose as his text Job 31:23 (Destruction from God was a terror to me) but his rhetoric was not in the jeremiad form of lament for the collective sins of the nation. Rather, the doctrine that "The fear of hell is a powerful restraint from sin" was used as a first step to conversion. The Jeremiad of impending doom was transformed into the millenarian hope of the New Life; instead of a lament for the past purity of the early church in Jerusalem or the first-generation meetinghouse in Boston, this was a straightforward attempt to present the fear of hell and "Destruction from God" as a help to good but unconverted men to "discover the dangerous nature of sin (Matt. 13:41, 42)" and their need of the Word (4–5). Not only did "the fear of hell" help man to see "the baseness of sin, but also it opened one's eyes to the "Light in Hell-fire" (8). While "the fear of hell helps men to see what practices are sinful" because "Natural conscience doth condemn many sins" (Rom 2:15) it also prepares them for the Word which "is as a two edged sword" (Heb 4:12). In his characteristic frontier homiletic, against lip service to Arminian moralism, Stoddard noted that "Fig leaves and sorry pretenses . . . will not serve their turn when God shall judge them" (9). Looking back on the past two decades since he began preaching converting ordinances, he admitted dismal failure: "the country hath been prosperous in other designs. There hath been an endeavor to promote [the cloth industry] and it hath . . . prospered; so there has been a design to promote learning and merchandize and there hath been success; but there have been great endeavors to promote reformation: laws have been enacted, sermons have been preached, covenants have been made but all endeavors have had a miscarrying womb; there has not been one sin generally reformed these twenty years. Instead of growing better and better the country grows worse and worse" (9). "The reason of it is," argued Stoddard, "they are not afraid of hell" (10). This was Stoddard's way of saying that until now he had really not applied doctrine alone in his preaching.

The entire thrust of the sermons in *The Efficacy of the Fear of Hell* was, therefore, Evangelistic: "of all the preachers that we read of in the Scriptures none was so frequent in warning the people to avoid hell as Jesus Christ" (14). This Gospel message applied to parents, ministers, rulers, under-officers, buyers and sellers, and young persons. If only parents and teachers would effectively counsel the young people, Stoddard exhorted, "a sense of Hell-fire would soon scare them out of those humors" of sin and lethargy. He knew of what he was talking since his recent harvest reaped several young people in Northampton. One technique he used was to apply the exhortation that "the misery of hell will be exceeding great," and that although it exceeded all others in scale, Stoddard permitted comparison to some other miseries like incarceration in "a dark dungeon" (Matt 8:12) or "a dark mirey hole (Jer. 38:6)" or when Sodom was set ablaze when "streams of fire and brimstone fell from heaven upon their houses and upon the ground and upon their bodies: men, women, children, all like torches; their bodies blazed; How did they scream out in that extremity!" (25). How much this sounds like the sermons of his successor Jonathan Edwards!

The next seven sermons in *The Efficacy* were entitled collectively as *The Benefit of the Gospel,* and they were all based on Luke 4:18, 19: "The Spirit of the Lord is upon me . . . to preach the acceptable year of the Lord" (32). The first sermon dealt with the third person of the Trinity as it related to preaching the Gospel message: "Ministers need have the spirit of the Lord upon them in order to the recovery of religion among his people" (34). Stoddard indicated his views on the psychology of revivalism: "Zeal will inflame the heart. . . . When men are sensible to the breaking out of fire . . . they will cry out earnestly" (37). While earlier he had argued that ministers need not be regenerate to preach the Word, now Stoddard reversed that opinion and argued that it was necessary for ministers to have the spirit, for only then would they be able to lead their people in reviving religion (39–46). Only if the people would "pray for the [converted] ministry" could present conditions be changed (51–55). The second sermon exhorted ministers "to preach the gospel to the poor" in spirit (56). It was Stoddard's appeal for ministers to go outside the churches to those not in communion and play the role of the Evangelical. He indicated this "the first good act that is done by the soul is [to] belong in Christ" and it is the poor in spirit who are best "prepared to receive the Gospel" (63–64). "So Paul was prepared (Acts 9:6)." "So the Jailor (Acts 16:30)." Stoddard reduced preparation to two stages: first, to see the want of salvation and, secondly, to see that only through the Gospel was it offered (66). He made it clear that preparation could come either in an instant as with Paul or slowly and imperceptibly as with the jailor or Lydia. Once again he indicated his opposition to the prescriptive, disciplinarian view of conversion held by strict Congregationalists.[5]

The third sermon, based on the text "He hath sent me to heal the broken hearted," was designed to show "the effect of preaching the Gospel to the poor" "to heal wounded consciences" (83). Stoddard's casuistry shifted here from that of the accusing conscience to the healing conscience. Thomas Hooker had been perhaps the first Puritan to insist that the conscience is not "primarily or exclusively" accusing but rather one must labor it to be on one's side. Stoddard followed Hooker in this insistence and thereby opposed the jeremiad casuists like Increase and Cotton Mather, endeavoring to show, as part of his Evangelical message, how "the Gospel applies its healing virtue by manifesting" "that God hath justified and accepted him" and "his conscience echoes the voice of God and pronounces him an heir of glory" (90–91). Similarly, Hooker had argued of *The Poor Doubting Christian* that "we should not only be content to have all our objections [about faith] answered, but [also] get them recorded in the court of conscience and there surely find the day and year when God's love was made sure to us." As George H. Williams has remarked, "Here surely we are at the springs of the New England retrospective conscience and the later revivalists insistance on the hour and the day of a saving experience." The fourth sermon, "To preach deliverance to the captives," was designed to show that "God offers deliverance to those that are in spiritual captivity" (107–108). Stoddard developed the Pauline law/grace dialectic based on the Epistle to the Romans, "Ye have your fruit unto happiness and the end, everlasting life" (Rom. 6:22). While, on the one hand, Paul indicated that "the law in his members brought him unto captivity (Rom. 7:23), through God's free grace in Christ man is redeemed" (115–17). "The gift of God is eternal life through Christ Jesus our Lord" (Rom. 6:23). Although effort was required of man, hope of salvation was free and depended on the arbitrary divine will.[6]

The fifth sermon further developed the hope of passing from a natural to a converted state by using metaphors of sight: "They that live under the preaching of the Gospel have an opportunity to have their eyes opened" (134). The Pauline nature/grace, light/darkness, flesh/spirit, visible/invisible dialectic was expanded from the text: "They that belong to the visible kingdom of darkness do also belong to the invisible kingdom of darkness, but they that have the light of the Gospel shining among them have an opportunity to have their eyes opened" (Col. 1:3). After enumerating those doctrines deemed essential to salvation from I Cor. 2:10, Stoddard reiterated the Pauline concern that it was necessary to "have a conviction set before them that they are blind" (Rom. 3:23) (136). It was not sufficient to merely articulate this "for form-sake" in a catechism. Rather, the light of the Gospel must be seen as "it is for the eyes to behold the Sun" (Eccl. 11:7) (143). Here Stoddard applied a nearly mystical language when describing the mediator, a language that would be developed and emulated in the Great Awakening: "The sight of Christ is a glorious sight. It is worth a while to go through a great deal of trouble for a sight of Jesus Christ. . . . It is worth the while to take a great journey for a sight of Jesus Christ" (Phil. 3:10). "Paul's heart was in it that he might know him and the power of his resurrection and the fellowship of his sufferings." "When the wise men saw the star that directed to Christ they rejoiced with exceeding great joy (Matt. 2:10). The sight of Jesus Christ is a beautiful vision" (144). Finally, Stoddard indicated how this revelation is perceived: "The greatest delight of man must needs be in the exercise of his superior faculties, understanding and will, upon the most glorious objects. It is a most pleasant thing to enjoy spiritual light" (145). This, for Stoddard, was true sanctification, not the bald adherence to rules of conduct and morality. It was a direct result of

his view that "The excellency of God has a magnetic power to draw
the heart" (145). The sixth sermon built upon this rhetoric of the
beauty and sensibility of the divine. Reflecting on the recent revival
at Northampton, Stoddard observed two varieties of religious awakening: "reviving is sometimes . . . more general when it is throughout a country were in all parts of the land" as in a Great Awakening,
"But sometimes this reviving is more particular when in some particular towns religion doth revive and flourish" (190). He went on to
observe that "sometimes it is not for long" and that "God is very
arbitrary in this matter" (191).

In these seven sermons Stoddard's revival techniques were aptly
applied. Increasing intensity of emotion, progression of rhetoric
from the general to the specific, and the outline of preparation with
a sudden and unexpected chasm between it and the converted state
demonstrate Stoddard's refined method fully. In these sermons we
have the elements that were to characterize the preachers of the
Great Awakening: the advocacy of a converted and almost an itinerant ministry, the elevation of a minister's authority above that of a
specific congregation, the dissolution of congregational autonomy
and the supremacy of council over specific churches in matters of
discipline, the Evangelical trusting of doctrine to the individual
soul, and finally the elevation of the aesthetic involvement with the
beauty of divine mystery, quite apart from the rational comprehension of creation's physical laws or religious conversion.

IV   A Guide to Christ (1714)

A Guide was the symbol of Stoddard's apparent success in the
Valley, since Increase Mather contributed a laudatory preface recognizing their past disagreements but their common purpose: "It is
known that in some parts (not fundamentals of religion) I differ from
the beloved author. Nevertheless (as when there was a difference of
opinion between Jerome and Au[gu]stine) Jerome said for all that I
cannot but love Christ in Au[gu]stine; so I say concerning my
brother Stoddard. Boston, Nov. 15, 1714" (xii). Yet Mather still did
disagree with Stoddard on the very issue discussed in this series of
sermons preached at Northampton, for in them Stoddard ham-
mered away at the theme of Man's total humiliation (42–43) and
God's supreme sovereignty (60) until Mather had to try to deny that
none of the founding fathers including Hooker and Shepard really
meant what they said about total self-negation. Stoddard on the

contrary called for total submission before the will of God (72–75). Stoddard's real enemies now were the supernatural rationalists springing up in Boston who asserted that the mechanism of salvation was orderly, smooth and predictable as any well-oiled machine. Natural gifts, they held, were the basis of one's heavenly reward. Stoddard recoiled in horror at this path theology was taking and devoted himself in these sermons to underscore the point that man's duty is preparation for salvation and he underscored John Norton's dictum that "There is not the like degree of humiliation in all that are converted." Furthermore, preparation was not conversion. God was wholly arbitrary in bestowing grace but man must strive in the work of preparation regardless. "There is no necessity in nature of any preparation before the infusion of grace. Christ changed water into wine and raised the dead to life without any previous preparation, so he can do in this case . . . and man when prepared can do nothing to help God in planting grace in them [nor] hinder God in implanting grace" (5). Once again Stoddard espoused the value of a converted ministry. He counseled that ministers should "not satisfy themselves with other points of learning but labor after that that . . . they may be instead eyes to them that are in the wilderness" (8). This was as much a general comment as it was a criticism of the Arminian direction Harvard had been taking under President Leverett.

In *A Guide* Stoddard firmly rejected his old theory of sacramental efficacy. He now claimed that man's spiritual voyage was entirely at God's mercy. It could be "like a ship that beats upon the coast day by day and can't get in" or it could be that "one ship may spend twice as much time as another in performing the same voyage" (48, 55). "God uses his sovereignty very much as to the degree of men's trouble," he warned, and it was the duty of ministers "to convince them that they cannot make their own hearts better. They find that afflications don't do it, nor ordinances, nor mercies" (49). Stoddard closed with the Christ-centered message "that there is enough in Christ. He is able to save to the uttermost" (Heb. 7:15). He argued that "If God do show man his own emptiness he may quickly after discover the excellency of Christ" (85), but the way was by no means certain: "It is no ways fit to tell a man that God will show mercy to him. He must wait upon God to open his eyes and show Jesus Christ to him" (86), to "plant a new heart" (87). *A Guide to Christ* was Stoddard's antidote to both the catechism and the communion manual, and it was issued as if it were Hampshire Association's book of devotions, being collected sermons many of which were presumably preached at the Hampshire Council's lecture series.

As the Association under Stoddard's leadership grew in power it required a constitution and by-laws. In 1714 its member churches ratified three proposals and in the next year they had their test case involving a dispute between a minister and a congregation. Also in these years other churches joined the group, West Springfield under John Woodbridge and Suffield under Ebenezer Devotion. The proposals revealed a similarity with Stoddard's pronouncements in the *Instituted Churches*. For instance, the first proposition revealed "That if any baptized persons living in our towns shall fall into any scandalous transgression" it was permissible to excommunicate them because, according to Stoddard, all those under the baptismal covenant were communicants and under the full disciplinary power of the church. The second proposition affirmed the disciplinary "power in ecclesiastical councils" and added evidence from the *Instituted Churches* to prove the point. Thirdly, the proposals indicated that Hampshire Association was, for the time being, the ecclesiastical court of last resort until a provincial council were established "unto which we may appeal." No such official synod was ever established.[7]

The first case brought before Hampshire Association involved members of the Enfield church who attempted to suspend their minister, Nathaniel Collins, from administering the Lord's Supper. Opponents to this faction appealed to the Association and Stoddard, acting for the group with John and William Williams, rebuked Collins's detractors, noting that his preaching was acceptable according to "several persons belonging to other places who have occasionally heard him abroad and at home":

But we are especially puzzled to conceive how you can justify your selves in not allowing the Lord's Supper to be administered, if he be fit to preach and baptize, surely he is fit to administer the Lord's Supper, can you satisfy your consciences to attend upon other parts of his ministry for a twelvemonth together, yet not give way to his administering the Lord's Supper. Surely he has power from Christ to dispense the ordinances of God, until he is in some way or order suspended from the execution of his office, you have not proved him scandalous, you have not pretended him to be insufficient, the world will be apt to judge two things upon it, one is that you don't thirst after the ordinances of God, the other is that you do it upon a design to affront him & weary him out.[8]

Stoddard concluded by threatening that unless the dispute were quelled, excommunication would follow:

You sent for a Council the last year, what you had to say was heard with patience, & a determination drawn up upon it, but you have acted since that as if you had a superior power, & sent for a Council to strengthen you in your way & not to direct in the mind of God. It renders your zeal much suspected that it doth precipitate you into unwarrantable methods, you will have no cause to wonder, if while you reject the Communion among yourselves, the *neighboring churches do withdraw communion from you.*[9]

When the Enfield group sought to participate in communion with the Springfield church, the Springfield Congregation asked the Association for a decision as to the propriety of this request. Once again the Association under Stoddard's leadership replied that:

We look upon it irregular, to admit them to participate with any of our Churches in that ordinance, since they may enjoy that privilege at home and meanwhile do neglect to submit to the determination of the Council.[10]

As late as 1718 the matter still was causing controversy in the Enfield church and a letter signed by Stoddard, John and William Williams indicated the state of affairs:

The discord is grown to so great an hight, & rejects all remedies, so that it proves an overbearing discouragement & impediment to Mr. Collins in his work, & a great hindrance to the people's edification & the edification of their children.[11]

They finally recommended that it was "not unwarrantable for Mr. Collins to lay down his work in that place" in view of the difficulty, and he finally left in 1724.

In the seven years from 1712 to 1718 the first phase of Stoddard's Pauline Evangelicalism was promulgated through the press and through the Hampshire Association lectures. John Woodward of Norwich was one of the first to issue the call by arguing *Civil Rulers are God's Ministers, for the Peoples Good* at the Connecticut election sermon in 1712, and a Hartford County Association was initiated to promulgate the Evangelical piety. Woodward had been secretary of the Saybrook Synod in the summer of 1708 and had tried to impose the Saybrook Platform on his own church by suppressing the clause allowing for dissent. When he was discovered in

this duplicity, Norwich dismissed him on September 13, 1716.[12]
Eliphalet Adams was much more of a steadying influence on his
church in New London where he was ordained in 1709. Adams had
been assistant minister at the Brattle Street Church, of all places,
from 1701 to 1704 with Benjamin Colman, but his Evangelistic zeal,
evinced when he was an Indian missionary, naturally conflicted with
Colman's Arminian rationalism. This was intimated in Adams's
Connecticut Election Sermon preached on May 11, 1710. Adams
defended with Stoddard and William Williams the central role of
the converted ministry in such sermons as *The Work of Ministers
Rightly to Divide the Word of Truth* (1725) and *Ministers Must Take
Heed to Their Ministry to Fulfill It* (1726). Isaac Chauncy of Hadley
also began his career in the midst of Stoddard's influence. Strict
Congregationalist John Russell had died at Hadley in 1692 and the
town expected a new preacher for a new age. On September 9,
1696, the year after he graduated from Harvard, A.M., Chauncy
was ordained at Hadley and Stoddard attended his first lecture.
Chauncy offered the religion his congregation yearned for, exemplified in an ordination sermon he delivered in 1724 for William
Rand at Sunderland, *The Faithful Evangelist, or the True Shepherd*
(1725). His son Isaac was chosen as Stoddard's first assistant in 1725.
Son-in-law Timothy Edwards, pastor of Windsor, supported Stoddard's concept of church associations. From his settlement in 1694
he preached for conversion of his parishioners' souls with a rhetoric
very similar to Stoddard's. His son, Jonathan, was chosen as the
second assistant at Northampton in 1726. Under Chauncy was
reared Jonathan Marsh, who graduated from Harvard in 1705 and
was ordained at Windsor in 1710. It was not until 1720 that he
promulgated publically Stoddardean Evangelicalism in *The Great
Care and Concern of Men under Gospel Light* (1720) and *A Sermon
Preached before the General Court of Election at Hartford* (1721).
Finally, Stoddard's son-in-law Samuel Whitman, a native of Hull,
and a graduate of Harvard, began promulgating Evangelicalism at
Farmington through such sermons as *Practical Godliness the Way to
Prosperity* (1714). Particularly in Whitman is evident that streak of
pragmatism that characterized Stoddard's own style of preaching.
Direct, forceful language was united to a rhetoric espousing com-
mon brotherhood in a public covenant.

William Williams of Hatfield was perhaps the most active in
promoting Stoddardean piety. On October 17, 1716, he warned his

nephew Stephen at his ordination at Longmeadow that when God sends "any into his harvest, it is not to loiter but to labor in it." How could "the ignorant be informed, the careless quickened, the erroneous refuted, the doubting resolved, the afflicted comforted, the self deceivers detected" unless the minister himself were converted? He counseled his nephew "to study men as well as books" if he were to be a successful experiential preacher. By 1717, therefore, Stoddard had a large ministerial following who were active in emphasizing conversion.

V The Duty of Gospel Ministers *(1717)*

Secure in his position as the leading figure of Hampshire Association, Stoddard now sought to publicize the broadening membership of the group by preaching ordination sermons to new members. Therefore, when Thomas Cheney was ordained as minister at Brookfield on October 16, 1717, Stoddard delivered the ordination sermon. Cheney (1692–1747), a native of Roxbury and a 1713 A.M. graduate of Harvard, was a product of President Leverett's liberalizing curriculum. Brookfield had extended a call to him on April 5, 1716, before the church was organized. Although he published nothing in his life, Cheney was respected during the Great Awakening as a nonseparatist. The text of the ordination sermon came from the Sermon on the Mount (Matt. 5:13), "Ye are the Salt of the Earth," and the doctrine drawn from the Scripture was that "The ministers are by their office to preserve the people from corruption" (1,3). This was Stoddard's plea to young ministers that the "principles of religion" must be preached with conviction or the church which is the "pillar and ground of truth" (I Tim. 3:15) will crumble into ruin (4–5). Looking at young Cheney and thinking of the growing worldliness of New England, Stoddard reflected "If the present generation be knowing men, in a few years many of them may die and the young generations, if they have not suitable means of instruction, will be very ignorant" (5). It was extremely important, therefore, that there be a converted minister since "If then teachers be blind and ignorant as the complaint is (Isaiah 56:10) no wonder if the people be ignorant" (6). People can grow corrupt either "In respect to the principles of religion" through ignorance or error or "In respect to practice" through formality or vice (5–7). Ministers can "preserve a people from corruption" "by instructing them in the principles of religion and the rule of God's Word," "by

solemn warnings," "by suitable encouragement," "by good government," and "by being good examples" (8–12). From the doctrine
Stoddard drew three uses: "A faithful minister in a land is a great
blessing"; "People had need be careful that they don't provoke God
to give them such a ministry as will be like unsavory salt"; and that
ministers were charged to "labor to convert as many as possible" to
keep them "in a flourishing condition" and to keep the consciences
of natural men tender "with a deep sense of the jealousy of God and
of the terrible judgements that God executes for sin" (13–24). It was
clear from this message that the whole purpose and thrust of Stoddard's Association was to promote revival religion not to act as a
disciplinary body. It also was clear that the Gospel and the Apostles of the church were the two instruments that Stoddard saw as
the only hope of bringing in the harvest. Therefore, the essential
key was the promotion of a converted ministry. The sermon called for
action in Stoddard's characteristic pose as a general among the soldiers of Christ.

VI   Three Sermons *(1717)*

This collection of actually four sermons presents in outline the
essential features of Stoddard's revised revival technique. In the
first three, the object is the understanding or the rational apprehension of the Gospel truths while the fourth is addressed to the will
and affections. Sermon I, *Shewing the Vertue of Christ's Blood to
Cleanse from Sin*, used as its text I John I:7 ("And the blood of Jesus
Christ his son cleanseth us from all sin.") and drew from it the
doctrine "There is mighty virtue in the blood of Christ to expiate the
guilt of sin." Having presented Christ as the Son of God and this as
the reason that his sufferings, "especially his bloody death" "has an
efficacy to cleanse us from sin," Stoddard went on to expose the
Pauline dialectic of sin and death in Rom. 6:23. Along with the Latin
Fathers he presented the atonement as a ransom or a pardon. Earlier, we may remember, he had spoken of it as the Greek Fathers
had, as a medicine of immortality. The dialectic in Stoddard's own
thought between the accusing and the assuring conscience seems to
reflect these two metaphors of atonement.

Arguments were marshaled to prove the Pauline point that "Wisdom is a defence and money is a defence, but the blood of Christ is a
defence against the curse of the Law: Gal. 3:13 ('He hath redeemed
us from the curse of the Law having made a curse for us.')." First,

Stoddard reasoned, "The father would not have put Christ on this service if death would not have prevailed for the pardon of sin" (3), "The dignity of his person is infinite," Stoddard reflected in awakening Christology, "and the love of his father exceeding great . . ." (4). Secondly, Stoddard argued, "God promised to Jesus Christ that his death should be accepted for doing away of sin" (4) and "the price of their redemption." Thirdly, Stoddard used the typological argument that "for four thousand years there were daily sacrifices" to God in the Temple and none could "purge away sin for they were all types and shadows of Christ (Col. 2:17)" (5–6). Stoddard's fourth argument must have astonished even his foes, for in it he renounced his earlier theory of sacramental efficacy. Baptism, for instance, held "forth our fellowship with Christ in his sufferings (Rom. 6:3). So many of us have been baptised into Jesus Christ were baptised into his death" (6). However, "Baptism," Stoddard now maintained, was "a seal of the doctrine of faith in the righteousness of Christ." Adult persons professed their faith in Christ before they were baptized (Acts 8:37, 38). . . . "So we are taught the same by the Lord's Supper" (7). The fifth argument presented the genuineness of divine love as the proof of trusting in the savior, "And surely God will not with seeming love draw us into a snare, will not with great appearance of love persuade us to build on a sandy foundation" (8).

Almost half of the sermon was designed to apply the doctrine Stoddard had presented, and this was in keeping with his emphasis on the will and affections in the process of preparation. Christ is "a great savior" (17), "he has fully paid our debts to the justice of God" (12), but unless man is truly humbled he could not "sense of the virtue of Christ's blood" (19). The second "use" was directed against "those that have a greater value for their own works than for the blood of Christ," because "Some men make their own works the great foundation of their hope" (19). Against these rationalists at Harvard who saw righteousness in man's achievements, Stoddard spoke out, "The best works of man are sinful (Isaiah 64:6) 'All our righteousnesses are as filthy rags' " (21). He exhorted the youthful audience to examine themselves if they were "delivered from the kingdom of darkness," explaining in a Pauline dialectic that "Light to discern the glory of Christ is the particular enjoyment of godly men (II Cor. 4:6) 'God hath shined in our hearts to give the light of the knowledge of the glory of God in the face of Jesus Christ' " (24). Throughout the sermon Stoddard succeeded in maintaining the tension between God's glory and Christ's love as dual aspects of faith.

Sermon II, *That Natural Men are Under the Government of Self Love*, was directed against the tendency in contemporary theology to relate or even identify one's self-love with selfless love. Taking as his text (II Tim. 3:2) "For men shall be lovers of their own selves" (34), Stoddard argued that the present age when men indulge in self-love runs counter to "the first and great command . . . 'to love the Lord thy God with all thy heart.' " (Matt. 22:37, 38). Hence, the doctrine "Natural men are under the government of self-love" (35). Using the Pauline dialectics throughout these sermons undid the complacent, liberal view that between nature and grace were orderly steps in a continuum of self-development. On the other hand, Stoddard maintained that between self-love and selfless love was a quantum jump. Love directed to the self was wholly other than love aimed at "the glory of God." "If men did aim at the glory of God, they could not neglect any duty of religion" the Northampton pastor urged (47). Those who "aim at no more religion than will promote their own interest" "come to the house of God but won't pray" or "bring their children to Baptism but neglect the Lord's Supper" (47). Total humiliation, total selfless love to God's glory, was the only point from which man could truly sense how Christian love really operates. The man of self-love rejected the afflicting wounds of his conscience but the man of true love was prepared for true religion. What he had said earlier about the fear of hell he now minimized. As with Edwards, Stoddard now maintained that the fear of hell was a product of self-love. While the Boston liberals were now beginning to frighten their congregations into the duties of religion, Stoddard with great psychological and social insight was arguing only true selfless love was the gate to heaven. Love of "the excellency of God," not fear of divine wrath was the basis of a genuine spiritual union (54).

Sermon III, *That the Gospel is the Means of Conversion*, was again based on a Pauline text (I Cor. 4: 15), "For in Jesus Christ I have begotten you through the Gospel," (65). Here was presented Stoddard's doctrine of the "New Creature" that totally denied the nature-grace continuity that was being espoused by Samuel Willard and Charles Chauncy. Paul, Stoddard noted, "doth not speak of a natural but spiritual begetting: that work whereby they were made New Creatures, New Men. This is the same that is intended by conversion. In Christ they are begotten; . . . this begetting did not make them men but Christians" (65–66). Stoddard noted that the "living instrument in this work" was man, "God was the principal agent" and the "doctrinal instrument" was the Gospel containing "the doctrine of the person and offices of Christ, his humiliation and exhaltation and the covenant of grace . . ." (66). The point of the sermon was that "The Gospel is the means of conversion," and this further eroded any hope in the saving nature of the sacraments that Stoddard had once preached, but he did notice that even in "the works of creation" (67) or the gracious works of men (72) "the glory of God" is shadowed forth. However, only the Gospel makes men "actually turn to God and leave a disposition on the heart that . . . despised" that " 'beauty in him, that we should desire him' " (Isaiah 53:2) (75). The Pauline reason/grace dialectic was clearly presented here: "Faith only [is] the condition of justification," selfless love is a condition of faith. The lesson was unmistakeably revivalistic: "where the Gospel is not known there is no conversion" (81). Furthermore, it was a specially damning idea that "many men among us that have lived thirty years under the preaching of the Gospel . . . are not yet converted" (83). Teaching the Gospel only advanced one in a state of education, but conversion was totally apart, for only in that state did men "turn to God" (90). Against the liberals, Stoddard stood firmly: "Peace with God passes all understanding" (91).

Sermon IV, *To Stir Up Young Men and Maidens in the Name of the Lord,* took as its text (Ps. 148: 12, 13), "Young men and maidens, let them praise the name of the Lord" (93). The structure of the four sermons recapitulated the Stoddardean preparation/conversion dialectic: the last sermon was devoted to "the excellency of His name," the religious affections in their desire to behold the spiritual beauty of "the majesty of God, and his divine truth and faithfulness" (96). So, Stoddard explained, "A religious attending on the preaching of the Word is a praising of God" just as a "a religious receiving the seals of the covenant" or "a religious singing of psalms is giving glory to God" (96). With regard to the Lord's's Supper, which had once been the keystone of his theology, Stoddard now could only call it "a thankful memorial of the redemption of Christ (I Cor. 11:26). The "Marvellous light" of the Gospel now outshone all the sacraments, for it, instead of they, illuminated the true nature of saving conversion. (97)

In these sermons Stoddard clearly articulated the tension between mystic quietism—the rejection of righteous living as a basis of religion—and pragmatic activism—the social demands of a reinvigorated national millenarianism. On the one hand Stoddard had demolished the idea of exclusive church compacts which reduced religion to psychological moralism. The aesthetics of religious emotion corresponded to the mystical quality of his concept of God. It was obviously an inner-directed doctrine. On the other hand, he railed against self-directed introspection that Arminian rationalists used as the basis of their moralistic religion. Self-less love extends to the ends of the nation, indeed, to the Millennium.

Here can be identified two later strains of thought. Jonathan Edwards would inherit this tension between the mystical and social implications of Stoddard's theology and is evident in his problem of locating the place of aesthetics (the mystical component) in the community (the social component.) Samuel Hopkins, a contemporary of Edwards, understood this tension and decided that the mystical emphasis in *True Virtue* nearly put practical religion in the clouds, for Edwards had invented an inferior, secondary order of virtue to discuss social morality. While Stoddard held the two orders in tension, albeit unresolved, Edwards, in effect, subordinated the social to the ontological. Hopkins, recognizing this, sought to redress the balance with his concept of disinterested benevolence as the essence of all virtue.

VII   The Presence of Christ *(1718)*

Continuing to expand the membership of the Council and to promulgate it through the press, Stoddard preached the ordination sermon for Joseph Willard at Swampfield (now Brookfield) on January 1, 1718. This was at the same time when the Enfield church was split over its minister, Nathaniel Collins, so Stoddard appended a sermon, "An Examination of the Power of Fraternity," which was intended to establish the authority of the Association that Enfield should follow minister Collins. The text chosen by Stoddard (Matt. 28:20), "And I am with you always even unto the end of the world," was applied to his abiding concern for a converted ministry as the doctrine drawn from it made evident: "Christ Jesus will be present with the ministers of the Gospel to the end of the world" (1–3). Stoddard noted that ministers need "the presence of Christ" "To furnish them with gifts for their work," "to receive all cases of conscience," "To strengthen them against temptation" "that there may be a reformation wrought in the land" (4–8). Clearly the chief task of this converted ministry was "to make the arrows of the Word stick in the hearts of men" (9). Stoddard assured Swampfield that the mediator was present in the "visible kingdom" with the elect "whose names are written in the Lamb's book of life" and with the ministers (10–13). The three "uses" drawn from this doctrine were designed to provoke "encouragement" and fear "for the ministers of the Christian world" (15). It was up to them to awaken the people: "Many men are in a fast sleep and whispering will not awaken them; the threatenings of God had need ring in their ears" (27). While earlier Stoddard had used Thomas Hooker's theory of the assuring conscience, now he balanced it with an appeal to the accusing conscience: "Preach in such a manner as is most proper to . . . the conscience. God's way is to bless suitable means. He doesn't bless healing plasters to eat away sound flesh. He doesn't bless cordials to take away stubborn humors. If ministers desire to convert men they had need speak piercing words" (27). Furthermore, the language in sermons should be plain, direct, and forceful: "Some ministers affect rhetorical strains of speech as if they were making an oration in the schools; this may tickle the fancies of men and scratch aching ears, but we have men's consciences to deal with: men need to be frightened and not be pleased" (I Cor. 2:4) (28).

Preached at a time when Boston rationalists were beginning to espouse the doctrine that God's benevolence extended to all moral men, this ordination sermon embodied a Pauline nature/grace dialectic in which the ministry was charged with awakening natural men to their true condition. The rhetoric Stoddard used was designed first to inculcate fear of the deity and encouragement for conversion, then called for man's total and unequivocal recognition that man was inextricably mired down in sin, and that only through total humiliation lay hope. While the accusing conscience was involved in the work of preparation, the assuring conscience was involved in conversion. Stoddardean Evangelicalism did not equate or even connect preparation with conversion: nature and grace were radically unlike each other. Man's initiative could only open him to the vision of that terrible, awesome sovereignty, while grace opened him to the excellency of Christ. Pray now, Stoddard warned, that you are among the chosen.

Added to the ordination sermon was Stoddard's defense of the *power of Fraternity* of associations. As we have noted, a case had been taken up by Hampshire Association concerning a church divided over their minister. The group had ordered the minister to assume his duties, but lingering objections persisted from the congregation. Stoddard viewed this as a more general problem of the relative authority of brethren and ministers that had been created in 1649 when the Cambridge Platform, he felt, gave too much power to the laity (2). He rejected the Platform's affirmation "that the brethren have power of judgement in matters of censure and power of admitting members" for this had led to the situation where they "see themselves advanced to a share of government: They have a greater fondness for power than ability to use it . . ." (3). Stoddard conceded that civil magistrates had the power to appoint fast and thanksgiving days, to call councils, to legislate laws maintaining ministers and to quell church disputes. He agreed that brethren had the power to choose officers, but he reserved to the elders, the spiritual descendants of the Apostles, all power of admitting members and censuring them formerly given to the brethren. The elders had this power of the keys directly from Christ. Furthermore, as "It was foretold in the prophesies of the Old Testament . . . the ministers of the Gospel should be judges in ecclesiastical controversies" (Ezek. 44:24) (12). Satisfied with his proof that Associations were binding over individual elders or brethren, he ended with the abrupt comment that "The matter being thus cleared, there is no occasion for that controversy . . ." (16). It was obvious from his authoritarian tone he considered himself supreme ruler of his own Association. It is questionable whether the young men and women recently received into the church at Northampton during the 1718 "harvest" agreed with Stoddard's claim to supreme authority in the church. The local historian Sylvester Judd summarized the social climate: "The attention in 1718 was not of long continuance and did not terminate happily. From 1718 was a time of stupidity and immorality among the young and contentiousness between the court and country party." He was, of course, referring to the competition of younger men for the valued positions within the tightly controlled oligarchic structure that had emerged in Northampton since 1661. As before, the young people involved in the 1718 revival belonged to families whose economic and political situation fell below that of the ruling group. In one sense, therefore, Stoddard managed to exploit the potentially disruptive anxieties of the youth in his town and channeled them into religious activity, but this very process threatened to break the chains of command in the community. As the youth now found that they no longer were the have-nots (at least spiritually), it seemed all too easy for them to also claim that they were the new leaders (at least in the church).

VIII   Treatise Concerning Conversion *(1719)*

Although Stoddard used the terminology of faculty psychology he did not rigidly compartmentalize the understanding, the will, and the affections. All three were, as they would be for Jonathan Edwards, modes of the self's engagement with reality, and all three modes had both a natural and a spiritual aspect. The understanding, therefore, was not a distinct faculty but rather a mode of the self's engagement with reality as being. Similarly, the will was the coordinate mode of the self in its engagement with reality as good or evil. The affections were not another separate mode of engagement of the self: they were the product of the interaction of the understanding and the will. When they were tuned on the sensibilities of natural man such as legal humiliation, their object was nature. When they were tuned on the sensibilities of spiritual man such as spiritual humiliation, their object was the spirit from which all true religious, gracious affections arose. On the one hand, therefore, Stoddard retained rational understanding while simultaneously presenting the coordinate sensible perceptions of the will. At the very juncture of understanding and will was the heart. The relationship among these elements can be represented by a simple diagram:

REALITY

Being   Good

AFFECTIONS

Under-   heart   will
standing

As Stoddard passed from his conception of God as absolute power to God as absolute beauty, gradually and erratically his rhetoric shifted from images of fear to images of beauty and his attention turned from ratiocination on being to an aesthetic perception of the good. Gradually reflections on the glory and excellence of God balanced the terrors of the unconverted state. This process in Stoddard's thought is not always clear, but by 1719 in *The Treatise Concerning Conversion* it was unmistakeable.

The *Treatise* of 1719 was really a fuller exposition of a theme that had only been summarily hinted at in sermons since 1712, that there were two books, that of nature and that of Scripture and that God can be apprehended in both if one had "spiritual understanding." Stoddard did not mean that man can know God by the study of nature or of the Bible. Rather, the spirit that breathed in the Scripture authors also breathes in its faithful hearers, just as the Creator's hand in nature touches those with faith:

When God opens the eyes of men and gives spiritual understanding to them, there are two ways wherein they may see the glory of God. 1. by reasoning from the works of creation and common providence. . . . When they behold the work of God, they readily see, if there eyes be opened, that these things were made by a God of infinite power and wisdom, and goodness. There is a self-evidencing light in these works of God, showing that they are the effects of a God of infinite glory. The world is a glass, reflecting the glory of God and when mens eyes are opened, they may plainly see it. . . . When men's eyes are opened, they see the force of the argument. . . . Reason enlightened by the Spirit of God teaches men convincingly what God is. 2. By reasoning from the Word of God. The Word of God had a self-evidencing light in it; it shews that it doth proceed from a God of infinite Glory. (37–38)

In this language Stoddard developed a theory of the beauty and sensibility of the divine that his grandson Jonathan Edwards would make as a cornerstone of his theology:

A man that has had the experience of the sweetness of honey is inclined thereby to judge so from time to time. . . . He that has understood the gloriousness of God, is prepared and disposed thereby to judge so from time to time. This discovery leaves such a sense and impression on the heart, as inclines it for ever to judge so concerning God. . . . Repeated discoveries strengthen the habit and dispose them to more readiness to judge so. (35–36)

Stoddard used the familiar metaphor that the glory of God is as a magnet and once it is put in contact with the heart (i.e., love or will) it irresistibly draws it to itself:

When men do see the glory of God they would act gainst their nature if they should not be holy. . . . When men know the excellency of God, they must chose him. The glory of God is such, that it capitulates the heart; where it is seen, it has a magnetic power; it irresistibly conquers the will; there is a necessity of loving God when he is seen. . . . There is no power in the will to resist holiness when the glory of God is seen. It is impossible in nature that men should know God and not be holy. . . . The excellency of God is a sufficient reason for men's loving and serving him. . . . The gloriousness of God has a commanding power on the heart. (32)

The sight of divine glory reinforced the feeling of God's absolute sovereignty, reasoned Stoddard, and thus he staunchly opposed the developing rationalism among eighteenth-century theologians that claimed man could initiate and participate in his own gradual ascent up the ladder of morality from nature to grace. Stoddard emphatically denied this; one was either converted or unconverted and there was no process between the two. Relying on the Pauline example, Stoddard claimed the transition to grace was instantaneous and complete:

Some have been of the opinion that saving grace and common grace differ only in degree, that Sorrow for sin increases until it becomes saving; and love to God increases till it becomes saving; But certainly, saving grace doth differ specifically from all that went before; gracious actions are of another nature than the religious actions of natural men. (5–6)

The impact of Stoddard's doctrine that man's imperfections are known only in the light of the sensed beauty of the perfection and glory of God found adherents among the younger ministers between 1720 and 1729. The son of aging Chief Justice Sewall, the Reverend Joseph (1688–1769), preached to the Old South Church in 1728 that every man should "look unto Jesus as pierced by their sins and mourn." However, not until the spirit brings "a feeling sense" to the "affections" could one exclaim "Now mine eye seeth thee, wherefore I abhor myself and repent in dust and ashes" (Job 42: 5,6). Sewall noted that while these truths were deducible from the light of nature, *experiential* knowledge of them came only from faith. Even Cotton Mather now became a spokesman for this Evangelical piety. What had once been a "legal union" with Christ now became a "vital union" in which "the redeemer and believer became one, both in point of interest and in point of influence." Conformity to Christ was the essence of spiritual union. For Stoddard, "union" had its institutional correlative and this made a lasting impact on Evangelical social theory. The true test of the regenerate ministry

became the establishment of that beautiful union of saints, *com-
munio sanctorum*. Stoddard and his followers now believed that the
grand design of redemption would be manifest not through some
long-awaited cataclysm as foretold in Revelation but through a
"Great Awakening" of all people, as Eliphalet Adams coined the
term at Windham's harvest. Stoddard, too, envisioned the day when
whole towns would unite in a public covenant, the reinvested symbol of Cotton's dream of a commonwealth sealed in a common
spiritual bond and destiny.

In a sense Stoddard had come full circle to the vision of the first
strict Puritans who followed the rigors of Cotton's Code, but he had
now predicated the basis of the vision on far different principles.
While Cotton had introduced a rationalistic and disciplinarian measure of religiosity into the colonial law of enfranchisement, Stoddard
removed them completely and replaced them with a personalistic
and doctrinal acceptance of religion. Yet, both prophets had the
ideal of their people united in a common destiny and moving in
some great spiritual renewal to a state in which all were spiritually
equal. Therefore, it is essential to the long and involved foreground
to the Great Awakening to realize that the Evangelicals began
thinking through the corporate dimensions of Christian life, press-
ing toward that concept of millenarian union that would penetrate
the Awakening's view of a totally equal society before God. In this
concept the revolutionary principles were implicit and obvious.[13]

Society had changed tremendously in the past one hundred years.
Whereas Cotton's Code was the creed of a tightly knit oligarchy that
controlled colonial government, using discipline as the weapon of
spiritual war, Stoddard's society had rejected this view of religion
and instead focused on the doctrinal, that is to say, the personalistic
and emotive qualities of religious life quite apart from their political
implications, for Cotton's Code was no longer viable. Some
Evangelicals insisted during the 1720s that the Kingdom was an
internal spiritual reality, not an external political one. Coinciden-
tally, other Evangelicals viewed the visible church as actually em-
bodying the Kingdom. Thus, the pre- and postmillenarian views
were held in this decade of uncertainty, and the tension later proved
to a crucial dynamic between New and Old Light Evangelicals in
the Great Awakening. For his part, Stoddard failed to resolve the
tension in his thought.[14]

IX The Way to Know Sincerity and Hypocrisy *(1719)*

Appended to the *Treatise Concerning Conversion* was a lecture sermon preached on July 2, 1719, "wherein the way to know sincerity and hypocrisy is cleared up." From its text (I John 4:7–8) was drawn the doctrine that "men may know their hypocrisy only by the course of life but their sincerity only by particular acts" (119). Stoddard's lecture was designed to undo the sense of false security of those hypocrites who professed faith on the basis of either their blameless conduct or their acts to fellow men. He argued, in line with the *Treatise*, that such outward appearances are totally apart and separate from being in a state of grace (137). Even though one might have led a good life, this meant nothing for one's spiritual state. Humiliation and the admission that one lived in sin were the first steps in any real preparation for a godly "conversation." From these "visible exercises of grace" would hopefully issue that assurance of the New Life (143).

Once again Stoddard had directed his message at the facile rationalists who placed their hope on man's goodness and rational progress, and once again he opposed Arminians and Latitudinarians, who elevated the role of reason and nearly equated religion with morality. The Evangelical impulse on the one hand demanded equality among all believers and on the other hand emphasized conversion as the sole road to equality. Early in his career Stoddard had sought sacramental support to assist in the crossing of conversion's chasm, but by 1719 he had become convinced that all means were futile except total resignation of one's being to God.

X Fifty-eight Sermons *(1719–1720)*

Throughout the period 1718–1722 Stoddard continued to preach his Pauline message of saving conversion and necessity of a converted ministry. During the period, Samuel Hall (1695–1776), a native of Wallingford, a graduate of Yale and a previous tutor there, "lived and studied with Mr. Stoddard." These years reflect the most complete record of Stoddard's preaching in the form of fifty-eight manuscript sermons recorded by Warham Williams from September 20, 1719, to May 15, 1720.[15] The unrest of the church at Enfield and the final dismissal of Nathaniel Collins there were symptomatic of the general social climate of unrest in the Connect-

icut River Valley. It is all too easy to dismiss Stoddard's criticism of
the drinking and loose living he saw around him as the reflections of
an excessively pious, white-laced intellectual. Stoddard was none of
these things: he was a frontier preacher who had a good education,
but knew its limits; he was a devoted husband and father of a large
family, and he was not afraid to soil his hands with daily labor, either
in the home garden or in the affairs of his expanding Council. Towns
in the Valley faced urgent problems of community solidarity. To
curb moral license tithingmen were created by the General Assembly of Connecticut and by the General Court of Massachusetts.
Churches also faced similar problems. The decline of strict Congregational control over church membership was accompanied by a loss
of ministerial power: when Stoddard opened the doors of his instituted church to anyone in the town, popular control of the church
became a reality. For instance, at nearby Norwich in August 1715
illiterates could vote by secret marked ballot against a minister if
they did not like him. Ministers in Stoddard's Association resisted this democratizing of their government.[16]

Stoddard's method of preaching at this time, as revealed by Hall,
was thus: "[He] chose his subject—in his mind divided [it] into
general and particular head—then taking his paper, left room for a
text and introduction—at proper distance wrote his doctrine and
first proposition—at another distance wrote another proposition,
etc., leaving spaces sufficient. Then he returned and wrote at
proper space particulars under the general—then went over the
whole again enlarging and finishing the particulars and adding texts
and proofs. Then he subjoined an improvement, etc. And last of all
he looked a text up and wrote it with an introduction to his doctrine."[17] This method helps explain the randomness of the texts
Stoddard chose between September 1719 and May 1720. Primary to
his concern was the subject, which remained fairly constant—conversion. Only at a secondary level was the choice of a text important.
This method of sermonizing was unlike the techniques of many first
and second generation ministers like John Cotton, Thomas Shepard
or Thomas Hooker, for instance, who would preach regularly
through whole books of Scripture and whose sermons can actually
be dated by the regularity of this approach. Stoddard on the other
hand, began with doctrine and fitted his selection of Scripture to it.
A listing of the doctrines Stoddard treated illustrates this:

Men's affections to spiritual things may be greater than any other affections to outward good things and yet not appear so. (10)

Holiness gives more contentment to the soul than any outward enjoyment. (11)

We ar bound to be thankful to God for His mercies to men. (14)

The first time the spiritual light is given to them the glory of God in the Gospel is discovered to them.(16)

God has chosen a certain number of particular men to eternal life.(18)

Although there be great difficulty in the conversion of sinners yet there be no impossibility in it.(20)

Sanctification and the belief of the Gospel do always go together.(22)

God has made all things out of nothing.(24)

Whatever changes any undergo between faith and sanctification they are no certain signs of election.(26)

The happiness of men and angels is in itself and in its own nature more desirable than their misery.(28)

A work of humiliation is no sure sign of election.(30)

Tis from the good pleasures of God that blessings of one kind or another are bestowed upon his people. (32)

Jesus of Nazareth was so-called or had that name given him for that reason because he saves his people from sin. (38)

These doctrines highlight the Pauline themes inherent in Stoddard's post-1712 writings, that between preparation and conversion there is a chasm only bridged by God's grace, that humiliation and the Word are basic to preparation but they are no sure way to election, that faith follows justification and true sanctification is a product of faith. This marks the point at which Stoddard discarded the last vestiges of his earlier sacramentalism. The chasm between sinner and saint, bridged only by the supernatural, was subject to no human means of facilitation. Because this doctrine represented a final turning point toward a harsher view of sin and salvation, Stoddard devoted himself to providing answers to questions that his congregation might have had about their own spiritual conditions, and he did this in a series of cases applied to the conscience.

XI   An Answer to Some Cases of Conscience *(1722)*

These *Cases of Conscience* were directed to the economic and political problems of Stoddard's Valley, which were the result of a deeper spiritual malaise. The demise of the beaver trade and the pecuniary pressures being applied by merchants and professional

men on a rural population dependent solely on the land for subsis-
tence were two cases in point. In answer to the question "Wherein
doth the oppression of the country principally consist?" Stoddard
answered that it was both in "an oppression of rulers" and in "an
oppression contrary to commutative justice" (1), giving examples of
unfair prices charged by apothecaries (as representative of merchants) and lawyers (as representative of professional men). He
complained of settlers who chose to dwell so far from the meetinghouse they could not attend worship (2) and publicly supported the
fixing of township size to between four and six square miles because
any larger area would threaten the nuclear nature of the Puritan
town (3). He complained of merchants who were trading 30s. in bills
for 20s. in silver (3). He complained of the wasteful expense and
vanity of recent customs such as wearing wigs and long hair (5–6).
He chastised those who chose to quit work early on Saturday by
claiming the Sabbath began at dusk (two or three hours before
sunset) rather than at sunset (7), a doctrine learned from William
Prynne, among others, underscoring his thoroughgoing work ethic.
Finally, he came to the underlying spiritual ills of the country. He
noted how Rhode Island "had fallen into heresy and some almost
into heathenism"—a reference to the Baptists, Quakers, and other
sectarians there (11)—and the failure of missions to the Indians. If
one compares this with the earlier statements he had made about
the aborigines, that they should be hunted with dogs for they were
no better than dogs, one can see the distance Stoddard had come in
the last three decades:

There has been a neglect to bring the Indians to the profession of the
Gospel. Something has been done through the piety of particular men and
at the cost of some in Old England; but we are reproached abroad for our
negligence. Many men have been more careful to make a prey of them than
to gain them to the knowledge of Christ. The King in the Charter says that
the undertakers did profess it to be their principal design to bring the
natives to the Knowledge of God. But we have very much failed to bring
that design to effect. We must bring them to civility and to learn our
language. Paul says to the Corinthians "I seek not yours but you." (II Cor.
12:14) The reverse is too true of New England. It may be on that account
God hath made them to be a scourge to us. . . . Did we any wrong to the
Indians in buying their land of small price?
A. There was some [vacant] part of the land that was not purchased [as]
when Abraham came into the land of Canaan he made use of vacant land as

he pleased, so did Isaac and Jacob. The Indians did eat the beasts of the forest and clothed themselves with their skins. They used the very wild cats and wolves and bears as well as the deer and beaver and other animals. With their bows and arrows and divers strategems they subdued and kept them under. By fowling and fishing they got a great part of their livelihood. The shell fish were their standing dish. They also made meals of Chestnuts, Beechnuts, Walnuts, Acorn, Strawberries, and groundnuts. They made themselves comfortable houses or huts, covering them with mats or barks of trees. These humble houses were adorned with the pictures of animals ingeniously drawn. But the chief ornament of them was their hospitality, which was truly excellent. They were [seated] and the fire being in the middle converg'd warmth to the inhabitants round about and helped [remove] the defects of their charity. That they might pass the rivers and bays, they made themselves boats or cannoos with the rind of birch trees ribb'd with cedar. Moreover they had pleasant fields of Indian corn and beans and squashes which being purchased by the English at their first coming was a relief to them. They had no oxen nor horses nor iron so that it may be rather wondered at that they went so far in their tillage than that they proceeded no further. Their sorrowful circumstances demanded pity. . . . It would be good for white men to follow the poet's advice *Nimium re crede colori.* (12–14)

Stoddard advocated a much more active mission to the Indians, in which his grandson would serve in due time, although he still viewed the primitive aborigine through the eyes of a colonizer bent on conforming their culture to the Puritans'. It was this altered attitude to missionary involvement that characterized the final phase of his development as an Evangelist. No longer merely concerned about the sacraments as means to an end within a single church or about conciliar government as a method of promulgating doctrine among many churches, he at last focused on the ever-expanding life of a truly colonial religion.

XII Defects of Preachers *(1723)*

Now, at eighty, Stoddard realized he must pass his mantle to a younger generation, and *Defects of Preachers,* delivered to the Northampton congregation on May 19, 1723, marked the final point of his Evangelicalism, the necessity of a regenerate ministry. With it, Stoddard came full circle in his theory of conversion: now he preached that it *was* necessary to know the exact moment of conversion because there were no degrees between nature and grace. In his congregation was one Salmon Treat, a product of a Harvard undergraduate education and a Yale A.M. who had settled as minister in Preston, Connecticut, in 1697.

Treat solicited the sermon for publication and revealed that as early as 1723 many younger men already were developing New Light sympathies which he outlined in a preface: "If by the reading [of] a passage in the ensuing sermon to this purpose, 'That it is frequent with persons that have attended to conversion to know the time of their conversion,' your soul should be cast into a darksome, dejected case . . . because you don't know the time of your conversion" (iii), Treat counseled, "Patiently wait upon [God] in his appointed ways, to know a time of a lively faith on Christ, a time of repentance of Love to God and to fellow Christians so as to know in time of your conversion" (iv). He argued that not only must a minister be in a converted state, he must also be able to preach from memory, not from notes, for formalism hindered "gesture in preaching and holy inspection of the congregation . . ." (v). With this one sermon all of Stoddard's career seemed to point to the one inescapable fact that he had finally his following as the "Reverend Leader and Father" of a new generation of emerging New Light ministers in the Valley (v). Ironically, during the Great Awakening, Treat was forced to resign by an Old Light faction in his own church, and since he was no separatist he lived out the remaining eighteen years of his life as his town burgeoned two separate societies.[18]

Stoddard used as his doctrine "There may be a great deal of good preaching in a country and yet a great want of good preaching" (2). By this he meant natural knowledge is not enough, it must also be experimental if one is to preach "convincingly and with good affection, . . . with great clearness and evidence . . ." (3). Moral duties were not the heart of religion, he warned, but regeneration is (4). He openly criticized the Arminians, their denial of election, original sin, and irresistible grace (6). Briefly stated, "Every learned and moral man," according to Stoddard, "is not a sincere convert" (9). In keeping with this Pauline theology of all post 1712 writings, Stoddard cited Paul's conversion experience, but this time he cited it as being normative for all true Christians: "Paul knew the time of his conversion"; "At midday, O King, I saw a light from heaven above the brightness of the Sun" (Act. 26:13) (10). "Conversion is a great change, from darkness to light," Stoddard maintained, and although it may not be that apparent outwardly, "as to the frame of men's hearts there is a very great difference" (10). "Conversion is the greatest change that men undergo in this world. . . . The prodigal knew well enough the time of his return to his father's house; the children of Israel knew the time of their passing over Jordan" (11). Secondly, as Stoddard had emphasized before, total humiliation was necessary before faith: "A self-righteous spirit is quite contrary to the Gospel" (12). Thirdly, the rhetoric of preaching must forcefully present "the danger of damnation" and "the terrors of the Lord": "It is well if thunder and lightning will awaken them: they had need to fear that they may work out their salvation with fear and trembling. . . . Ministers should be the sons of thunder: men had need have storms in their hearts before they will betake themselves to Christ for refuge. . . . Reason will govern men in other things, but it is fear that must make them diligently to seek salvation" (14–15). Fourthly, justifying faith cannot be preached from hearsay evidence; it must be preached from within, but fifthly, men must not be too strict in searching for the outward signs of grace (18), as would the more extreme New Lights who, under the Reverends Jonathan Edwards and George Whitefield, would preach the doctrine of sanctification by faith alone.

Returning to the theme of the *Guide to Christ*, Stoddard reasserted Calvin's doctrine that "the foundation of believing the divine authority of the Scripture is the manifestation of the divine glory in them. There is a self-evidencing light in the works of God: the creation of the world shows God's power and God-head (Rom. 1:20). It is impossible that the world should be made by any but an infinite God. So there is a self-evidencing light in the Word of God; there are such things revealed there as can be made known by none but God (I Cor. 2:9)" (19).

The *Defects of Preachers* marks the final evolution in Stoddard's theology. With it he openly espoused the revival doctrines that prepared the way for the Great Awakening, embued with the Pauline dialectic of nature and grace and the Calvinistic doctrine of the self-evidencing light in the works and Word of God. Central to this revival theology were the religious affections—love of God and man—not an enlightened mind or righteous living and moral precepts. Rational enlightenment was viewed as original sin made manifest. Natural man was no guide to holiness. Both the Godhead and religious experience were inscrutable. Therefore, self-directed knowledge was an expression of self-love, not Christ-love. There was also a political sense of these religious metaphors. Self-love

operated to the exclusion of national or corporate love. The nation
was bound in covenant as a people with a common transcendent
destiny, not as exclusive churches. Christ-love when translated to
the political sphere implied equality, fraternity, and a common
transcendent destiny. In other words, it was doctrinal, not disciplinarian, equalitarian, not hierarchical.

XIII   Question whether God is Not Angry with The Country for Doing so Little towards the Conversion of Indians (1723)

This, the last of Stoddard's published works, was released on
August 9, 1723. It represents the furthest development of his theory
of Evangelical missions. In it he argued that "When the Jews rejected the Gospel, God sent it to the Gentiles and they received it"
(3). He charged the ministers with having failed "for not preaching
the Gospel to the heathen" and this had resulted in the pestilence
and war that ravaged New England (6). He warned them to break
out of their spiritual slumber and blind worldliness. Even though
the Indian population had acted in "a very brutish and sottish spirit"
that did not excuse the New Englanders for ignoring them (6).
Throughout the history of Christianity it had always been the duty of
the church to bring the Gospel to the heathen, as indeed it had been
brought originally to Britain. In the contemporary world, Stoddard
noted, the German pietists and the Danes were zealous in promoting missions in the Far East (9). Indeed, even the Catholic world
under the Spanish in Mexico, the Portugese in Brazil and the
French in Canada had made great progress in converting the native
populations. Always the practical frontiersman, Stoddard concluded
that it was better to convert the Indians in the cause of peace than to
destroy them in the cause of war.

Stoddard's Evangelicalism would find expression in the careers of
revival missionaries to the Indians, and it crystallized the extent to
which he envisioned the centrifugally impelled selfless love among
all men—reaching beyond the bounds of parishes into the vast un-
tamed wilderness, the converted ministry was bound to carry the
Word. And, in place of the praying villages established on the earlier Congregational model of autonomous churches, each with its
minister, as John Eliot had indicated in his own treatise on church
government, written in 1649 and published in 1660, Stoddard now

advocated what appeared to be an essentially itinerant ministry, both among the Indians and among the churches of Hampshire Association. It is easy to see how extreme revivalists in the Great Awakening could look back to Stoddard for the foundation of an itinerant ministry.

However, the association movement that Stoddard championed did not erode clerical authority. Quite the contrary. Associations, unlike councils, excluded the laity from the decision-making process and thereby elevated the authority of ministers who performed, *de facto*, the functions of councils such as settling church disputes, approving and settling ministers, regularizing the exchange of pulpits and providing missionaries. In Connecticut the rise of preachers' power was dramatic, since traditionally the laity had cooperated with ministers as a result of Hooker's moderate Congregationalism. The association movement in Hooker's colony undermined the official church government of consociations that had been developed in the Saybrook Platform and it removed the laity's traditional role in church government. Yet, the laity did gain something, since the regular exchange of pulpits among each county's association members opened the doors of meeting houses to new ideas. Because it appealed to both the laity and to ministers, the association movement spread like wildfire across New England in the first four decades of the eighteenth century. Stoddard's Association, the largest of any, extended the length of the Connecticut River Valley encompassing two dozen towns. A Sherborne Association in central Massachusetts contained twenty three members. In the east four associations (Salem, Bradford, Cambridge-Boston and Plymouth) included thirty two churches. Cotton Mather, realizing that the movement was another step closer to destroying his *Magnalia's* myth of monolithic strict Congregationalism, was forced to confess in 1726 that "the Country is full of *Associations,* formed by Pastors in their several vicinities for the prosecution of *Evangelical Purposes.*" Through the exchange of pulpits, the county associations of Connecticut and the regional associations of Massachusetts and Plymouth facilitated the reception of Stoddardean revivalist ideas.[19]

CHAPTER 5

Epilogue

A T eighty Stoddard's health began to fail, making it impossible for him to make the annual pilgrimage to Harvard commencement, to the lecture before the General Court, and to visit with his old friend Samuel Sewall, who, because of his own infirmities would permanently relinquish his post on the Governor's Council in 1725. Forever ended were the long horseback rides across the rolling hills of Hampshire County to Boston Bay, where friends and relatives, almost too numerous to remember, would offer the weary wilderness pastor traditional seasonal gifts of a Harvard thesis printed on stiff rag paper, a morsel of commencement cake, and a bag of raisins and almonds for the long journey back. Stoddard's physical strength impaired, his mind remained keen, his sermons uttered forcefully. Visiting friends and relatives such as son Anthony and nephew Thomas Hawley, however, now often relieved him of preaching duties on Sunday.[1]

Townsmen realized that a ministry of over five decades was coming to an end, when, on April 4, 1725, the third-generation oligarchy (including son John Stoddard, son-in-law Joseph Hawley, Joseph Parsons, Capt. Ebenezer Pomeroy, Deacons Ebenezer Wright, John Clark, and Samuel Allen), resolved "to get some meet person to assist him in the work." Deacon Clark journeyed to Hartford but returned alone. After deliberation they chose Israel Chauncey, son of Stoddard's close friend, the Reverend Isaac Chauncey of Hadley. Israel a graduate of Harvard, suffered from acute mental depression, and mental illness appears to have affected at least one other member of the Chauncey family. Israel remained less than a year, moved to Housatonnuck, and then returned to live in one of his father's out-buildings in Hadley where he was consumed in a fire later. Once again the leading men deliberated and this time they finally agreed to test their candidate's fitness before

176

accepting him, so they requested the precocious son of Windsor's minister to deliver sermons for the month of August 1726. The candidate, Jonathan Edwards, was Stoddard's grandson and it is possible that the leading men hesitated selecting him in 1725: he had been available then (although had had an illness from the fall of 1725 to the spring of 1726) having already rejected several other "calls" to pastorates. His eagerness to accept the Northampton position was revealed when he resigned his position as Yale tutor a month before the official offer of November 20, 1726, was received. Stoddard selected the Reverend John Williams of Deerfield, step-sister Eunice's husband, to deliver the ordination sermon, and on February 22, 1727, he recorded at last that "Mr. Jonathan Edwards was ordained a pastor of the church of Northampton."[2]

For the next two years grandfather and grandson worked side by side in the old meetinghouse, and it was obvious to anyone in attendance on Sunday that the two were compatible, but it remained problematic as to whether or not this extended to their theologies. As a conversationalist Stoddard, for instance, "was grave but delightful, and very profitable, with a very sweet affability and freedom from moroseness." Edwards, too, had that practical bent of a frontiersman: as a husbandman he could discourse on the superiority of the milk of brindled cows and as a gardener he knew how to stagger the planting of cucumbers, beets, and lettuce. He agreed with Stoddard's favorite saying that "We should study things to the bottom." At Yale he had begun notebooks on science and "the mind" to penetrate the wonders of creation. In Northampton, however, Stoddard had Edwards turn to that other book, Scriptures, and revealed to him in his sermons of the last two years the secrets of his Evangelicalism.[3]

For instance, on a Sunday in September 1727 Stoddard preached from Jer. 17:9 that "the heart of natural men is exceeding wicked. If the hearts of natural men are so very bad, it is not to be wondered at that there is so much corruption and swearing in the hearts of the godly. 'Wretched man that I am,' says Paul, 'who shall deliver me from the body of this death?'" To the question that "Some godly men have been converted young," perhaps like Edwards, who was converted in 1717, "and have had a long time to grow in grace," Stoddard answered that just "as there are times of divine help by special discoveries so there are divine withdrawings." While there may be stages of preparation, a man's conversion remained known

only to God. Stoddard rejected the subtle shift to moralism that
many Harvard-educated ministers were espousing from pulpits in
eastern and even in central Massachusetts. Against the Arminian
view that God was "reasonable," Stoddard exhorted, "let him have
the glory of his sovereignty." However, the chief attribute that the
aged minister dwelled on in his last sermons was God's love.
Preaching in December 1727 he put forth the doctrine "that it is a
great condemnation of men not to have the love of God in 'em. . . .
Loving God is the first and great Commandment. . . . If men have
no love to God, it is a certain sign that they have no spiritual knowledge of God. All that know God are upright in heart . . . because
love to God is the root of all the graces. . . . If a man have zeal, if it
don't flow out from love, it is no grace." This, indeed, was the final
point of Stoddard's theology as he blended the Johannine message
that God is love with the Pauline dialectic of nature and grace.

On the other side of the pulpit Jonathan Edwards heeded the
faltering speech, its rhetoric, its images. He saw before him the
people of Northampton, the wealthier sort in front and the less
well-to-do, perhaps even unchurched, crowding into the far corners
of the meetinghouse. Stoddard gave the morning prayer, a Psalm
was sung, and with some trepidation Edwards walked up to the
pulpit and delivered his sermon. "Luke 13:24th 'For many, I say
unto you, will seek to enter in and shall not be able. I say unto you
that there are many that seek eternal life that never will be able.'
First question: Who are those that seek so as never to obtain? Answer: Such as only seek and strive. Question: What is it to strive?
'Tis to make it our chief concern . . . the duties of the second
Table." This was not the point of Evangelicalism, Stoddard probably
thought, as he listened to his young assistant: first humiliation, then
the glory of God and the mystery of His ways. That afternoon at
lecture Edwards tried again. This time he preached from Isaiah
1:18–20 and drew the doctrine "that all God's ways of dealing with
men are most reasonable." As the golden leaves swirled in the brisk
fall air that afternoon on meetinghouse hill, Stoddard had cause to
reflect. Would his grandson learn the lessons of his long career in
time before he met his Creator? If he had ever learned anything, it
was that God's ways were inscrutable and most unreasonable and
that the sight of the Lord's body was most excellent to behold.[4]

Edwards followed Stoddard's implicit criticisms, and in his
sermons immediately following he began utilizing Stoddardean
rhetoric which emphasized the awful distance between God and

man. Instead of resorting to the casuistry of the healing conscience that extended comfort to the listener, Edwards returned to the accusing conscience, reiterating divine inscrutability and human ignorance. "Great men," he quipped as he looked into the Northampton pews on a Sunday in 1728, are only "bigger worms" in God's sight, who is "infinitely high above you." Yet, like grandfather Solomon, Jonathan tantalized his auditors with a hope to lead them out of total frustration—that Christ was instrumental to salvation just as the sacraments had been used earlier as an aid to assurance by Stoddard. This was done through the imagery of the parent-child relationship: "all along [He] conversed with them with the most friendly familiarity, as a father amongst a company of children." Facilely stated, yet here the conundrum, for the "children" were not nature's but God's, not the unregenerate but the elect. Familial imagery in the hands of grandfather and grandson actually intensified anguish rather than abating it. Here, too, the passage from Stoddardean sacramentalism to Stoddardean Evangelicalism was complete. Christ had become the central means to conversion and the community to which hope was offered was that of the elect, not nature's nation. Yet, both grandfather and grandson retained a Pauline dialectic which resisted this oversimplification: Christ was both lion and lamb, God and man, majestic and miserable, glorious and ghastly: similarly, His community numbered both saint and sinner, elect and damned.[5]

From Northampton the winds of change were blowing strong to the south and to the east. William Williams had taken the initiative in preaching for a converted ministry at the 1723 ordination of his relative, and Stoddard's amanuensis, the Reverend Warham Williams of Waltham, the brother of the Reverend John Williams, the redeemed Indian captive of Deerfield. The Williamses were leading supporters of Stoddard and not shy of their allegiance. At the 1726 convention of ministers in Boston William Williams preached a characteristically Evangelical Stoddardean message that *The Great Duty of Ministers* [is] *to Advance the Kingdom of God and Then Comfort in Fellow Helpers to This Work.* In it he emphasized the necessity for a converted ministry to lay low the sinner and expose the overwhelming excellency of the Savior. The nascent New Light movement in the Valley was symbolized by the 1726 installation of Nehemiah Bull as Edward Taylor's assistant at Westfield by William Williams, who preached the ordination sermon and by the 1727 installation of Williams's sister-in-law's son, Jonathan Edwards as

Stoddard's assistant. In Westfield, Taylor watched in dismay as Bull opened communion because as an Evangelical Bull believed with Stoddard that not sacraments but the experience of conversion and pursuit of personal piety were the marrow of religion. With heaviness of heart, the aged poet-priest could only mourn the "Realms of Prelate's Arch"

> Where open Sinners vile masked indeed
> Are welcome guests (if they can say the creed)
> Unto Christ's table.[6]

Once concerned that failure to attend the Lord's Supper was due to the excessive legalism caused by the Winthrop-Cotton code of regenerate citizenship, Stoddard had tried to open communion to the progeny of believers. This sacramentalism failed and he found by experience that the Pauline dialectic of nature and grace provided the Evangelical message people in the Valley seemed to respond to. Stoddard had developed a new doctrine and his followers rejoiced in his message extolling piety over order. In this sense the two old foes were united in the end. The very thing that Taylor sought to protect throughout his life, the inviolate purity of the Lord's Supper, had now been destroyed in the year before his death. Yet when Stoddard and Taylor, John Williams and Samuel Sewall died in 1729, they were closer, ironically, than they had ever been.

Stoddard's death on the second of November 1729 occasioned wide tribute from the clergy who respected the ideals for which he had labored so long. It was only fitting that William Williams be called to deliver the funeral sermon in which, with great emotion, he lamented "the loss of a father and a prophet, of a great and a good man that has fallen among us." A memorial was given at Harvard commencement the following July by aging Benjamin Colman, leader of the Brattle group. Since 1707, when Stoddard jettisoned the theory of the instituted church, the ground on which they found initial agreement, they had drifted silently apart into remarkably different views. Remembering the earlier Stoddard, the pope of the instituted church, Colman recalled that he was "as a Peter here among the disciples, . . . very much our primate and a prince among us, in an Evangelical and truly apostolical sense".[7]

The reinvigorated faith inspired by Stoddard the Evangelical taught a reborn millenarian expectation of Christ's coming to earth on clouds of glory to establish his Kingdom: the New Age was close at hand. Stoddard's friends and relatives reflected this religiosity. Samuel Sewall had sent a copy of his reprinted *Phaenomena Quaedam Apocalyptica* to Stoddard's son-in-law as soon as it was off the press in 1727, and Williams immediately praised Sewall's vision of the "beauty and grandeur of the New Jerusalem" that was New England. Not since that golden age of Cotton and Hooker had such a wave of mystical expectancy enveloped the senses of the people: "may we not hope that the true and pious zeal that God put into the hearts of many that transplanted themselves and families into this then uncultivated wilderness was on a design of mercy to their posterity," Williams rejoiced, when the Millennium, the thousand-year Reign of Christ, would ring forth from the hills of Hampshire County.

A gradually expanding equalitarianism emerged in each of the communities subject to Stoddard's influence. Originally towns had been ruled by nuclei of oligarchic men who dominated both church and town meeting, applying their particular ideologies of strict or moderate Congregationalism. However, the internal dynamics of community life were changing in subtle and profound ways as a correlation of sexuality and religion reveals. By periodicizing the life of communities on the basis of dullness and revival of religion, new social patterns are revealed. During periods of little or no revival of religion, converts in Stoddardean churches (such as Deerfield, Longmeadow, Northampton, Springfield and Suffield) tended to be more likely married and older than their counterparts in the years of harvests of souls. For instance, from 1718 to 1726, 50 percent of the total known admissions were unmarried averaging 27 years old, but in the two years following, 1726–1727, a period of a hitherto unnoticed harvest—the first in young Edward's career—70 percent were unmarried averaging 24 years old. In the following period of dullness (1729–1734) 45 percent were unmarried, averaging 32 years old, but in the period of the 1735 awakening 70 percent were unmarried, averaging 23 years old. In the following dull period from 1736 to 1740, 37 percent were unmarried, averaging 29 years old, while in the subsequent two years of the Great Awakening 80 percent were unmarried, averaging 22 years old. The Awakening in New England, therefore, was a process, not an event. It was accomplished over three generations of struggle, and its product was, ostensibly, a more equalitarian society—at least for the believers, who were now invested with a common transcendent basis of their hard won personhood.

APPENDIX 1

Elegy, 1664

Sighs are the symtoms of a soule distresst,
And hence demonstrate hearts as o're prest.
Then let's in sorrow weep while tears remaine,
and lest we want we'l weep them o're again.
groans make best harmony to sighs forth,   5
that greife which bears proportion to his worth,
such musick is one refuge wherein none
except a Thracian would deny to join.
See eye of all these parts is ye most tender
how then is it possible without a wonder,   10
to 'abstaine from floods of tears (nor surprise,
to see a bridegroom wedded to his tomb.
Circe her selfe the worst of feinds would crie
at this sad spectacle for company.
To number up the virtuous acts whereby   15
his name shall flourish to eternity,
the effluxes of his graces while yet quicke
is a taske exceeding my Arithmetick.
Knew I ye stars to number in ye skie
I'd make a shift to make a guesse thereby.   20
He was the darling of ye graces light,
both learning's patron and her favorite.
His years soon sold o're yet in them he gat,
Ye basis of a never fading state,
his heaven born soule aspiring him unto,   25
who gave it rise & leaving earth below,
ascends those heavenly mansions of above
to eternity and renders earth his due.
lest then we seem too foolish let's likewise
Rejoice with him who hath obtain'd ye prize)   30
breath is the terme of life, If motion rest,
then let us end, since consionomatia est.
his active mind (alas the more our woe)
like keen sword soon hath cut the scabbard through.   34

Tripos Verse, 1665

Utrum Deus puniat peccata necessitate naturae.
Affirmat Respondens Solomon Stoddardus.

O tu, quae sapis alta numis, Sapientia prima,	1
Quaeque Gigantaeis ausibus astra petis,	2
Aut velut Icariis assumptis, tolleris, alis	3
In Coelum, similem non metuendo casum,	4
Disce Φρονέιν & σωφροχέιν—NON subdere fata	5
Concipe nos ausos, nec voluisse Deum:	6
Justitiam at punire malos natura requirit,	7
Peccatum pugnat cum bonitate Dei.	8
Ω βαθός! hic clama miser, & mirare videndo	9
Peccati salvos posse tot esse reos.	10

Translation

O thou, Primal Wisdom, who knowest the things most high,	1
And who with the Gigantes stormest the stars,	2
Or are taken up into heaven, as it were,	3
By the wings of Icarus, yet having no fear of a similar fall.	4
Teach us to reflect and to be prudent—perceive that we have not dared	5
To subdue the Fates for God has so willed it	6
That nature demands justice by punishing those who are evil:	7
Nature battles sin with the goodness of God.	8
O Bathos! Here, call them out, ye wretches, and be amazed	9
That so many guilty of sin can be saved.	10

APPENDIX 3

Solomon Stoddard's Library, 1664

It is rare to be able to reconstruct the entire library of a graduate student at Harvard in the seventeenth century. After a thorough search of university libraries only one item has actually been located, Keckerman's 1603 *Systema Theologiae*, at Yale University, Beinecke Rare Book and Manuscript Library. The source for this list is Stoddard's college notebook. For a discussion of the importance of these sources see Chapter 1, §§ II and III, and Chapter 3, §VII.

The convention adopted in this bibliography is that brackets indicate the first date of publication of a title while parentheses indicate that this date is the probable one for Stoddard's copy as inferred from the number of volumes or some other distinguishing feature of an edition.

Perhaps many of these books were taken by Stoddard to Northampton and were among those left in his estate in 1729. However, although his library was dispersed at his death no catalog of the items was made. It seems unlikely that any were claimed by his grandson Jonathan Edwards, since none are listed in Edward's library "Catalogue" (*ca.* 1723–1753) deposited at Yale.

1. Ainsworth, Henry, 1571–1622? Annotations upon the Book of Psalms [1617].

2. Allen, Thomas, 1608–1673. A Chain of Scripture Chronology [1658].

6. Alting, Heinrich, fl. 1646–1664. Theologia Elencha Nova [1654].

7. Ames, William, 1576–1633. Bellarminus Ennervatus [1629].

8. ——. Christianae Catechesis Sciagraphia [1635].

9. ——. Coronis [1618].

10. ——. Medulla Theologica [1642].

11. ——. Technometria [1633].

12. ——. A Treatise on Conscience [1643].

3. Apollonius, Willem, 1603?–1657. Consideratio Quarundam Controversiarum, ad Regimen Ecclesiae [1644].

14. Arnold, Nicholaus, 1618–1680. Religio Sociniana sev Catechesis Racoviana Maior

Publicis Disputationibus Refutata [1654].

15. Arrowsmith, John, 1602–1659. Tactica Sacra, seu de Milite Spirituali [1647].

17. Baker, Sir Richard, ca. 1568–1645. Chronicle of the Kings of England from the Time of the Romans Government unto the Death of King James [1641].

19. Bible. English. The Holy Bible.

20. Bible. Hebrew. The Old Testament in 4 parts.

21. Bible. Latin. Septuagint. 3 copies.

22. Boyd, Robert, 1578–1627. In Epistolam ad Ephesios Praelectiones [1652].

23. Brightman, Thomas, 1557–1607. On the Revelation of St. John [1644].

24. ——. Scholia in Cantica Cantorum. Explicatio partis Ultimae et Difficillimae Prophetae Danielis [1614].

25. Broughton, Hugh, 1549–1612. The Works of the Great Albionean Divine, Renowned in Many Nations for Rare Skill in Salem's and Athen's Tongues [1662] 4v.

26. Bucanus, William. Institutiones Theologicae [1606].

27. Buchler, Johann, ca. 1570–ca. 1640. Thesaurus Phrasium Poeticarum [1627].

28. Burgersdijck, Franco. Institutionum Logicarum [1644].

30. Calderwood, David, 1575–1650. Altare Damascenum seu Politia Ecclesiae Anglicanae [1623].

31. Calvin, John, 1509–1564. Institutes of the Christian Religion [1634].

32. ——. Institution Christianae Religionis [1545].

35. Cartwright, Thomas, ca. 1535–1603. Commentaria Practica in Totam Historiam Evangelicam [1630].

36. ——. Commentarii in Proverbia Solomonis [1617].

37. Cawdry, Daniel, 1588–1664. Sabbatum Redividum, or the Christian's Sabbath Vindicated [1645].

38. Chemnitz, Martin, 1522–1586. Harmonia Evangelicorum [1583].

39. Cicero, Marcus Tullius. De Officiis [1465].

40. ——. Orationes [1471].

41. ——. Sententiae [1471].

42. Cocceius, Johann, 1603–1669. De Foedere et Testamento Dei [1648].

43. ——. Versio et Commentatio in xii Prophetas Minores [1652].

44. Cotton, John, 1585–1652. A

Brief Exposition with a Practical Commentary upon the Whole Book of Ecclesiastes [1654].

45. Curtius, Rufus Quintus. Historia Alexandri Magni [1471].

46. Davenant, John, bp., d. 1641. De Judice Controversarium et Justitia [1631].

47. ——. Determinationes XLIX. Quaestionum Quarundam Theologicarum [1634].

48. ——. Expositio Epistolae D. Pauli ad Colossenses Praelectiones de Duobus in Theologia [1631].

49. Day, John, 1566–1628. Commentary on Isaiah.

50. Descartes, René, 1596–1650. A Discourse of a Method [1649].

51. ——. Meditationes de Prima Philosophia [1664].

52. Digby, Sir Kenelm, 1603–1648. Of Bodies and of Man's Soul [1657].

53. Diodati, Giovanni, 1576–1638. Annotations upon the Holy Bible [1643].

54. Donne, John, 1573–1631.

55. Dort, Synod of. [?The Judgement of the Synode Concerning the Five Articles 1619].

57. Draxe, Thomas, d.1618. Calleopeia, or a Rich Store-house of Proper, Choise amd Elegant Latin [1613].

58. Erasmus, Desiderius, 1467–1536. Adages [1519].

59. ——. Colloquies [1519].

60. Estienne, Carolous, d.1564. Dictionarium Historico-Geographico-Poeticum [1556].

61. Eustachius, St., bp. of Antioch. Divinity. 2 parts.

62. Eusebius, Pamphilius, 267–338 ca. Ecclesiastical History [1474].

63. Farnaby, Thomas, ca. 1575–1647. Index Rhetoricus [1640].

64. Fenner, Dudley, 1558?–1587 Sacra Theologia [1632].

65. Fidelius, Ludovicus Nervius. Opuscula Theologia [1550].

66. Foxe, John, 1516–1587. The Acts and Monuments [1563].

68. Gerhard, Johann, 1582–1637. Locorum Communium Theologicorum (1610–22) 9v.

69. Golius, Theophastus. Epitome Doctrinae Moralis et Libris Ethicorum Aristotelis [1592].

70. Gouge, William, 1575–1653. Commentary on the Hebrews. 2v. [1655]

71. Guillim, John, ca.1560–1621. A Display of Heraldry [1610].

72. Hammond, Henry, 1605–1660. Paraphrases and Annotations on the New Testament [1653].

76. Herodian. Historia [1493].

77. Hessles, Jean, 1522–1566. Brevis Catholica Decalogi [1567].

80. Homer. Iliad [1474].

82. Hommius, Festus. Disputationes Theologicae, Adversus Pontificos [1614].

83. Horace. Opera [1474].

85. Isocrates. Opera [1550].

86. Jachaeus, Gilbertus, 1585 ca.– 1648. Metaphysicae [1650].

87. Jackson, Arthur, 1593–1666. Annotations on the Five Books [1658].

88. Jackson, Thomas, 1579–1640. Diverse Sermons [1637].

89. Janua Linguarum [1611].

90. Jeanes, Henry, fl. 1653–6C Want of Church Government No Warrant for Total Omission of the Lord's Supper [1653].

91. Keckerman, Bartholomew, 1571–1609. Systema Theologiae. 1603. Location: Yale University, Beinecke Rare Book and Manuscript Library.

92. Leigh, Edward, 1602–1671. A Body of Divinity [1654].

93. ——. Critica Sacra, or Observations on the Hebrew Words of the Old and the Greek of the New Testaments [1639].

94. Lycosthenes, Conrad, 1518– 1561 Apophthegmata. (1635)

96. Makowski, Jan, Distinctiones et Regulae Theologicae ac Philiosophicae [1656].

97. ——. Loci Communes [1650].

99. ——. Redivivus, seu Manuscripta Ejus Typis Exscripta Opera Nic. Arnoldi [1647].

100. Meisner, Balthasar, 1587– 1626 Philosophia Sobria [1611].

102. Musculus, Wolfgang, 1497– 1563 In Euangelistam Lucam

103. Norton, John, 1606–1663 The Orthodox Evangelist [1654].

104. ——. Responsio ad Guillemi Apollonii Syllogen [1648].

105. ——. Three Choice and Profitable Sermons. [1651]

106. Ovid. Metamorphoses. [1474].

107. Owen, John, 1616–1683 Diatribe de Justitia Divina [1653]

108. ——. Of Communion with God. (1657)

109. ——. Doctrine of the Saints Perseverance (1659)

111. Palmer, Herbert, 1601–1647 Sabbatum Redivivum [1648].

112. Paraeus, David, 1548–1622 Commentarii in Matth et in Joelem, Amos, Haggai, et Duas Epistolas Petri [1631].

113. ——. Corpus Theologiae Orthodoxum [1647]

115. Parker, Thomas, 1595–1677

The Visions and Prophecies of Daniel Expounded [1646].

116. Pemble, William, 1591–1623 Works [1635].

117. Piscator, Johann, 1546–1625 Commentarii in Omnes Libros Novi Testamenti [1658].

118. Polanus, Amandus, 1561–1610 Syntagma Theologiae Christianae [1612].

119. Polycarp, St., bp. of Smyrna, d. 167

120. Prideaux, John, bp. of Worcester, 1578–1650. Scholasticae Theologicae [1651]

123. Rivet, Andreas, 1572–1647. Catholicus Orthodoxus. 2v.

124. ——. Isagoge. [1627]

125. Rutherford, Samuel, 1600?–1661. Exercitationes pro Divina Gratia [1636].

126. ——. Disputatio Scholastica De Divina Providentia [1650].

127. ——. The Divine Right of Church Government [1646].

128. ——. The Due Right of Presbyteries [1645].

129. ——. The Spiritual Antichrist [1648].

130. Scapula, Johann, fl.1580 Lexicon Graeco-Latinum [1579].

132. Scheibler, Christoph, 1589–1653 Metaphysica [1657].

133. Scultetius, Abraham, 1556–

1625 Exercitationes Evangelica. [1624]

134. ——. Idea Concionum in Isaiam.

135. Sibbes, Richard, 1577–1635. The Soule's Conflict [1651].

136. Spanheim, Freidrich, 1600–1649. Disputatione Syntagma.

137. ——. Dubiorum Evangelicorum in Tres Partes [1639].

138. ——. Exercitationes De Gratia Universati (1646) 4v.

140. Stresonius, Caspar, fl. 1660. Commentarius Practicus in Actorum Apostolicorum [1658].

141. Suarez, Francisco, 1548–1617. Disputationes Metaphysicae [1605].

142. Tarnovius, Paul, 1562–1633. Commentarium in Sancti Johannis Evangelium [1629].

143. Taylor, Jeremy, bp. of Down and Connor. [? A Choice Manual, 1664].

144. Taylor, Thomas, fl. 1612–1653. [? Moses and Aaron: or, the Types of the Old Testament, 1653].

146. Thomas Aquinas, St. De Ente et Arte.

147. ——. Quaestiones Disputatae [1476].

148. Tilen, Daniel, 1563–1633. Lexicon Theologiae.

150. Twisse, William, 1575–1646. Works [1652].

151. Ursinus, Zachariah, 1534–1583 Catechismus [1591].

152. Usher, James, 1580–1656. Annales Vet. et Nov. Test. ab Orbe [1650].

153. ——. Body of Divinity [1645].

154. ——. Chronologia Sacra, seu Annorum [1660].

155. Valerius Maximus. De Dictus [1470].

156. Vossius, Gerard, 1577–1649. De Origine et Progressu Idolatriae [1641].

157. Walaeus, Anthony, 1573–1639. Opera [1647].

158. Walaeus, Baldasar. Novum Testamentum Libri Historici Graeci et Latini [1653].

159. Ward, Samuel, d. 1643. Opera Nonnulla, viz. Determinationes Theologicae [1658].

160. ——. Tractatus de Justificatione et Praelectione de Peccato Originali [1658].

161. Weemse, John, 1573?–1636. Exposition of the Laws of Moses [1632].

162. White, Thomas, 1582–1676. Euclides Metaphysicus sive de Principiis Sapientiae Stoccheideae [1658].

164. Willet, Andrew, 1562–1621 [?Synopsis Papismi, 1592].

165. ——. Hexapla, or a Sixfold Commentary on Daniel [1610].

166. ——. Hexapla upon the Epistle to the Romans [1611].

168. Wilson, Thomas, 1563–1622. A Christian Dictionary [1612].

Solomon Stoddard's Kin and Family: I

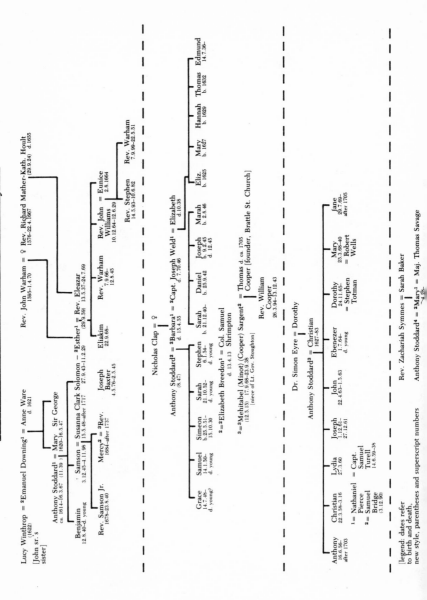

[legend: dates refer
to birth and death.
new style, parentheses and superscript numbers]

Solomon Stoddard's Kin and Family: II

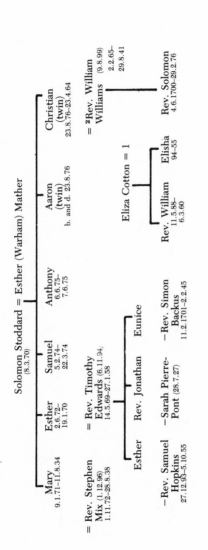

Solomon Stoddard = Esther (Warham) Mather
(8.3.70)

Mary
9.1.71–11.8.34

= Rev. Stephen
Mix (1.12.96)
1.11.72–28.8.38

Esther
2.6.72–
19.1.70

= Rev. Timothy
Edwards (6.11.94;
14.5.69–27.1.58

Esther   Rev. Jonathan   Eunice

–Rev. Samuel
Hopkins
27.12.93–5.10.55

–Sarah Pierre-
Pont (28.7.27)

Samuel
5.2.74–
22.3.74

Anthony
6.6.75–
7.6.75

–Rev. Simon
Backus
11.2.1701–2.2.45

Aaron
(twin)
b. and d. 23.8.76

Christian
(twin)
23.8.76–23.4.64

= ²Rev. William
Williams   (9.8.99)
2.2.65–
29.8.41

Eliza Cotton = 1

Rev. William
11.5.88–
6.3.60

Elisha
94–55

Rev. Solomon
4.6.1700–29.2.76

Rev. Anthony
9.8.78–6.9.60

¹= Prudence Wells
82–14 (3.1701)

²= Mary Sherman
b. 20.3.92
12.1.20 (15.1.16)

³= Hannah
d. 26.11.47

Sarah
1.5.80–
10.9.58

= Rev. Samuel
Whitman
(19.3.1707)
1676–31.7.51

Col. John
17.2.82–
19.6.48

= Prudence Chester
(13.12.71)
4.3.99–
11.7.80

Israel
10.5.84–1703

Rebecca
1686–2.1.66

= Lt. Joseph
Hawley (brother
of Rev. Thomas
of Ridgefield)
(16.11.22)
1682–1.6.35

Hannah
21.4.88–
29.12.45

= Rev.
William
Williams
(6.7.10)
11.5.88–
6.3.60

The Northampton Oligarchy, 1661–1669

NAME	lnd. pos.	estate in £	lit.	occu- pation	cm	fm	sm		dep co	militia	prev. town
John Strong	1	51	yes	tanner	X	[x]	X(62)		ruling elder	Lt.	D
David Wilton	2	976	yes	trader	X	X	X(62)	X		Ens.	D
William Clark	3	131	yes	miller inn- keeper	X	[x]	X	X		Lt.	D
Aaron Cooke	4	526	yes	farmer	X	X	X(62)	X		Capt.	D
William Holton	5	67	yes	farmer	X	X	X	X	deacon		H
Joseph Parsons	6	2088	yes	trader	X	[x]	X			Cornet	H-S
Richard Lyman	7	426	yes	farmer	[x]	[x]	X				H
Robert Bartlett	10	658	yes	farmer	X	X	X				H
Joseph Fitch (Mr)	11	?	yes	farmer	X	[x]	X				H
Henry Woodward	12	184	yes	phy- sician	X	X	X			Quartr- Mstr.	D
Samuel Wright, Sr.	13	344	yes	farmer	[x]	[x]	X		deacon		S
John Lyman	14	922	yes	cobbler	[x]	[x]	X			Ens.	H

NAME	lnd. pos.	estate in £	lit.	occu- pation	cm	fm	sm	dep co	militia	prev. town
Thomas Root, Sr.	15	440	yes	farmer weaver	[x]	[x]	X			H
William Miller	16	551	?	tanner	[x]	[x]	X			?
John King	38	?	yes	tanner	[x]	[x]	X		serg.	W
Henry Curnleff	39	96	yes	lawyer	X	X				D
Josias Dewey	60	?	yes	farmer	X	X	X			
Thomas Hanchett	61	?	yes	farmer	X	[x]	X	deacon		New Haven

Legend: lnd. pos.—landed position; estate—from inventory at death; lit.—literacy as judged from a) possession of Bible in will, b) signature on will, town records, or church covenant; occupation—as judged from percent of inventory devoted to land (i.e., farming) and from occupation indicated in town records or will; cm—church member; fm—freeman; sm—selectman; dep—deputy; co—church office; militia—rank in covenanted militia; prev. town—residence just prior to Northampton (i.e., D=Dorchester, W = Windsor, H = Hartford, S = Springfield).
Brackets indicate probable category not definitely proved from records.

APPENDIX 7

The Northampton Oligarchy, Second-Third Generations, 1670–1726

	land in rods 2d/3d/4th div.	estate in £	1st gen. Oligarchic family?	cm	sm	other
Allen, Samuel	24/25/29			'83	'93	sgt.
Allen, Samuel, Jr.	34	120		after '06		deacon '25
Baker, Joseph	00/67/20	1477			'92	ens.
Bartlett, Samuel			X	by '06	'85–'06	
Bridgman, John, Sr.	49			'72 (½)	'83	
Clapp, Preserved				'72 (½)	'84–'07	ens.
Clapp, Preserved, Jr.	00/16/8			after '06	'21–'25	sgt., ruling eld. '20
Clapp, Samuel					'10, '19	
Clark, John	28	540	X	'78	'89–'04	deacon '91
Clark, John Jr.		649	X	after '06	'14–'26	
Clark, Samuel	26/29/30	103	X	by '06	'06–'20	
Edwards, Benjamin	00/20/20			by '06	'00–'14	
Hawley, Joseph	22/17/15	341		'79	'79–'25	schoolmaster, preacher lt.

Name						
Holton, William Jr.	00/34/28		X	'83	'91–'94	
Hunt, Jonathan Jr.				after '06	'09, '13	
Hutchinson, Judah		46			'20	
Judd, Thomas					'81	deacon
King, John	59/33/20	908	X	'72 (½)	'70–'05	sgt., lt.
King, John, Jr.			X	ca. '88		
King, William			X		'99	
Kingsley, Enos	26	400		'80	'94	
Kingsley, John					'21	sgt.
Lyman, Benjamin, Jr.	00/10/6	1147	X	after '06	'21	
Lyman, John Jr.	37/16/8	460	X	by '06	'99	ens., lt.
Lyman, Thomas	25/11/11	392	X		'96	ens.
Marshall, Samuel	32/14/14	486		after '06	'00, '13–5	
Parsons, John			X	by '06	'90, '11	capt.
Parsons, Eben			X	after '06	'21–'26	
Parsons, Joseph Jr.	40/23/23	430	X	'72 (½)	'82–'20	
Parsons, Samuel	31	220	X	by '06	'94–'00	capt.
Phelps, Nathaniel	4/30/19	276		by '77	'90	deacon '90
Phelps, Nat. Jr.				by '06	'06	
Pomeroy, Medad	22/11/11	347		'71	'69–'04	deacon '75
Pomeroy, Eben				by '06	'99–'26	capt.
Root, Thomas Jr.	17/5/5	259	X		'59–'76	
Sheldon, Isaac Jr.	14/7/7	219		by '06	'04–'10	
Sheldon, Thomas	12/5/5			ca. '88	'95–'19	deacon '04

	land in rods 2d/3d/4th div.	estate in £	1st gen. Oligarchic family?	cm	sm	other
Southwell, William	11	182		ca. '88	'05-'15	
Stebbins, John					'71-'86	
Stoddard, John			X	by '06	'05-'25	maj., col.
Stoddard, Solomon	30/14/14	460	X			minister
Strong, Eben	37/22/22	558	X	'72 (½)	'87-'91	deacon
Strong, Eben Jr.			X	after '06	'01-'25	
Strong, Nathaniel			X		'22-'25	
Strong, Thomas	41/20/20	426	X	'72 (½)	'80-'84	
Strong, Thomas Jr.		166	X	by '06	'11	
Weller, Richard					'70	
Wright, Eben		153	X	by '06	'03-'25	deacon '04, sgt.
Wright, James	23/20/14		X	'72 (½)	'83	
Wright, Judah	21/12/25		X	'72 (½)	'75'79-'03	
Wright, Samuel	66	326	X	ca. '88	'87-'18	

For legend see Appendix 6.

APPENDIX 8

Biographical Glossary

ELIPHALET ADAMS. b. Dedham, Mar. 26, 1677, son of Rev. William and Mary (Manning) Adams; Harvard, 1694, A.B., A.M.; preached at Little Compton, R.I., 1696–1698; Indian Missionary, 1698–1700; sett. Boston, (Brattle St. Chh., asst. min.), 1701–1704; Ord. New London, Ct., Feb. 9, 1708/9; sett. New London, Ct., 1708–1753; missionary to the Indians, 1725–1746; Trustee, Yale, 1720–1738; Ct. Election Sermons, 1710, 1734; d. New London, Ct., Oct. 4, 1753.

SIMON BACKUS. b. Norwich, Ct., Feb 11, 1700/1, son of Joseph and Elizabeth (Huntington) Backus; Yale, 1724, A.B., A.M.; Ord. Newington Ct., (2nd Chh. in Wethersfield), Jan. 25, 1727; sett. Newington, Ct. 1726–1745; Chaplain at Louisburg, Cape Breton, 1745; d. Cape Breton, Feb. 2, 1744/5.

JOSEPH BAXTER. b. Braintree, June 4, 1676, son of Lieut. John and Hannah (White) Baxter; Harvard, 1693, A.B., A.M.; Ord. Medfield, Apr. 21, 1697; sett. Medfield, 1694–1745; Artillery Election Sermon, 1716; Election Sermon, 1727; d. Medfield, May 2, 1745.

DANIEL BREWER. b. Roxbury, Feb. 7, 1669, son of Daniel and Hannah (Morrill) Brewer; Harvard, 1687, A.B., A.M.; Ord. Springfield, May 16, 1694; sett. Springfield, 1694–1733, d. Springfield, Nov. 5, 1733.

NEHEMIAH BULL. b. Farmington, Ct., 1701, son of John and Esther (Royce) Bull; Yale., 1723, A.B., A.M.; Ord. Westfield, Oct. 26, 1726; sett. Westfield, 1725–1740; d. Westfield, Apr. 12, 1740.

CHARLES CHAUNCY. b. Boston, Jan 1, 1705, son of Charles and Sarah (Walley) Chauncy; Harvard, 1721, A.B., A.M.; S.T.D., U. of Edinburgh, 1742; Ord. Boston, (1st Chh.) Oct. 25, 1727; sett. Boston, 1727–1787; founder of the Am. Acad. of Arts and Sciences; defender of liberal (Arminian) Congregationalism; Artillery Election Sermon, 1734; Election Sermon, 1747; Convention Sermon, 1744, 1765; Dudleian Lecture, 1762; d. Boston, Feb. 10, 1787.

ISAAC CHAUNCY. b. Stratford, Ct., Oct. 5, 1670, son of Rev. Israel and Mary (Nichols) Chauncy; Harvard 1693, A.B., A.M.; Ord. Hadley, Sept. 9, 1696; sett. Hadley, 1695–1745; d. Hadley, May 2, 1745.

NATHANIEL COLLINS. b. Middletown, Ct., June 13, 1677, son of Rev.

Nathaniel and Mary (Whiting) Collins; Harvard, 1697, A.B.; Ord. Enfield, Ct., June 3, 1699, as the first minister; sett. Enfield Ct., 1697–1724; dism. Mar 1/24; Rep. Gen. Ct. of Mass., 1726–1728; 1734–1736; d. Glastonbury, Ct., Dec. 31, 1756.

BENJAMIN COLMAN, b. Boston, Oct. 19, 1673, son of William and Elizabeth Colman; Harvard, 1692, A.B., A.M.; S.T.D., U. of Glasgow, 1731; chosen President of Harvard, but did not accept; Fellow, Harvard, 1717–1728; Ord. London, England, by the Presbytery, Aug. 4, 1699; sett. Boston (Brattle St. Chh.) 1699–1747; Commissioner of the Society for the Propagation of the Gospel in N.E. and for Parts Adjacent; Artillery Election Sermons, 1702, 1738; Election Sermons 1718, 1723; d. Boston, Aug. 29, 1747.

WILLIAM COOPER. b. Boston, Mar. 20, 1694, son of Thomas and Mehitable (Minot) Cooper; Harvard, 1712, A.B., A.M.; Ord. Boston, (Brattle St. Chh.) May 23, 1716; sett. Boston, 1715–1743; chosen Pres. of Harvard; did not accept; Artillery Election Sermon, 1722; Election Sermon, 1740; d. Boston, Dec. 13, 1743.

JOHN COTTON. b. Derby, England, Dec. 4, 1585, son of Roland, Esq., and Mary (Hulbert) Cotton; Trinity Coll. Camb., A.B., 1602/3; A.M. Emmanuel Coll., Camb., 1606; B.D., Emmanuel Coll., Camb., 1613; Fellow, 1606, Head Lecturer, Dean and Catechist of Emmanuel Coll., Camb.; Ord. Lincoln, Eng. July 13, 1610; Vicar of St. Botolph's Chh., Boston, Lincolnshire, 1612–1633; emigrated 1633; Trimount renamed Boston in his honor; Ord. Boston, (1st Chh.), Oct. 10, 1633; instituted strict Congregational code for colony, 1633; sett. Boston, 1633–1652; Election Sermon, 1634; Artillery Election Sermon, 1651; his portrait is owned by the Conn. Hist. Soc.; d. Boston, Dec. 23, 1652.

JONATHAN EDWARDS. b. East Windsor, Ct., Oct. 5, 1703, son of Rev. Timothy and Esther (Stoddard) Edwards; Yale, 1720, A.B., A.M.; Tutor, 1724–1726; Ord. Northampton, Feb. 15, 1726/7, as colleague with his grandfather, Rev. Solomon Stoddard; sett. Northampton, 1727–1750; dism. June 22, 1750; sett. Stockbridge, 1750–1758; preacher to the Indians; inst. Princeton U., as President, Jan. 1758; d. Princeton, N.J., Mar. 22, 1758.

TIMOTHY EDWARDS. b. Hartford, Ct., May 14, 1669, son of Richard and Elizabeth (Tuttle) Edwards; Harvard, 1691, A.B., A.M.; Ord. South Windsor, Ct., (2nd Chh.) May 28, 1698; sett. Windsor Farms, Ct., 1694–1758; Chaplain, 1711; Ct. Election Sermons, 1708, 1732; d. Windsor, Ct., Jan 27, 1758.

JOSEPH ELIOT. b. Roxbury, Dec. 20, 1638, son of Rev. John and Hannah (Mountford) Eliot; Harvard, 1658, A.B., A.M.; Indian missionary, 1658–1662; sett. Northampton, Mass., 1662–1664; Ord. Guilford, Ct., 1664; sett. Guilford, Ct., 1664–1694; d. Guilford, Ct., May 24, 1694.

SAMUEL HALL. b. Wallingford, Ct., Oct. 5, 1695, son of Hon. John and Mary (Lyman) Hall; Yale., 1716. A.B., A.M.; Tutor, Yale, 1716–1718; sett. as unofficial assistant to Solomon Stoddard, 1718–1721; Ord. Cheshire, Ct., Dec. 9, 1724; sett. Cheshire, Ct., 1722–1766; Ct. Election Sermon, 1746; d. Cheshire, Ct., Feb 26, 1776.

JOSEPH HAWLEY. b. Roxbury, June 7, 1654, son of Thomas and Dorothy (Harbottle) (Lamb) Hawley; Harvard, 1674, A.B.; teacher, preacher at Northampton; not ordained; surveyor; Lt., Capt.; Rep. Gen. Ct., 1683–1692; d. Northampton, May 19, 1711.

THOMAS HOOKER. b. Birstall, Leicestershire, Eng., July 7, 1586, son of Thomas Hooker; Emmanuel Coll., Camb., A.B., 1607/8; A.M., 1611; Fellow of the U., 1609–1618; Curate of Esher, Surrey, and lecturer at Chelmsford, Essex, 1620–1629; preached at Chelmsford, Essex, 1625–1629; silenced by Archbishop Laud, 1630; kept a private school at Little Baddow, Essex, where John Eliot was his asst., 1629–1631; in Holland, 1631–1633; emigrated, 1633; Ord. Cambridge, Oct. 11, 1633, as first minister; sett. Cambridge, 1633–1636; disagreed with Cotton's code of strict Congregationalism; removed to Hartford, Ct., 1636; sett. Hartford, Ct., 1636–1647; d. Hartford, Ct., July 7, 1647.

JOHN LEVERETT. b. Boston, Aug. 25, 1662, son of Hudson and Sarah (Payton) Leverett; Harvard, 1680, A.B., A.M.; S.T.B., 1692; F.R.S., 1713; Tutor and Fellow, H.C.; preached 1680–1684; Judge of Superior Court; Judge of Probate; Member of the Corp., H.C., 1692; Rep. in the Legislature; Speaker, 1700; Member of the Governor's Council; President of Harvard College, 1707–1724; d. Boston, May 3, 1724.

COTTON MATHER. b. Boston, Feb. 12, 1662/3, son of Rev. Dr. Increase and Maria (Cotton) Mather; Harvard, 1678, A.B., A.M.; S.T.D. U. of Glasgow, 1710; Fellow, Harvard, 1690–1703; Fellow Royal Society, 1717; Ord. Boston, (2nd Chh.), May 13, 1685; sett. Boston, 1683–1728; his *Magnalia Christi Americana* (1702) defends strict Congregationalism; Artillery Election Sermons, 1691, 1707; Election Sermons 1689, 1690, 1696, 1700; Convention Sermons, 1690, 1721; d. Boston, Feb. 13, 1728.

INCREASE MATHER. b. Dorchester, June 21, 1639, son of Rev. Richard and Katharine (Hoult) Mather; Harvard, 1656, A.B.; A.M., Trinity Coll., Dublin, 1658; S.T.D., Harvard, 1692, (first ever given at Harvard); Fellow, Harvard, 1675–1685; Ord. Boston, (2nd Chh.) May 27, 1664; sett. Boston, 1661–1723; sixth President of Harvard, June 11, 1658; served as President, 1685–1701; voluminous writer against Stoddard; Artillery Election Sermons, 1677, 1693, 1699, 1702; d. Boston, Aug. 23, 1723.

RICHARD MATHER. b. Lowton, Winwick, Lancashire, England, 1596, son of Thomas and Margaret Mather; Brazenose Coll., Oxford, matric. May 6, 1618; Ord. Toxteth, Co. Lancaster, 1618; sett. Toxteth and

Prescott, Lancashire, 1618–1633; suspended 1633, for non-conformity; came to N.E. 1635; disagrees with Cotton's Code and is prevented from founding church in spring of 1636; sett. Dorchester, Aug. 1636–1669; published the Bay Psalm Book and other works; Artillery Election Sermon, 1656; Election Sermons, 1660, 1664; d. Dorchester, Apr. 22, 1669.

SAMUEL MATHER. b. Dublin, Ireland, May 13, 1626, son of Rev. Richard and Katharine (Hoult) Mather; came to N.E. 1635; Harvard 1643, A.B., A.M.; A.M., at Cambridge, Oxford and Dublin, First Fellow of Harvard, 1650; asst. to Mr. Rogers at Rowley; sett Boston, (1st Chh.) June 5, 1650, but was not ordained here; returned to England, 1650; minister at Leith, Scotland; Chaplain to the Lord Mayor of London, 1650; Chaplain, Magdalen Coll., Oxford, 1650–1653; Senior Fellow of Trinity Coll., Dublin, 1655; minister of St. Nicholas' Chh., Dublin, 1655; d. Dublin, Ireland, Oct. 29, 1671.

SAMUEL MATHER, b. Dorchester, Sept. 5, 1651, son of Timothy and Elizabeth (Atherton) Mather; Harvard, 1671, A.B.; Trustee, Yale, 1701; sett. Deerfield, 1673–1675; sett. Branford, Ct., 1680; Ord. Windsor, Ct., 1684/5; sett. Windsor, Ct., 1682–1728; d. Windsor, Ct., Mar. 18, 1727/8.

WARHAM MATHER. b. Northampton, Sept. 7, 1666, son of Rev. Eleazer and Esther (Warham) Mather; Harvard, 1685, A.B., A.M.; sett. West Chester, N.Y., 1684; sett. Northfield, 1688–1690; sett. Killingworth, Ct., 1691–1693; sett. Farmington, Ct., 1704; not ordained; Justice of the Peace and of Quorum in Ct., 1710–1716; Justice of Probate, 1716–1727; d. New Haven, Ct., Aug 12, 1745.

JOHN MAVERICK. bapt. Awliscombe, Devon, Oct. 27, 1578, son of Rev. Peter and Dorothy (Tucke) Maverick; Exeter Coll., Oxford, A.B., 1599; A.M., 1603; Ord. deacon at Exeter, July 26, 1597; inst. Beaworthy, Devon, Aug. 30, 1615, by the Bishop of Exeter; sett. Beaworthy, Devon, 1615–1629; Ord. Plymouth, Devon, Mar. 30, 1630; emigrated on the *Mary and John*; disagreed with Cotton's Code of strict Congregationalism; d. 1636, at Dorchester, before he could emigrate to Connecticut.

JONATHAN MITCHELL. b. Halifax, Yorkshire, England, 1624, son of Matthew and Susan Mitchell; came to Boston, 1635; Harvard, 1647, A.B., A.M.; Tutor and Fellow, Harvard, 1650–1668; Ord. Cambridge, Aug. 21, 1650; sett. Cambridge, 1650–1668; Election Sermons, 1658, 1667; major channel of moderate Congregationalism for Stoddard; d. Cambridge, July 9, 1668.

STEPHEN MIX. b. New Haven, Ct., Nov. 1, 1672, son of Thomas and Rebecca (Turner) Mix; Harvard, 1690, A.B., A.M.; Ord. Wethersfield, Ct., 1694; sett. Wethersfield, Ct., 1694–1738; Ct. Election Sermon, 1735; d. Wethersfield, Ct., Aug. 28, 1738.

GEORGE MOXON. bapt. Wakefield, Yorkshire, England, Apr. 28, 1602, son of James Moxon; Sidney Sussex Coll., Camb., A.B., 1623/4; Ord. as an Anglican clergyman in England, 1626; sett. St. Helen's Chester, England; cited for nonconformity, 1637; fled to N.E., 1637, sett. Springfield (1st Chh.), 1637–1651, as the first minister; returned to England, 1651 with William Pynchon, Esq.; minister at Newbold-Ashbury, Cheshire, 1653–1661; also at Rushton Spencer, Staffordshire; nonconformist preacher at Congleton, 1667–1687; d. England, Sept. 15, 1687.

JOHN NORTON. b. Bishop's Stortford, Hertfordshire, England, May 6, 1606, son of William and Alice (Browest) Norton; Peterhouse, Cambridge, A.B., 1623/4; A.M., 1627; Curate at Bishop's Stortford; Chaplain to Sir William Masham at High Lever, Essex; came to N.E. Oct. 1635; Ord. Ipswich (1st Chh.), Feb. 20, 1638; sett. Ipswich, 1636–1653; inst. Boston (1st Chh.), July 23, 1656; sett. Boston, 1653–1663; Election Sermons, 1645, 1657, 1661; Artillery Election Sermon, 1659; active in drawing up "The Platform of Church Discipline," 1646; Overseer, Harvard; Envoy to England, 1662; d. Boston, Apr. 5, 1663, a. 57.

JOHN OXENBRIDGE. b. Daventry, Northamptonshire, England, Jan. 30, 1608/9, son of Dr. Daniel and Katherine (Harby) Oxenbridge; matriculated Emmanuel Coll., Camb., 1626; Magdalen Hall, Oxford, A.B., 1628; A.M., 1631; Tutor at Magdalen Hall, Oxford, but deprived by Archbishop Laud, 1634; influenced Thomas Bliss of Daventry, settler of Northampton; Fellow of Eaton Coll., 1653; sett. Bermuda, 1634–1641; sett. Beverly, England, 1642–1662; lecturer at Berwick-on-Tweed, 1650–1651; silenced 1662; sett. Surinam, 1662–1667; sett. Barbadoes, 1667–1669, met Stoddard; inst. Boston, (1st chh.) Apr. 10, 1670; sett. Boston, 1670–1674; Artillery Election Sermon, 1670; Election Sermon, 1671; d. Boston, Dec. 28, 1674.

GURDON SALTONSTALL. b. Haverhill, Mar. 27, 1666, son of Nathaniel and Elizabeth (Ward) Saltonstall; Harvard, 1684, A.B., A.M.; ord. New London, Ct., Nov. 25, 1691; sett. New London, 1687–1707; supported Stoddard in sermons, 1703–1707; Gov. of Ct., 1707–1724; supported Saybrook Platform, 1708; d. New London, Sept. 20, 1724.

ANTHONY STODDARD. b. Northampton, Aug. 9, 1678, son of Rev. Solomon and Esther (Warham) Stoddard; Harvard, 1697; A.B.; A.M., 1715; Trustee, Yale., 1738; Ord. Woodbury, Ct., (1st Chh.), May 27, 1702; sett. Woodbury, Ct., 1700–1760; Ct. Election Sermon, 1716; d. Woodbury, Ct., Sept. 6, 1760.

SAMSON STODDARD, b. Boston, *ca.* 1680, son of Samson Stoddard; Harvard, 1701, A.B., A.M.; Ord. Chelmsford, Nov. 6, 1706; sett. Chelmsford, 1706–1740; Artillery Election Sermon, 1713; d. Chelmsford, Aug. 23, 1740.

SIMEON STODDARD. b. Woodbury, Ct., Mar. 1, 1734/5, son of Capt. Dea.

Gideon and Olive (Curtiss) Stoddard; Yale, 1755, A.B., A.M.; Ord. Chester, Ct., (4th Chh. in Saybrook), Oct. 31, 1759; sett. Chester, Ct., 1759–1765; d. Chester, Ct., Oct. 27, 1765.

SAMUEL STONE. b. Hertford, July 30, 1602, son of John Stone; Emmanuel Coll., Camb., A.B., 1623/4; A.M., 1627; Ord. by the Bishop of Peterborough, July 8, 1626; Curate at Stisted, Essex, 1623–1630; suspended for nonconformity; Lecturer at Towcester, Northamptonshire, 1630; emigrated, 1633 with Thomas Hooker; Ord. Cambridge, Oct. 11, 1633; disagreed with Cotton's code of strict Congregationalism; sett. Cambridge, 1633–1636, as the first minister; sett. Hartford, Ct., 1636–1663; Chaplain, Pequot expedition, 1637; wrote moderate congregational treatise on church government, ca. 1655; d. Hartford, Ct., July 26, 1663.

EDWARD TAYLOR. b. Sketelby, Leicestershire, England, ca. 1642, came to N.E. 1663; Harvard, 1671, A.B.; A.M., 1720, Ord. Westfield, Aug. 27, 1679, as the first minister, sett. Westfield, 1671–1729; major opponent of Stoddard; d. Westfield, June 24, 1729.

SALMON TREAT. b. Wethersfield, Ct., ca. 1673, son of Lieut. James and Rebecca (Lattimer) Treat; Harvard, 1694, A.B.; Yale, 1702, A.M.; sett. Greenwich, Ct., (1st Chh.) 1695–1697; Ord. Preston, Ct., Nov. 16, 1698; sett. Preston, Ct., 1697–1744; resigned, Mar. 14, 1743/4, d. Preston, Ct., Jan. 6, 1762.

SAMUEL WHITMAN. b. Hull, 1676, son of Rev. Zechariah and Sarah (Alcock) Whitman; Harvard, 1696, A.B., A.M.; Trustee and Fellow, Yale; preached at Lancaster and Salem; Ord. Farmington, Ct., Dec. 10, 1706; sett. Farmington, Ct., 1705–1751; Ct. Election Sermon, 1714; d. Farmington, Ct., July 31, 1751.

JOSEPH WILLARD. b. Saybrook, Ct., July 23, 1696, son of Samuel and Sarah (Clark) Willard; Yale., 1714, A.B., A.M.; Harvard, A.M., (Hon.), 1723; Ord. Sunderland, Jan. 1, 1718/9; sett. Sunderland, 1718–1721; sett. Rutland, July 2, 1721–1723; killed by the Indians at Rutland, Aug. 14, 1723.

JOHN WARHAM. b. 1595. Moderate Puritan opposed to Cotton's Code of strict Congregationalism. A.B., A.M. Oxford, 1618. Lecturer at St. Sidwell's parish, Exeter, Devon; protegé of the Rev. John White, moderate Puritan leader of the Dorchester Company; emigrated 1630; sett. Dorchester as junior minister to John Maverick; 1636, rem. to Windsor, Ct., with Hooker. Eleazar Mather's father-in-law, Warham Mather's grandfather. d. Windsor, Ct., Apr. 1, 1670.

SAMUEL WILLARD. b. Concord, Jan. 31, 1639/40, son of Major Simon and Mary (Sharpe) Willard; Harvard, 1659, A.B., A.M.; Fellow, Harvard 1692–1707; Ord. Groton, July 13, 1664; sett. Groton, 1663–1676; inst. Boston, (Old South Chh) Mar. 31, 1678; sett. Boston, 1676–1707; Vice President of Harvard, then acting President, inst., Sept. 6, 1701–1707;

author of *Body of Divinity*; Artillery Election Sermons, 1686, 1699; Election Sermons, 1682, 1694; d. Boston, Sept. 12, 1707.

ELISHA WILLIAMS. b. Hatfield, Aug. 24, 1694, son of Rev. William and Eliza (Cotton) Williams; Harvard, 1711, A.B., A.M.; Ord. Newington, Ct., (2nd Chh. in Wethersfield), Oct. 17, 1722, as the first minister; sett. Newington, Ct. 1722–1726; Rector (or President), Yale, 1726–1739; Rep. Gen. Assembly; Judge, Superior Court of Ct.; Colonel; Chaplain, Cape Breton Expedition, 1746; d. Wethersfield, Ct., July 24, 1755.

JOHN WILLIAMS. b. Roxbury, Dec. 10, 1664, son of Dea. Samuel and Theoda (Park) Williams; Harvard, 1683, A.B., A.M.; taught school at Dorchester, 1684–1685; Ord. Deerfield, Oct. 17, 1688, as the first minister; est. Deerfield, 1686–1729; Convention Sermon, 1728; with his oldest son and daughter was captive, held in Canada, 1704–1706, wife was massacred at Deerfield at the time of their capture; published narrative "The Redeemed Captive," 1706; d. Deerfield, June 12, 1729.

SOLOMON WILLIAMS. b. Hatfield, June 4, 1700, son of Rev. William and Christian (Stoddard) Williams; Harvard 1719, A.B., A.M.; S.T.D., Yale, 1773; Fellow, Yale, 1749–1769; Ord. Lebanon, Ct. (1st Chh.) Dec. 5, 1722; sett. Lebanon, Ct., 1722–1776; Ct. Election Sermon, 1741; d. Lebanon, Ct., Feb. 29, 1776.

STEPHEN WILLIAMS. b. Deerfield, May 14, 1693, son of Rev. John and Eunice (Mather) Williams; Harvard, 1713, A.B., A.M.; S.T.D., Dart. Coll. 1773; Ord. Longmeadow, Oct. 17, 1716, sett. Longmeadow, 1714–1782; Convention Sermon, 1754; was carried captive with his father to Canada, 1704: in 1734, he established an Indian mission at Stockbridge, served as Chaplain at Louisburg, 1745; in the Northern army, 1756; d. Longmeadow, June 10, 1782.

WARHAM WILLIAMS. b. Deerfield, Sept. 7, 1699, son of Rev. John and Eunice (Mather) Williams; Harvard, 1719, A.B., A.M.; Ord. Waltham, June 11, 1723; sett. Waltham, 1723–1751: carried captive to Canada with his father, 1704; d. Waltham, June 22, 1751.

WILLIAM WILLIAMS. b. Newton, Feb. 2, 1665, son of Capt. Isaac and Martha (Parke) Williams; Harvard., 1683, A.B., A.M.; Ord. Hatfield, 1685 or 1686; sett. Hatfield, 1685–1741; Election Sermon, 1719; Convention Sermon, 1726; d. Hatfield, Aug. 29, 1741, a. 76.

WILLIAM WILLIAMS, JR. b. Hatfield, May 11, 1688, son of Rev. William and Eliza (Cotton) Williams; Harvard, 1705, A.B., A.M.; Ord. Weston, Nov. 1, 1709; sett. Weston, 1709–1750; dism. Oct. 24, 1750; Artillery Election Sermon, 1737; Election Sermon, 1741; d. Weston, Mar. 6, 1760.

TIMOTHY WOODBRIDGE. b. Burford St. Martin's, Wiltshire, England, 1656, son of Rev. John and Mercy (Dudley) Woodbridge; Harvard, 1675, A.B., A.M.; Founder, Trustee, and Fellow, Yale, 1700–1732; Ord.,

Hartford Ct. (1st Chh.) Nov. 18, 1685; sett. Hartford, Ct., 1683–1732; sett. Kittery, Me., 1680–1682; Ct. Election Sermons, 1698, 1727; d. Hartford, Ct., Apr. 30, 1732.

Notes and References

Preface

1. Quoted in William B. Sprague, *Annals of the American Pulpit* (New York, 1857–1864), I:343–344.

2. Cotton Mather, *Magnalia Christi Americana, Books I and II*, ed. Kenneth B. Murdock (Cambridge, Mass.: the Belknap Press of Harvard University Press, 1977), p. 111. For secondary literature cited see "Selected Bibliography, Secondary Sources" at end.

Chapter One

1. Frederick Johnson Simmons, *A Narrative Outline for a Biography of Emmanuel Downinge*, 1585–1660 [N.p., *ca.* 1960], pp. 5, 48, including his MS. correspondence bound in the copy of the New England Historic Genealogical Society Library, Boston.

2. *Ibid.*, pp. 50–51.

3. Henry F. Waters, *Genealogical Gleanings in England* (1901; rpt. 2 vols., Baltimore, 1969), I, 654; G.A. Raikes, ed., *The Ancient Vellum Book of the Honourable Artillery Company* (London, 1890), p. 35.

4. R.J. Coffman, "Gardens in the Wilderness" (Ph.D. diss., Harvard Univ.), Table 36, p. 294.

5. "The Apologia of Robert Keayne," ed. Bernard Bailyn, *Colonial Society of Massachusetts Publications*, XLII (1964), 72–73.

6. Alford, Lincs., Parish Register in Reginald Dudding, *History of the Parish and Manor of Alford* (Horncastle, 1930), p. 148; John Cotton, Sermon (Sept. 26, 1640) in Robert Keayne, *Notebook*, Massachusetts Historical Society; "The Records of the first Church in Boston, 1630–1868," ed. Richard D. Pierce, *Colonial Society of Massachusetts Publications*, XXXIX (1969), 34.

7. Zachariah Whitman, *The History of the Ancient and Honorable Artillery Company* (Boston, 1842), p. 98; *The Records of the Governor and Company of Massachusetts Bay*, ed. Nathaniel Shurtleff (5 vols., Boston, 1853–54), II, 335 (hereinafter cited as *Mass. Recs.*); E.W. Stoddard, *Anthony Stoddard of Boston, Mass.* (New York, 1873) p. 101; cf. John Winthrop, *Journal*, ed. James K. Hosmer (2 vols., Boston, 1908), II, 40.

8. John Cotton, *Milk for Babes* (1646), rpt. in Everett Emerson, *John*

Cotton, Twayne's U.S. Authors Series (Boston: G. K. Hall, 1965), p. 127.

9. E. W. Stoddard, *Anthony Stoddard,* p. 102; Massachusetts Archives, State House, Boston, MS. IX, fols. 8, 11, 14.

10. *The Laws and Liberties of Massachusetts,* ed. Max Farrand (1648, rpt. Cambridge, Mass., 1929), pp. 11, 12, 47; *Mass Recs.,* II 6–9.

11. Cotton, *Milk,* pp. 130–31.

12. Samuel Eliot Morison, *The Founding of Harvard College* (Cambridge, Mass., 1963), p. 373; *Mass. Recs.,* IV, pt. 1, 397; *New England's First Fruits* (London, 1643), p. 13; G.E. Littlefield, "Elijah Corlet," *Colonial Society of Massachusetts Publications,* XVIII (1915), 135.

13. William Pynchon, *The Meritorious Price of Our Redemption* (London, 1650), pp. 84–85; Samuel Eliot Morison, *Builders of the Bay Colony* (1930, rpt., Boston, 1964), pp. 368–75; Bernard Bailyn, *New England Merchants in the Seventeenth Century* (New York, 1964), p. 108.

14. R. J. Crandall and R. J. Coffman, "From Emigrants to Rulers: The Charlestown Oligarchy in the Great Migration," *New England Historical and Genealogical Register,* CXXXI (1977), 2–5; Coffman, "Gardens," ch. 3; George H. Williams et al., "Thomas Hooker," *Harvard Theological Studies,* XXVIII (1976), 159.

15. Donald Lines Jacobus and Edgar Francis Waterman, *Hale, House and Related Families* (Hartford, 1952), p. 739; *New England Historical and Genealogical Register,* LXIX (1913), 248–250; "Harvard College Records," *Colonial Society of Massachusetts Publications,* XXXI (1928), 329.

16. "Harvard College Records," p. 333.

17. Solomon Stoddard, *Notebook 1660–1664,* Union Theological Seminary, New York.

18. Quoted in Richard M. Gummere, *The American Colonial Mind and the Classical Tradition* (Cambridge, Mass., 1963), pp. 38, 39; R. R. Bolgar, *The Classical Heritage* (New York, 1964), p. 121; Israel Chauncy. *An Almanac* (Boston, 1664).

19. Walter J. Ong, *Ramus, Method and the Decay of Dialog* (Cambridge, Mass., 1958); Wilbur K. Howell, *Logic and Rhetoric in Seventeenth Century England* (1956, rpt. New York, 1970).

20. Perry Miller, *The New England Mind: The Seventeenth Century* (1939, rpt., Boston, 1967), pp. 116–53; Babette May Levy, *Preaching in the First Half Century of New England History* (1945, rpt. New York, *ca.* 1960), 18–19.

21. Alexandre Koyré, *From the Closed World to the Infinite Universe* (Baltimore, 1957), pp. 5, 37, 110–12.

22. John Hull, "The Diaries of John Hull," *American Antiquarian Society Transactions,* III (1857), 198; cf. Robert Pope, *The Half-Way Covenant* (Princeton, 1969), p. 36.

23. Williston Walker, *Creeds and Platforms of Congregationalism* (Boston, 1960).

24. Stoddard, Notebook; Thomas Erastus, *Explicatio Questionis, Utrum*

Excommunicatio . . . a Sacramentorum Usu (Peoclavii, apud Bracium Sub-tacetterum [sic], 1589), pp. 1–3; Erastus, *The Nullity of Church Censures* (London, 1659), pp. 2–5; William Prynne, *Foure Serious Questions of Grand Importance, Excommunication and Suspension from the Sacrament* [London ? 1643 ?], pp. 4–5; Prynne, *A Vindication of Foure Serious Questions* (London, 1645), pp. 40–42; John Humphrey, *A Rejoynder to Mr. Drake* (London, 1654), pp. 65–66; Wilfred W. Biggs, "The Controversy concerning Free Admission to the Lord's Supper, 1652–1660," *Congregational Historical Society Transactions*, XVI (1951), 178–89; for the influence of New England on England see Stephen Mayer, *The Lord's Supper in Early English Dissent* (London, 1972), pp. 85–92; Brian G. Armstrong, *Calvinism and the Amyraut Controversy* (Madison, 1969), pp. 47–55.

25. Stoddard, Notebook.

26. *Ibid.*, fols. [101–103]

27. *Ibid.*, fol. [105]; Cotton, *The Way of Congregational Churches Cleared*, 1658, in *John Cotton on the Churches of New England*, ed. Larzer Ziff, the John Harvard Library (Cambridge, Mass., 1968), pp. 330–61; Daniel Cawdry, *Vindiciae Clavium* (London, 1645); see *Ibid.*, p. 307.

28. Edwin S. Fussell, "Benjamin Tompson, Public Poet," *New England Quarterly*, XXVI (1953), 503–504. All known funeral elegies except Stoddard's are cited in Astrid Schmitt-von Muhlenfels, *Die 'Funeral Elegy' Neuenglands* (Heidelberg, 1973), pp. 139–47; Alexander Richardson *The Logician's Schoolmaster; Or, a Comment upon Ramus Logic* (London, 1657), p. 70; see Darrett B. Rutman, *American Puritanism* (p., 1970), pp. 99–105; see Samuel Mather, *The Figures or Types of the Old Testament* (1705; rpt. New York, 1969), pp. xii–xiii, 1–3.

29. Cf. John Langdon Sibley, *Graduates of Harvard University* (3 vols. 1873; rpt. New York, 1974), II, 60–61, 144–45.

30. John Wilson, "Anagram: Into Honnor," II. 141–144 in Kenneth Murdock, *Handkerchiefs from Paul* (Cambridge, Mass., 1927), p. 98.

31. Cf. Jean Seznec, *The Survival of the Pagan Gods*, tr. Barbara F. Sessions (New York, 1961), p. 303.

32. Samuel Eliot Morison, *Harvard College in the Seventeenth Century* (2 vols., Cambridge, Mass, 1936), I, 256.

33. Harvard College, "Quaestiones in Philosophia Discutiendae, sub Carolo Chaunceo SS. Theol. Bac. Praeside Col. Harvard. Cantabridgea Nov-Angl. In Comitia per inceptoris in Artibus die Octavo sextiles M.DC.LXV." [Cantabridgiae: Impensis S. Green, 1665] Broadside. [Evans 108].

34. Sibley, *Graduates*, II, 145.

35. *Ibid.*, IV, 71.

Chapter Two

1. Joseph G. Holland, *History of Western Massachusetts* (Springfield, Mass., 1855), pp. 13–14.

2. John Pynchon, Account Book, Connecticut Valley Historical Museum, Springfield, vol. 1, fols. 152–261, 306. John Insley Coddington, "The Stebbing Family of Co. Essex, England . . . ," *The American Genealogist*, XXXI (1955), 193–211; Roxbury, Town Records; Springfield, Town Records.

3. W. H. Wright and G. Wright Ketcham, *History of the Wright Family* (Denver: Williamson-Haffner, 1936), pp. 25–34, 42–43; William K. Wright, "The Wrights of Northampton, Mass.," *The New England Historical and Genealogical Register*, XL (1886), 280–84; *Records of the First Church at Dorchester*, ed. G. H. Ellis (Boston, 1891), pp. 149ff.

4. Essex Records office, High Ongar Parish Records; Lyman Coleman, *Genealogy of the Lyman Family* (n.p., n.d.), pp. 32–39.

5. Willard S. Allen, *A Genealogy of Samuel Allen of Windsor, Connecticut* (Boston: privately printed, 1876), p. 6; John Spargo, *Notes on the Ancestry and Immediate Descendants of Ethan and Ira Allen* (Bennington, Vt., 1948), p. 3.

6. Samuel G. Drake, *Result of Researches among British Archives* (1860; rpt.; Baltimore: Genealogical Pub. Co., 1963) pp. 85–87; Henry M. Burt, *Cornet Joseph Parsons* (Garden City: Albert Ross Parsons n.d.), pp. 90–93.

7. Anon., "The Parsons Family," *The New England Historical and Genealogical Register*, I(1847), 266; Black Torrington, Protestation Returns, 1641, Devon Records Office; Great Torrington, Parish Registers (Bishops' Transcripts), *Ibid.*; Thomas Shepard to Richard Mather, A. MS (1635–1636), Massachusetts Historical Society.

8. R. Sharpe France, Lancashire Records Office, personal correspondence (May 6, 1976): parish register searches, Clark (Cockersham, Garstang, Lancaster, Manchester), Cunliffe (Blackburn, Burnley, Bury), Hayward (Childwall); (March 1, 1976); Woodward (Childwall).

9. I.P. Collins, Somerset Records Office, personal correspondence (May 2, 1976); (Mrs.) Jeanne Strong, Los Altos Hills, California, personal correspondence (April 14, 1976) and her "Evidence Supporting the Ancestry of Elder John Strong" (n.p., 1976), typescript "Somerset Assize Orders, 1629–1640," ed. T. G. Barnes, Somerset Records Society Publications, LXV(1959), 30; Edward Strong, "Elder John Strong and His Descendants," *The New England Historical and Genealogical Register*, XXIII (1869), 294–96.

10. Charles Hoppin, *The Bliss Book* (Hartford: privately printed, 1913), pp. 156–69; John Dod to John Cotton, MS (1636), Boston Public Library.

11. *Northamptonshire Quarter Sessions Records*, pp. xlv, 58–60; L. Q. C. Elmer, *Genealogy of the Elmer and More Families* (Boston, 1930); James Pierce Root, *Root Genealogical Records, 1600–1870* (New York: R. C. Root, 1870), p. 101 and chart III.

12. See R. J. Coffman, "Gardens in the Wilderness" (1976) *passim*.

13. Burt N. Bridgman and Joseph Clark Bridgman, *Genealogy of the Bridgman Family, Descendants of James Bridgman* (Hyde Park, Mass., 1894), pp. 1–10; Springfield Town Records, Land Records, City Clerk's Office, Springfield, Massachusetts.

14. Springfield, Mass., Town Records; John Pynchon, Account Books; Symon Beamon to John Pynchon (Sept. 19, 1656), Widener Treasure Room, Harvard University; John Demos, "Underlying Themes in the Witchcraft of Seventeenth Century New England," *American Historical Review*, LXXV (1970), 13–24.

15. Eleazar Mather to John Davenport in Trumbull, *History*, I: 201–202; Pope, *Half-Way Covenant*, pp. 18–20, 49. Three natives of Lancashire, Richard Mather's county: Cunliffe was baptized at Bury 10 December 1609 (Lancashire Record Office); and in his will he called Mather his grandfather; Clark was baptized at Cockersham 20 February 1615/16 and Woodward was baptized at Much Woolton, Childwall, 4 September 1611. I am indebted to Mr. R. Sharpe France, Lancashire County Archivist for these identifications.

16. Northampton, Mass., First Church Records, 1661–1924, Forbes Library, Northampton, p. 7.

17. Trumbull, *History*, 1:211.

18. Norman Pettit, "Lydia's Conversion; An Issue in Hooker's Departure," *Cambridge Historical Society Proceedings* (1964–1966), 59–83; William Williams, *The Death of a Prophet Lamented* (Boston, 1729), p. 25; Stoddard to John Strong, Caleb Strong Papers, Massachusetts Historical Society, Boston, vol. 1.

19. I. N. Tarbox, "Jonathan Edwards as a Man and the Ministers of the Last Century," *The New Englander*, XXXXIII (1884) 625–26.

20. Northampton, First Church Records.

21. Northampton Covenant, November 5, 1672, in Ezra Stiles, *Extracts from the Itineraries* (New Haven, 1916), p. 201.

22. Hampshire County Probate Records, Hampshire County Court House, Springfield, I:158–59; John Pynchon, Waste Book, Hampshire County Ct. House, p. 120; *Recs. of Ct. of Assts.*, I, 31, 33.

23. Edward Taylor, Commonplace Book, Massachusetts Historical Society, pp. [26], [23]; See Dean Hall and Thomas M. Davis, "The Two Versions of Edward Taylor's Foundation Day Sermon" *Resources for American Literary Study*, V (1975), 199–216.

24. *Ibid.*, pp. 29, 32.

25. Francis Jennings, *The Invasion of America* (Chapel Hill, 1975), p. 298, 319. Cf. Douglas Edward Leach, *Flintlock and Tomahawk* (New York, 1960), pp. viii, 206.

26. It was Rev. John Russell Hadley and not Stoddard who supplied the account of Indian affairs in Increase Mather, *A Brief History of the War with the Indians in New England* (Boston, 1676), pp. 9–11.

27. Massachusetts Archives, State House, Boston, LXVIII, fol. 182.

28. Trumbull, *History*, I:320–21.

29. Stoddard to Governor Dudley, 1703, in "The Dudley Papers," Collections of the Massachusetts Historical Society, ser. 4, II, 235–37.

30. Massachusetts Archives, XXX, fols. 382, 384–86. For another account see Sylvester Judd, *History of Hadley* (Springfield, 1905; rpt., Somersworth, N.H., 1976), p. 256.

31. *Ibid.*, XXX, fol. 400; *Ibid.*, X, fol. 277.

32. Great Britain, *Calendar of State Papers, Colonial Series, 1675–1676*, #1067; Leach, *Flintlock*, p. 243., *Mass. Recs.*, V: 106, 130–31.

33. Massachusetts Historical Society, *Proceedings*, 4th Ser., VIII (1868), 587; Edward Randolph, "The Present State of New England," British Museum, London, Add. Ms. 280–89, fols. 6–20; David S. Lovejoy, *The Glorious Revolution in America* (New York, 1972), p. 139; Karl Keller, "The Example of Solomon Stoddard: A Review Essay," *Seventeenth Century Notes* (Summer-Fall 1976), p. 58.

34. Hampshire County Probate Court Records, Hampshire County Court House, Springfield, I: 158–59; John Pynchon, Waste Book for Hampshire County, Hampshire County Court House, p. 120; Records of the Court of Assistants, I: 31, 33; Cf., Smith, *Colonial Justice;* Massachusetts Archives, LXI, fol. 204 (June 11, 1679); *Ibid.*, X, fol. 199, *Ibid.*, X, 198. Signed by John Eliot, Increase Mather, Samuel Torrey, Samuel Willard, Moses Fiske, Josiah Flint, Thomas Clark, James Sherman, Joseph Whiting, Samuel Cheever, Samuel Phillips, Solomon Stoddard, Samuel Whiting, Sr., Thomas Cobbet, Edward Bulkeley, John Sherman, John Higginson, John Hull, Samuel Whiting, Jr., John Wilson.

35. Increase Mather, "Autobiography," *American Antiquarian Society Proceedings*, LXXXI (1969), 302–303.

36. See Dean Hall and Thomas M. Davis, "The Two Versions of Edward Taylor's Foundation Day Sermon" *Resources for American Literary Study*, V (1975), 199–216.

37. Henry Martyn Dexter, *The Congregationalism of the Last Three Hundred Years* (New York, 1880), pp. 477–81; Walker *Creeds*, pp. 418–19; Cf. Miller, *Stoddard*, p. 282.

38. Edward Taylor to Solomon Stoddard in Norman S. Grabo, "The Poet to the Pope: Edward Taylor to Solomon Stoddard," *American Literature*, XXXII (1960), 198, 201; Peter Thacher, *Diary*, in Walker, *Creeds*, pp. 417–19. Solomon Stoddard, *An Appeal to the Learned* (Boston, 1709), pp. 93–94.

39. Solomon Stoddard, "Nine Arguments," edited by Thomas M. Davis, *American Antiquarian Society Proceedings*, LXXXVI (1976). Citations from the text refer to the paginations of the manuscript that Davis preserved. See also Mason Lowance and Everett Emerson, "Increase Mather's Confutation of Solomon Stoddard's Observation Respecting the Lord's Supper, 1680,"

American Antiquarian Society Proceedings, LXXXIII (1973), 29–65, from a transcription of the original by Cotton Mather. The original exists at the Society, having been discovered by William Joyce, curator. Citations from the text refer to the original pagination of the manuscript as it is indicated in the version published by the American Antiquarian Society.

40. William Ames, *Conscience with the Power and Cases Thereof, Divided into Five Books* (London, 1643), Bk. 1, p. 3; Cf. Keith Sprunger, *The Learned Doctor William Ames: Dutch Backgrounds of English and American Puritanism* (Urbana, III., 1972), pp. 166–82.

41. Ames, *Conscience*, Bk. IV, pp. 84–85.

42. Answer, 1662, p. 21; Mather, "Confutation," p. 45.

43. *Ibid.*, pp. 46–47.

44. *Ibid.*, p. 49.

45. *Ibid.*, p. 50.

46. *Ibid.*

47. *Ibid.*, p. 51.

48. *Ibid.*

49. *Ibid.*, p. 57.

50. *Ibid.*

51. Increase Mather, quoted in William L. Joyce and Michael G. Hall, "Three Manuscripts of Increase Mather," *American Antiquarian Society Proceedings*, LXXXVI (1976), 115.

52. Boston Synod, *The Necessity of Reformation* (Boston, 1679), printed in Walker, *Creeds*, p. 433.

53. Mass. Historical Society Proceedings, 4th ser. VIII (1868), 587; *Mass. Recs.*, V: 244; Increase Mather *Parentator* (Boston, pp. 85–87).

54. John Russell to Increase Mather (March 2, 1681), in Massachusetts Historical Society, *Collections*, 4th ser. VIII (46), 83–84. See Russell's 1680 essay transcribed in Edward Taylor MS. *Commonplace Book*, Boston Public Library.

55. Samuel Green, ["Voluntary System in the Maintenance of Elders"] *American Antiquarian Society Proceedings* (1886), 86–126; Massachusetts Archives X. fols. 151, 151a.

56. Solomon Stoddard to Increase Mather (December 19, 1685), Massachusetts Historical Society, MS. LXI.I.60; Miller, "Solomon Stoddard," pp. 285–86; Miller, *The New England Mind: From Colony to Province* (Cambridge, Mass., 1953), p. 233; Benjamin Coleman, *The Faithful Ministers of Christ Mindful of Their Own Death* (Boston, 1729), p. 24.

57. Samuel Willard, *A Compleat Body of Divinity* (Boston, 1726), p. 255.

58. James G. Blight, "Solomon Stoddard's 'Safety of Appearing' and the Dissolution of the Puritan Faculty Psychology," *Journal of the History of the Behavioral Sciences*, X (1974), 249–50.

59. Edward Taylor, MS. Commonplace Book, Massachusetts Historical Society, pp. 61–63. My own transcription. For the full text, see Norman

Grabo, "The Poet to the Pope: Edward Taylor to Solomon Stoddard," *American Literature*, XXXII (1961), 197–201.

60. Edward Taylor, MS. Animadversions, Boston Public Library, Prince Collection, Taylor Extracts no. 12.

61. Edward Taylor, MS. Commonplace Book, pp. 65–67.

62. Edward Taylor, *The Poems*, ed. Donald E. Stanford (New Haven, 1966), p. 243.

63. Miller, *New England Mind: From Colony to Province*, p. 226; Cotton Mather, *Diary*, 2 vols. (New York, 1957) I: 137; Cotton Mather, *A Companion for Communicants* (Boston, 1690), pp. 29, 30, 43.

64. Increase Mather, *Ecclesiastes or the Life of the Reverend and Excellent Jonathan Mitchel* (Boston, 1697), pp. 1–3; Increase Mather in Cotton Mather, *Magnalia Christi Americana* (Boston, 1708), Bk. IV, pp. 159–60; Bk. V, pp. 43–44; Bk. VII, pp. 103–104.

65. Samuel K. Lothrop, *A History of the Church in Brattle Street, Boston* (Boston, 1851), pp. 45–50; Miller, *The New England Mind: From Colony to Province*, p. 256.

66. Mather, *Diary*, I 325–26.

Chapter Three

1. James De Normandie, "The Manifesto Church," *Proceedings of the Massachusetts Historical Society*, XLVII (1913–1914), p. 274.

2. Lothrop, *The Brattle Street Church*, p. 22.

3. Mather, *Diary*, VII, 325–26.

4. French Papers. MSS., Massachusetts Historical Society. John Demos, *A Little Commonwealth* (New York, 1970), p. 67; Philip Greven, *Four Generations* (Ithaca, 1970), p. 111.

5. Cf. Harry G. Swanhart, "Solomon Stoddard" (Ph.D. Diss.; Boston University, 1960).

6. [Cotton and Increase Mather], "A Defense of the Evangelical Churches," in John Quick, *The Young Man's Claim Unto the Sacrament of the Lord's Supper* (Boston, 1700), p. 1.

7. Increase Mather, *A Treatise on The Order of the Gospel* (Boston, 1701), p.v.

8. *Ibid.*, pp. 143–44.

9. Lothrop, *The Brattle Street Church*, pp. 28–37.

10. [Cotton and Increase Mather], "A Defense," in Quick, *The Young Man's Claim*, p. 64.

11. Morison, *Seventeenth-Century Harvard*, II: 505–507.

12. *Ibid.*, II: 530–35.

13. Richard Warch, *School of the Prophets: Yale College, 1701–1740* (New Haven, 1973), pp. 19, 305.

14. Morison, *Seventeenth-Century Harvard*, II: 545.

15. R. W. Henderson, *The Teaching Office in the Reformed Tradition: A History of the Doctoral Ministry* (Philadelphia, 1962), p. 133.

16. See Bernard Bailyn, "The Origins of American Politics," *Perspectives in American History*, I (1967), 56; Timothy H. Breen, *The Character of the Good Ruler: Puritan Political Ideas in New England, 1630-1730* (New Haven, 1970) pp. 224–25.

17. Gurdon Saltonstall, MS Sermons, Massachusetts Historical Society.

18. The original five-page document is entitled "At the Assn. of Ministers at Cambridge, the first Monday in August, 1705," and is in the Colman MSS. Massachusetts Historical Society; cf. Walker, *Creeds and Platforms*, p. 488.

19. Williston Walker, "Why Did Not Massachusetts Have a Saybrook Platform?" *Yale Review*, I (1892–1893), 85; cf. Miller, *The New England Mind: From Colony to Province*, p. 266; cf. Alan Heimert, "Introduction," *The Great Awakening, Documents Illustrating the Crisis and Its Consequences* (New York, 1967), p. xxxi.

20. Increase Mather, *A Dissertation* (Boston, 1708), p. iv.

21. Coleman MSS., Massachusetts Historical Society.

22. Sibley, *Harvard Graduates*, III, 263–69; Perry Miller, *Jonathan Edwards* (New York, 1949), pp. 14–15; S. W. Williams, *Genealogy and History of the Family of Williams* (1847).

23. William Williams, *The Danger of Not Reforming Known Evils . . . April 16, 1707* (Boston, 1707), pp. 5–7, 17–18.

24. *An Appeal of Some of the Unlearned* (Boston, 1709), pp. 2, 11, 27.

25. Edward Taylor, The Appeal Tried, MS. H. 20a, 27, 14, p. [90], Boston Public Library.

Chapter Four

1. Connecticut, *Court Records*, V: 5, 51, 86–87.

2. William Williams, *Notebook*, 1712, Massachusetts Historical Society.

3. John Warner Barber, *Historical Collection* (Worcester, Mass., 1839), p. 332.

4. Cf. John S. Coolidge, *The Pauline Renaissance in England: Puritanism and the Bible* (Oxford, 1970), pp. 145–47.

5. Cf. Edmund S. Morgan, *Visible Saints: The History of a Puritan Idea* (New York, 1963), pp. 93–99.

6. Thomas Hooker, "Writings in England and Holland, 1626–1633," edited by George H. Williams *et al.*, *Harvard Theological Studies*, XXVIII (1975), 15–16.

7. Northampton Church Record, First Church of Christ, Northampton, p. 21.

8. Solomon Stoddard *et al.* to the Reverend Mr. Nathaniel Collins,

pastor to the church of Enfield, "to be communicated to the church and congregation there," Forbes Library, Northampton, Mass.

9. Solomon Stoddard *et al.*, "to the minister of Springfield to be communicated to the church and congregation there," Dreer American Clergy MSS., The Historical Society of Pennsylvania.

10. Solomon Stoddard *et al.* to———, Dreer American Clergy MSS., The Historical Society of Pennsylvania.

11. Williston Walker, *The History of the First Church of Hartford* (Hartford, 1884), pp. 258–60; cf. C. C. Goen, *Revivalism and Separatism in New England, 1740–1800* (Hamden, Conn., 1969), p. 3.

12. Williams, *A Painful Ministry, the Peculiar Gift of the Lord of the Harvest* (Boston, 1717), pp. 10, 12, 21.

13. Sewall, *The Holy Spirit the Gift of God Our Father* (Boston, 1728), p. 25; Mather, *Mystical Marriage* (Boston, 1728), p. 6; Adams, *A Sermon Preached at Windham* (New London, 1721), pp. ii–iv.

14. See Ernest L. Tuveson, *Redeemer Nation* (Chicago, 1968), pp. 27–30.

15. Ezra Stiles, *Extracts from the Itineraries*, ed. by Franklin Bowditch Dexter (New Haven, 1916), p. 274; Warch, *School of Prophets*, pp. 75, 77; Warham Williams, Notebook, 1719–1720, Massachusetts Historical Society, Boston, Mass.

16. Bruce C. Daniels, "Connecticut's Villages Become Mature Towns: The Complexity of Local Institutions, 1676–1776," *William and Mary Quarterly* XXXIV (1977), 95, 98.

17. Stiles, *Extracts*, 273–74.

18. Goen, *Revivalism*, p. 307.

19. Cotton Mather, *Ratio Disciplinae* (Boston, 1726), p. 176.

Chapter Five

1. Sewall, *Diary, passim.*

2. Trumbell, *Northampton*, II, 42; Northampton, Church Records.

3. Williams, *Death of a Prophet*, p. 24; Colman, *Faithful Ministers of Christ* (Boston, 1730), p. 2; Edwards, Notes, MS. no. 5, Edwards Collection, Andover Newton Theological School.

4. Stoddard, Sermons, MS. 1720–1729A (2), Edwards Collection, Andover Newton Theological School.

5. Jonathan Edwards, "The Excellency of Christ (1728)," in *The Works of President Edwards*, ed. Samuel Austin (8 Vols.; Worcester, Mass., 1808–1809), VII, 267–307.

6. Quoted in Miller, "Stoddard," p. 302.

10. "Sewall-Williams Correspondence," *Mass. Historical Soc. Coll.*, 6th ser. II, 250–52.

Selected Bibliography

PRIMARY SOURCES

1. Published

The following chronological list is based on the American Antiquarian Society Readex Microprint edition of Charles Evans, *American Bibliography 1639–1800* (13 vols., 2 vol. rpt. Metuchen, N.J., 1967) and the opaque microtext reprints of all titles listed in Evans. Many college and university libraries have access to this American Antiquarian Society Readex microtext collection. Only works by Stoddard are listed here. For other authors see Evans's *Bibliography*.

1679   "Nine Arguments against Examinations Concerning a Work of Grace." Printed in Thomas M. Davis and Jeff Jeske, "Solomon Stoddard's 'Arguments Concerning Admission to the Lord's Supper.' " *American Antiquarian Society Proceedings*, LXXXVI (1976), 75–111. Pagination cited is to the MS., and it is indicated herein.

1681   Letter to Increase Mather. Printed in Norman Grabo, "The Poet to the Pope," *American Literature*, XXXII (1960), 197–201.

1687   *The Safety of Appearing.* 1687; rpt. Worcester, 1963. Evans no. 434.

1688   *The Tryal of Assurance.* 1698; rpt. Worcester, 1963. Evans no. 853.

1690   The Sermon on Paul's Epistle to the Galatians. Printed in Thomas M. Davis, "Solomon Stoddard's Sermon on the Lord's Supper as a Converting Ordinance." Resources for *American Literary Study* IV (1975), 205–24. Pagination cited is to the MS., and it is indicated herein.

1700   *The Doctrine of the Instituted Churches.* 1700; rpt. New York, 1970.

1701   *The Necessity of Acknowledgement of Offenses.* 1701; rpt. Worcester, 1963. Evans no. 1026.

1703   *God's Frown on the Death of Useful Men.* 1703; rpt. Worcester, 1963. Evans no. 1146.
       The Way for a People to Live. 1703; rpt. Worcester, 1963. Evans no. 1148.
       [*The Sufficiency of One Good Sign.* Boston: B. Green and J. Allen, 1703] No copy extant.

1705 *The Danger of Speedy Degeneracy.* 1705; rpt. Worcester, 1963.
      Evans no. 1234.
1707 *The Inexcusableness of Neglecting the Worship of God.* 1708; rpt.
      Worcester, 1963. Evans 1372.
1708 *The Falseness of the Hopes of Many Professors.* 1708; rpt. Worces-
      ter, 1963. Evans no. 1371.
1709 *The Appeal to the Learned.* 1709; rpt. Worcester, 1963. Evans no.
      1433.
1712 *Those Taught by God the Father.* 1712; rpt. Worcester, 1963. Evans
      no. 1584.
      *The Efficacy of the Fear of Hell . . . together with The Benefit of the
      Gospel.* 1713; rpt. Worcester, 1963. Evans no. 1651.
1714 *A Guide to Christ.* 1714; rpt. Worcester, 1963. Evans no. 1716.
1717 *Three Sermons Lately Preached.* 1717; rpt. Worcester, 1963, Evans
      no. 1930.
1718 *The Presence of Christ.* 1718; rpt. Worcester, 1963. Evans no. 1999.
1719 *The Way to Know Sincerity* [included with] *A Treatise Concerning
      Conversion* [reprinted in 1735 as *The Nature of Saving Conversion*].
      1719; rpt. Worcester, 1963. Evans no. 2072.
1722 *An Answer to Some Cases of Conscience.* 1722; rpt. Worcester,
      1963. Evans no. 2387.
1723 *The Defects of Preachers Reproved.* 1724; rpt. Worcester, 1963.
      Evans no. 2585.
      Question: Whether God Is Not Angry. 1723; rpt. Worcester, 1963.
      Evans no. 2479.

2. Unpublished

The wealth of manuscript sermons by Stoddard provides a rich supply of
material for the serious student. Since most are not dated but are arranged
in some sequential thematic order, scrutiny of them may reward the re-
searcher who has the patience to decipher Stoddard's holograph. The sermons recorded by Warham Williams are easily read.

STODDARD, SOLOMON. Inscription of his gift of "God's Frown," 1703, to
      Edward Taylor of Westfield. Massachusetts Historical Society. Boston,
      Massachusetts.
————. Letter to Benjamin Colman, Northampton, Massachusetts, Feb-
      ruary 7, 1707/8. Massachusetts Historical Society.
————. Letter to Elder John Strong, Boston, Massachusetts, February 7,
      1671/2. Massachusetts Historical Society.
————. Letter to John Earle's Master, August 25, 1673. Massachusetts
      Historical Society.
————. Letter to William Williams of Hadley. N.d. Dartmouth College
      Library.

————. Letter to Increase Mather, Northampton, Massachusetts, October 19, 1685. Massachusetts Historical Society.

————. Letter to Mr. Nathaniel Collins. Dreer MSS., Historical Society of Pennsylvania.

————. Letter to Rev. Mr. Nathaniel Collins, Pastor of the Church of Enfield, Northampton, Massachusetts, 1715. Forbes Library, Northampton, Massachusetts.

————. Letter to the minister of Springfield. Dreer MSS., Historical Society of Pennsylvania.

————. Notebook, 1660–1664. Union Theological Seminary, New York, New York.

————. Sermon on Ezra 8:13 [1660–1664 ?]. Houghton Library, Harvard University.

————. Sermons. Dr. Williams' Library, London.

————. Sermons. American Antiquarian Society, Worcester, Mass.

————. 58 Sermons recorded by William Williams. 1719–1720; 5 preached in Cambridge May 10–31, 1719; 61 preached at Northampton, 20 September–15 May 1720.

————. 8 Sermons recorded by "J. D." August 16–September 1720. MS. 1720–1729A (1a), Edwards Collection, Andover Newton Theological School, Newton Center, Mass.

————. Sermons Recorded October–December 1720. Includes sermons by Anthony Stoddard, William Williams and Joseph Hawley. MS. 1720–1729A (1b), Edwards Collection, Andover Newton,

————. Sermons recorded by Joseph Hawley, September 1725, September 1727. MS. 1720–1729A (2), Edwards Collection, Andover Newton.

SECONDARY SOURCES

BLIGHT, JAMES G. "Solomon Stoddard's 'Safety of Appearing' and the Dissolution of Puritan Faculty Psychology," *Journal of the History of the Behavioral Science*, X (1974), 238–50. One of the few attempts to relate how faculty psychology was rejected by Stoddard.

EMERSON, EVERETT, and MASON I. LOWANCE. "Increase Mather's Confutation of Solomon Stoddard's [1679] Observations Respecting the Lord's Supper, 1680." *Proceedings of the American Antiquarian Society*, n.s., LXXXIII (1973), 29–65. Reveals Mather's tactics to undermine Stoddard's position paper at the 1679 Reforming Synod.

HALL, DEAN, and THOMAS M. DAVIS. "The Two Versions of Edward Taylor's Foundation Day Sermon." *Resources for American Literary Study*, V (1975), 199–216. Illustrates the effect of Stoddard's changing position on Taylor's own development.

HOLIFIELD, E. BROOKS. *The Covenant Sealed: The Development of Puritan Sacramental Theology in Old and New England, 1570–1720.* New

Haven: Yale University Press, 1974. Offers a major reinterpretation of the centrality of sacraments to Puritan worship in general and to Stoddard's place within that tradition.

———. "The Intellectual Sources of Stoddardeanism." *New England Quarterly*, XLV (1972), 373–92. Should be compared with Stoddard's Notebook entries and his later statements.

JOYCE, WILLIAM. "Note on Increase Mather's Observations Respecting the Lord's Supper." *Proceedings of the American Antiquarian Society*, n.s., LXXXIII (1973), 343–44. Revises Emerson's article above.

KELLER, KARL. *The Example of Edward Taylor*. Amherst: University of Massachusetts Press, 1975. A finely written, sympathetic portrait of a sensitive poet-preacher who steadfastly opposed Stoddard's early sacramental theory.

———. "The Example of Solomon Stoddard: A Review Essay." *Seventeenth Century Notes* (Summer-Fall 1976), 56–65. A review of recent research on Stoddard.

LOWANCE, MASON I. *Increase Mather*. Twayne's United States Authors Series, no. 246. Boston: G. K. Hall, 1975. The most recent full study of Mather since Kenneth B. Murdock's biography (1925). Examines Stoddard's archrival in illuminating thematic analyses of his contributions to history, science, homiletics, and doctrine.

LUCAS, PAUL R. " 'An Appeal to the Learned': The Mind of Solomon Stoddard." *William and Mary Quarterly*, 3d ser., XXX (1973), 257–92. Argues that Stoddard's main issue was doctrine and this has eluded his contemporaries as well as the modern scholar through his uses of deception and contradiction. Points to Stoddard's rejection of the instituted church idea for preaching Evangelicalism in 1708.

———. *Valley of Discord: Church and Society along the Connecticut River, 1636–1725*. Hanover, New Hampshire: University Press of New England, 1976. A provocative reinterpretation of Stoddard and the society that advocated moderate Congregational and Presbyterian ideas in the century before the Great Awakening. Questions the pervasiveness of Stoddard's influence in the valley.

MILLER, PERRY. *The New England Mind: From Colony to Province*. 1951; rpt. Boston: Beacon Press, 1963. A major work by a master of Puritan thought.

———. "Solomon Stoddard, 1643–1729," *Harvard Theological Review*, XXXIV (1941), 277–320. The first modern treatment of Stoddard and still a seminal article.

MORGAN, EDMUND. *Visible Saints: The History of a Puritan Idea*. New York: New York University Press, 1963. Treats the origin of strict Congregational church polity with reference to Stoddard.

PETTIT, NORMAN. *The Heart Prepared: Grace and Conversion in Puritan Spiritual Life*. New Haven: Yale University Press, 1966. Describes the varieties of Puritan preparation theology with reference to Stoddard and to its Reformed background.

POPE, ROBERT G. *The Half-Way Covenant: Church Membership in Puritan New England.* Princeton: Princeton University Press, 1969. Questions the view of declining piety in the last half of the seventeenth century with reference to the revival experiences of individual churches.

SCHAEFER, THOMAS. "Solomon Stoddard and the Theology of Revival." In Stuard C. Henry, ed., *A Miscellany of American Christianity: Essays in Honor of H. Shelton Smith.* Durham, North Carolina. Duke University Press, 1963. Treats Stoddard's rejection of covenant theology and his implicit contribution to the Great Awakening.

STUART, ROBERT LEE. " 'Mr. Stoddard's Way': Church and Sacraments in Northampton," *American Quarterly,* XXIV (1972), 243–53. Argues that Jonathan Edwards was unaware of Stoddard's distinction between preparation and conversion and was closer to Stoddard's mature theology than he ever realized.

WALSH, JAMES P. "Solomon Stoddard's Open Communion: A Reexamination," *New England Quarterly,* XLIII (1970), 97–114. Argues that the major issue in Northampton was discipline. Compare Lucas above.

WHITE, EUGENE E. *Puritan Rhetoric: The Issue of Emotion in Religion.* Carbondale, Ill.; Southern Illinois University Press, 1972. A comparison of Evangelical and rationalist homiletics during the Great Awakening, with some reference to Stoddard.

———. "Solomon Stoddard's Theories of Persuasion," *Speech Monographs,* XXIX (1962), 235–59. Deals with Stoddard's revivalistic rhetoric but without reference to the development of his theology and thought.

Index

220